Carlota Joaquina Queen of Portugal

DONA CARLOTA JOAQUINA
from a portrait at Queluz

CARLOTA JOAQUINA

Queen of Portugal

BY MARCUS CHEKE

Select Bibliographies Reprint Series

BOOKS FOR LIBRARIES PRESS
FREEPORT, NEW YORK

STANDARD BOOK NUMBER:
8369-5040-2

LIBRARY OF CONGRESS CATALOG CARD NUMBER:
70-94266

PRINTED IN THE UNITED STATES OF AMERICA

UXORI CARISSIMAE
DEDICAT
M.C.
SEXENNII MEMOR
TAGI FLUMINIS AD RIPAS
SUAVISSIME PERACTI

PREFACE

THE indulgence shown by the public to my " Life of the Marquis of Pombal,"* a book which followed the course of Portuguese history from 1699 to 1782, encouraged me to prepare the present volume covering the half-century subsequent to Pombal's death.

My choice of the Queen Carlota Joaquina as my central theme may appear a curious one, for she did not exert a substantial influence on events until the last decade of her life. Moreover during ten years (1811 to 1821) she lived in complete retirement. For these reasons there are chapters in the first part of this book in which her name makes only fitful appearances. And indeed, for a long time after I had begun my researches into the history of her time, I hesitated between the three alternatives of embarking on a biography of the Queen, of writing a life of the Duke of Palmella, and of writing a biography of Dom Miguel. But I subsequently realized that if the first of these subjects presented certain difficulties to an historian wishing to write a history in the framework of a biography, the two others presented many more. During the first part of his life the diplomatist Duke of Palmella was not in Portugal at all, and was a more familiar figure in St. James's Street and the Rue Saint Honoré than he was in Black Horse Square. Dom Miguel, on the other hand, flared like a comet in the Lisbon sky for only two short periods in his long lifetime—between 1821 and 1824 (from the time of his return with the Portuguese Court from Brazil to his exile in Vienna as a result of the revolution known as the Abrilada), and between 1827 and 1835 (when he usurped the Portuguese throne and reigned as Absolute King). But Queen Carlota Joaquina, as long as she lived, whether in Rio de Janeiro or in Lisbon, was always on the Portuguese scene, while the year of her death, 1830, was marked by political convulsions all over Europe which swept away the last vestiges of that eighteenth century whose spirit she incarnated. The life-time of Queen Carlota Joaquina is therefore a clearly definable period.

The epoch with which my book deals is not a glorious one in Portuguese annals. Portugal has been famous in history for two types of heroes—her sailors and her priests. But in the period under review she threw up no truly heroic men. On the contrary, it was a period of national calamity, of civil discord, of economic distress. Nevertheless it richly repays study for two reasons. In the first place, the bitter struggle between the Constitutionalists and the Absolutists which began in Dona Carlota Joaquina's lifetime and which she infused with

---

*Published by Sidgwick and Jackson, 1938, under the title " Dictator of Portugal."

her own fanaticism left deep scars on Portuguese political life. By exhausting Portugal's vitality, by inflaming intestine hatreds, and by canalising the energies of the Portuguese into sterile political squabbles, it was directly responsible for her stagnation in the nineteenth century. The scars are not effaced even today. Therefore some knowledge of the epoch of Queen Carlota Joaquina is essential to anyone who desires to understand modern Portugal. In the second place, the history of that epoch presents an interesting and typical example of what happens, all the world over and at all eras, when an attempt is made to transplant alien political institutions (in this case, institutions based upon the Liberal principles of the French Revolution) into a country of ancient traditions unprepared to receive them, and inhabited by a people to whose national temperament they may be entirely unsuited. The moral of the tale has been admirably pointed in L. T. Chen's "History of Chinese Political Thought." "When an institution," he writes, "whose roots are not among the people, is introduced from the top, it is like plucking the flowers of a neighbour's garden to embellish the dying branches of one's own tree : there can be no life . . . the reconstruction of a nation's thought is not to be accomplished by the wholesale transplantation of the thoughts of another society : it must follow the natural development and must begin with the proper retention of elements of the old social heritage."

Only if the above truth is grasped is it possible to explain the progress which the existing government of General Carmona and Dr. Salazar has been able to achieve in the introduction of wide reforms through traditional Portuguese channels of paternal government. And the story of Queen Carlota Joaquina's life may serve also as a warning to foreign theorists who may be tempted to cry that this or that country "ought to" embrace this or that system of government foreign to its soil and air.

I owe thanks to Mr. Noel Blakiston for assistance in consulting diplomatic despatches in His Majesty's Record Office ; to Colonel da Costa Vriga of the National Library in Lisbon ; to Professor Prestage and Mrs. Garland Jayne for their indication and loan of useful books of reference ; and to the helpful Secretariado de Propaganda National in Lisbon for facilities in taking photographs of portraits in the Palace of Queluz. I owe thanks, too, to many Portuguese friends whose courteous inquiries as to the progress of the book have prodded me to renew my oft-interrupted labours. Last but not least, I feel I owe a debt of gratitude to all the Portuguese people, for if I have conducted long and enjoyable inquiries into their past history, the inspiration of my work has always been the affectionate regard which few of them have ever failed to arouse in me, since the day I first sprang on to the Lisbon quay.

MARCUS CHEKE

Chapter I

SOME five miles from Lisbon the palace of Queluz nestles among low hills to the left of the Cintra road. Built by the King of Portugal at the close of the seventeenth century, it is a charming example of those royal residences that were designed to imitate Versailles. But it has none of the monumental grandeur of the original. Queluz is a pavilion rather than a palace, a pavilion of coral pink faced with grey stone, seeming scarcely more permanent in substance than the painted scenery of a theatre. The principal façade facing south is flanked by two low wings of irregular length decorated in the baroque style. It overlooks a formal garden with flower-beds bordered with clipped yew hedges, fountains and statuary. Here a decaying Neptune attended by his nymphs presides over a little stone-edged basin stocked with gold-fish and carp. Here a divinity dressed like Madame de Pompadour reclines uneasily on the scales of a sea-monster; and beyond is a coppice of old elms dissected by wide straight paths leading to orna-mental gates, grottos encrusted with sea-shells, or fountains half hidden by camellia trees and magnolia. Beyond, again, are the rounded hills where the people of Lisbon used to gather in old days to watch the fireworks in the gardens on Saint Peter's night. It is a place which forcibly evokes the past. No great effort of the imagination is needed to conjure up to the mind's eye the Portuguese infantas in their brocade hooped skirts moving among the box hedges or loitering in a grotto's shade.

This palace and its little park are indissolubly associated with the memory of the Queen Carlota Joaquina, famous as the mother of the two Portuguese princes Dom Pedro and Dom Miguel whose exploits exerted a profound influence on the history of Brazil and Portugal, but deserving to be famous also for the part she herself played in the events of her epoch.

She was the daughter of King Charles the Fourth of Spain and of his Queen Maria Louisa of Parma. Her parentage is in itself important: the deformity, the decadence and the sensuality of the Spanish Bourbons can be read in Goya's canvases. She arrived in Portugal when she was only ten years old, to be solemnly married, in June, 1785, to the eighteen-year-old Prince John of Portugal. The marriage had been arranged seven years earlier, when the Princess was hardly out of her cradle, but when one of those treaties of friendship with Spain so common in Portuguese history—so common, and generally so short-lived—had needed to be cemented by a double betrothal, Dom John's sister Mariana Victoria being betrothed at the same time to Carlota Joaquina's uncle, Don Gabriel of Spain. The Portuguese Princess was taller and altogether more comely than the Spanish, and the people of

Lisbon, when they first set eyes on Dona Carlota Joaquina, exclaimed that they had given Spain a whiting in exchange for a sardine.

Whatever the Portuguese Ambassador at Madrid might write in praise of her white teeth and the perfection of her features, Carlota Joaquina was in fact an ugly duckling. She was undersized, and marked with smallpox. According, however, to the limited standards by which the royal personages of the period were judged, she was intelligent. Shortly before being sent to Portugal she underwent an examination in front of the Spanish court, and astonished everybody (it must be admitted that court etiquette would insist on astonishment being shown) by her knowledge of French and Latin and the Old and New Testaments. She especially delighted her audience by her style in dancing a minuet and an " English dance."

She was certainly precocious ; in some strange way her character must have become set before she said farewell to Madrid, for, as will be seen, she remained throughout her life Spanish rather than Portuguese and was never assimilated to her adopted country. Her distinguishing characteristic was her extreme vivacity. She showed an extraordinary passion for music and every kind of dance. She arrived in Lisbon accompanied by a bevy of chattering Spanish ladies who at a given signal would seize upon their castanets and break into breathless jotas and boleros. When, one afternoon in later years, she received William Beckford of Fonthill in the gardens of Queluz, she first made him run a race down the avenue with these nymphs, and then insisted on his giving an exhibition of his skill in the fandango. In short, she was a restless, mischievous child, giving evidence from her earliest years of an insatiable craving for amusement and excitement.

It was unfortunate that the Portuguese court provided a dismal contrast to the gaiety of her parents' court at Aranjuez. In order to understand why this should have been so it is necessary to throw a glance at the history of Portugal during the preceding half-century.

King John the Fifth, who died in 1750, was the Solomon of his age. He lavished the immense wealth which his kingdom derived from the gold and diamond mines of Brazil in maintaining a splendour second only to that of the court of France, and in establishing at the Lisbon cathedral a patriarchate which imitated in every detail the pomp and magnificence of Saint Peter's. As pious as he was ostentatious, he permitted the Church to acquire a wealth and influence that probably has no parallel in the history of any other Christian country. He transformed Lisbon into a kind of Holy City like Benares, an ant-hill of monks. He was succeeded on the throne by King Joseph the First, whose reign of twenty-seven years was distinguished by the enlightened but ferocious rule of his famous minister, the Marquis of Pombal. This extraordinary man rebuilt Lisbon, which had been reduced to ashes by a great earthquake. He then proceeded to make a calculated and systematic attack upon the influence of the Portuguese nobles and, having pretended to establish the complicity of the aged Marquis of Tavora in a mysterious attempt on the King's life, he caused him, together with his entire family, to be tortured and put to death on the scaffold. Pombal then conducted a hardly less terrible assault on the power of the clergy. He was the first statesman to expel the Jesuits, his example being followed shortly afterwards by the rest of Europe. During the last fifteen years of Pombal's rule, Portugal lived under a reign of terror. The prisons were crowded with noblemen and priests, and when his carriage rolled through the streets of Lisbon every window was slammed at his approach.

In cowing the aristocracy and brow-beating the clergy, it had been Pombal's aim to modernize his country. Much of his legislation was praiseworthy ; but his almost insane ferocity was abhorrent to the sentimental temperament of his countrymen. When King Joseph died, eight years before this story opens, and was succeeded by his daughter, Queen Maria the First, Pombal was hastily exiled to his country estates. The whole policy of the previous reign was reversed. The Queen, in harmony with the feelings of her subjects, immediately on her accession opened the prison doors, and invited the Church and the nobles to resume their part in the administration. But her healing efforts were too late. Pombal's drastic reforms had left Portugal exhausted. The mills and factories he had established fell into decay. The country had been reduced to a condition akin to paralysis. The memory of Pombal was like the memory of some horrible nightmare.

Queen Maria the First was a woman of fanatical religious convictions, whose actions were propelled by her confessors or by the priests who swarmed at her court. Her chief aim as Queen was to repair the insults inflicted on the Church by her father's minister. Workmen were called off rebuilding the earthquake-shattered capital to erect an elaborate temple dedicated to her favourite emblem, the heart of Jesus. When thieves broke into a church and scattered the consecrated wafers, she put her court into nine days' mourning, postponed all public business, and took part on foot, holding a candle, in a penitential procession up and down Lisbon. A true grand-daughter of King John the Fifth, whose inveterate passion it was to arrange ever more sumptuous religious processions, it was her preferred pastime to preside at Church ceremonies to celebrate the salvation of various obscure individuals who had been persuaded, generally in return for a court pension, to declare themselves converted to the true faith. But nothing could calm the pangs that she felt at the thought that her father's soul might be suffering eternal torment for having permitted the Marquis of Pombal to persecute Christ's representatives on earth. This dreadful apprehension preyed on her mind. As early as 1785, when the little Princess Carlota Joaquina arrived in Portugal, the Queen's behaviour was becoming increasingly odd. As the years passed her mind grew disordered. She fancied she saw her father's image " a calcined mass of cinder " (such was the description given to Beckford by her minister, the Marquis of Angeja) " in colour black and horrible, erected on a pedestal of molten iron, which a crowd of ghastly phantoms were in the act of dragging down."

In 1795, a fire having destroyed the Ajuda palace, the royal residence in Lisbon, the whole court moved to Queluz. Here the Queen lay all day behind closed shutters, and the silence of the gardens was sometimes broken by her agonizing shriek : " Ai Jesus ! Ai Jesus !" The ministers, the priests and courtiers who comprised her court were perhaps not unsuited for attendance on a demented sovereign. Indeed, they might have been chosen by a skilled *metteur en scène* as the chorus to some macabre play. Many, such as the Marquis of Alorna and other kinsmen of the unhappy Tavoras, having incurred Pombal's enmity, had lain rotting for years in the Junqueira prison. When the Queen had ordered them to be released they had emerged, as one eye-witness described them, like " living corpses," obsessed by two passions : a burning desire to be revenged on the fallen minister and a still fiercer ambition to recover their confiscated estates. The minds of some, such as the merry Count of San Lourenço, had become unhinged by their sufferings. It is easily understandable that these half-crazed and vengeance-obsessed courtiers did not contribute much towards dispelling the atmosphere of melancholia and insanity that hung over Queluz.

The society of her young husband offered Dona Carlota Joaquina no resources. Dom John was a clumsily built, lethargic, awkward youth who yawned at parties. It is true that he was amiable and good-natured, and had never been known to lose his temper with anybody, except on one occasion when he lifted his cane to chastise his mother's impertinent black dwarf Dona Anna who had baited him—though she scuttled out of reach. But his temperament was as different to his bride's as water is to fire. It must be borne in mind that his mother, Queen Maria, and his father, the Prince Consort Dom Pedro, who died in 1789, were respectively niece and uncle to each other, King Joseph, who had no sons, having solved the problem of the succession by marrying his eldest daughter to his own brother. Dom John was essentially a Braganza, and he represented to the point of caricature the Portuguese temperament, so different to the Spanish. He was a Portuguese Braganza, and she was a Spanish Bourbon : this simple fact is sufficient to explain the fatal incompatibility of their characters. Though their countries are neighbours the one to the other, the Portuguese and the Spanish agree in nothing. Nowhere in the world has geography made bedfellows so ill-assorted as in the Iberian Peninsula.

The more time passed, the more irritated did Dona Carlota Joaquina feel with Dom John. She did not share her husband's relish for ecclesiastical ceremonies. She was disgusted by his physical timidity, his indolence and his obstinacy. She was revolted by his traits of eccentricity ; for instance, his habit of carrying in his pocket two small boxes, the one containing snuff and the other grilled chicken's legs to gnaw at idle moments. He on his side was sensitive to her dislike, and as the years passed he spent an increasing portion of his time away from her, in retirement at Mafra—the vast and sombre palace raised at Dom John the Fifth's command, in an attempt to outbuild the Escurial, on the wide plain between Cintra and the

Torres Vedras hills. Here he lived in a circle of boon companions, monks and friars, spending long hours dozing in the incense-loaded twilight of the royal chapel.

Few and meagre were the amusements at the disposal of his child-bride. To convert a saloon at Queluz into a cocoon-hung house for silk-worms; to pinch and tease Dona Anna; to play her guitar among her Spanish ladies, whose restless castanets created a small oasis of Andalusian high-spirits in the surrounding boredom; to accompany, on stated anniversaries, a picnic pilgrimage to some local shrine—such were her diversions at Queluz. And the only gossip to break the monotony would be the occasional news of how some new miracle had occurred in one of the Lisbon churches—how the image of Our Saviour at San Rocque had spouted blood, or how the image of Saint Anthony had come to life and had been found by the priests blessing beggar-children in the aisle.

Four years after Dona Carlota Joaquina's coming to Portugal her marriage to Dom John was consummated, and in the following fifteen years she bore him a numerous family. In 1793, the Infanta Maria Isobel; in 1795, the Prince Dom Antonio, who died in infancy; in 1797, the Infanta Isabel Maria; in 1798, Dom Pedro, afterwards celebrated as the first Emperor of Brazil; in 1800, the Infanta Maria Francisca, who later married the Spanish Infante Dom Carlos, the central figure of the first Carlist war. In 1802 was born the most remarkable of all her children, Dom Miguel, whose very name was destined in future years to excite the enthusiasm and animosity of Europe. A last child was born to Dona Carlota Joaquina in 1805, the Infanta Maria d'Assuncâo.

During these years Dona Carlota Joaquina's character was developing, but it was not changing; its traits were growing steadily more accentuated. Mischievous and restless as a child, she was intensely vital, malicious and vindictive as a woman. She had a strange gift for hatred (as an old woman she used to fondle a mule which she had purchased and made her favourite because it had kicked Sir William Clinton), and her placid, indolent, ungainly husband was the first whom she grew to hate, hating him with the peculiar intensity that a person can feel for another whom he despises but on whom he is dependent.

As she grew up, her passion for hunting and shooting—she loved to let fly at partridges from the saddle with a heavy musket—was a symptom of her exuberant vitality. Both she and her husband lived in familiarity with the common people, but for different reasons. Dom John chose his cronies among friars and grooms because he distrusted more worldly men. Dona Carlota Joaquina loved the people simply because their amusements were hers. She loved the very smell of the stables, the dust of a country fair, the rough excitements of the bull-ring. But neither dancing all night nor galloping across country all day could calm her eternal gnawing restlessness and ennui. A gypsy woman who had once told her character had written a verse for her to sing—

" En porfías soy manchega
Y en malicia soy gitana
Mis intentos y mis planes
No se me quitan del alma."

(" Stubborn in my quarrels, with the malice of a gypsy, my schemes and plans never leave me in peace.") The rhyme described her perfectly.

During her years of child-bearing two events took place which exercised a lasting influence over Dona Carlota Joaquina's life. Dom John was Queen Maria's second son, the heir to the throne being Dom José, the Prince of Brazil, a delicate, rather priggish boy who had been carefully educated by masters chosen by Pombal. When Dona Carlota Joaquina first came to Portugal, therefore, she had nothing to look forward to at court save the tedious existence of the wife of a younger son. But in 1788, at the age of twenty-seven, the Prince of Brazil succumbed to the smallpox. He had been married, at King Joseph's death-bed, to his own aunt, the Infanta Maria Benedicta, who was fifteen years older than he was. He died childless. Dona Carlota now found herself the wife of the prince who stood in direct line of succession to the Portuguese throne. Four years afterwards the Queen's mental derangement increased to such an extent that a council of physicians declared there was no hope of her recovery, and Dom John, by a decree signed by him on the 10th February, 1792, became Prince Regent of Portugal.

It was these two turns in the wheel of fortune that first directed Dona Carlota Joaquina's thoughts towards political intrigue. She determined to play a part as leader of the Portuguese court. Her first essay was innocent enough—the foundation of an order of nobility for the gratification of her ladies-in-waiting. The insignia of this " Order of Noble Ladies of the Queen Saint Isabel " was a gold medallion displaying an image of the royal saint, with the device *pauperum solacio* in blue enamel, suspended across the right shoulder by a rose-pink ribbon edged with white.

Her second enterprise was something very much more serious and more dangerous. In 1806 Dom John fell ill, and was cloistered for several months at Mafra. Dona Carlota Joaquina in his absence wove a plot to have him declared insane like his mother, and to have herself made Regent in his stead. Considerable mystery surrounds this affair, whose consequences, in spite of the fact that the plot failed and never, indeed, had any prospects of success, were destined to be far-reaching. It is said that the Princess's treachery was betrayed to the Prince Regent by the Marquis of Loulé, the unfortunate nobleman whose murder at Villa Vicosa seventeen years afterwards she was supposed to have contrived. Certainly information reached Dom John's ears from some courtier-spy passing to and fro between Queluz and Mafra, and it is probable that he learned also the substance of the letter which the Princess sent by secret messenger to Madrid to implore aid from the Spanish court.

"I appeal to you in the greatest consternation," she wrote on the 13th August to her father, King Charles the Fourth (the letter survives in the Spanish historical archives), "to inform you that the prince is every day becoming more deranged, and as a consequence I am in danger of ruin, for those men (she is evidently referring to some of the Prince's circle at Mafra hostile to her) are becoming daily more powerful. The time has come for you to help me, and your grand-children. . . . The only remedy is for you to send intimation that you wish me to enter the government, and that you will not accept a refusal, or else your reply will be to take up arms to avenge the affronts and insults to which you know I am constantly exposed. . . . This is the only means of preventing the spilling of much blood in this Kingdom, because the Court wants to draw sword on my behalf, and the people also . . . for it is obvious to all that the Prince is out of his mind. . . ." On the same day she wrote a similar letter, in an even more piteous strain, to her mother.

It was an absurd, almost childish plot, revealing her immaturity and inexperience. The letters were thoroughly mendacious. The Prince was not mad; the court and the people were not, and never were, disposed to take up arms on her behalf against Dom John, whose imperturbable good-nature and unfailing kindness made him universally popular.

It may be said of this Prince that, though indecision and indolence were his most obvious characteristics, he was not devoid of a certain shrewd sense which enabled him again and again to take the right decision in a political as well as in a domestic crisis. As a result, though he lived in an epoch of unparalleled political convulsions when most of the sovereigns of Europe lost their crowns, Dom John, who succeeded in due time to the Portuguese throne, lived and died a King.

The effects of Dona Carlota Joaquina's first political intrigue were important because they marked a turning point in her relations with her husband. Already there had been quarrels between them in which he had been made to feel the lash of her Spanish tongue. Already he had been made to listen to outrageous charges based on the idlest tittle-tattle about his supposed infatuation for a lady-in-waiting called Dona Eugenia de Menezes. Already she had upbraided him coarsely on the score of the boundless confidence he was placing in his hair-dresser, Francisco Lobato. The Prince had listened to her in obstinate silence, too slow-witted to parry her wounding thrusts, and choosing therefore another method of self-defence—passively shutting himself up at Mafra, where her rasping Spanish accents could not reach him, leaving her to vent her exasperation and hatred in spiteful jokes among her Spanish ladies. But in 1806, when the proof of disloyalty was added to the utter incompatibility of their natures, the breach between Dom John and Dona Carlota Joaquina became complete. At this crisis in their relationship they adopted the roles that neither relin-quished until separated by death. They lived their own lives in private, meeting only on ceremonial occasions, which grew rarer as time passed.

Their fierce hostility, mute on his side and articulate on hers, was to be a cardinal factor in Portuguese history for the next twenty years.

The memoirs of Madame Junot, afterwards Duchess of Abrantes, provide us with a picture of the royal pair as they were at this period. " My God ! How ugly he is !" Junot exclaimed when he returned from presenting his credentials as French Ambassador. " How ugly the Princess is ! How ugly they both are !" And Madame Junot herself, when she was received in her turn, was no more complimentary. It must be admitted that she was French, and being French she found everything outside France ridiculous. She was a product of Paris, where time had lately been moving at a terrific velocity. So it is scarcely surprising that she was shocked by the antiquated, Moresco-Gothic manners of the court, and by finding Dona Carlota Joaquina's ladies-in-waiting all seated cross-legged on the floor, even if she did not, like another visitor, surprise them employed removing insects from each other's ornately bejewelled heads. But though the portraits which Madame Junot has left us may have been prejudiced, they were certainly drawn from the life. She describes the Prince Regent as stout and swarthy, with a thick and pendant lip, a head too big for his body, and a shock of hair like a negro's. Contemporary paintings (which, when they portray princes, are generally as flattering as possible) do not do much to contradict Madame Junot. Nevertheless it is only fair to add that Dom John had a certain natural dignity, combined in normal circumstances with a sort of winning benignity of expression, which impressed most foreigners favourably.

It is really not possible, on the other hand, to find any contemporary evidence to correct her portrait of the Princess. Already at this time, in 1805, Dona Carlota was perhaps the ugliest royal personage that has ever existed. She stood hardly more than four feet six inches in height, with bloodshot, malevolent eyes. She had a hooked nose, a nut-cracker chin, and bluish lips that opened to reveal teeth like great bones, " uneven like Pan's flute." Madame Junot describes this singular figure dressed in a rich robe of Indian muslin, embroidered with gold and silver, attached at the throat and shoulders with magnificent diamonds. " Her unruly and dirty hair," she writes, " was bound with pearls and diamonds of extraordinary beauty. Her dress was also sewn with pearls of an inestimable value. She wore in her ears a pair of ear-rings such as I have never seen on any other person ; a pair of pear-shaped diamonds, as long as my thumb and of a water as limpid as crystal. These were superb and most beautiful ornaments. But the face they framed was so horrible that their beauty was eclipsed. I had the impression that I was looking at some strange being not of our own species."

This was the garb of Dona Carlota Joaquina dressed to receive an ambassadress at Queluz. Her appearance on less exceptional occasions, equipped for riding or hunting, was even more bizarre. She wore an old coat like a man's, cut in green cloth with gold lace frogs, a split skirt of the same material, and a man's cocked hat. Her horse having once fallen on her, she fractured a leg and was permanently lamed, but this accident did not impair her horsemanship. She always rode astride. " I was once at Queluz," writes Madame Junot, " when she was starting out. When I saw this figure, so strange in itself, now so weirdly dressed, I felt as if I were gazing on some fantastic apparition. She was sitting astride a little black horse, small like all Portuguese horses, but bad-tempered enough to make a good rider nervous. The Princess gave her mount several cuts with her whip over its neck and shoulders and made it manœuvre round the courtyard in front of the palace. Then she set off at a gallop like a fifteen-year-old schoolboy out of college. At first she struck me as so ridiculous that I had great difficulty in remembering that my diplomatic status made gravity imperative. But immediately my impulse to laugh gave way to feelings of a very different sort. I could not see this personage whom nature had deformed in every part without feeling a disgust so strong that it extinguished my first instinct of gaiety, and I turned my eyes away. I could not think of her as a woman, and yet I knew at the time facts which abundantly proved she was one."   ·

This last sly stroke refers to something which seems so utterly at variance with the Infanta's exterior appearance that it would be incredible were it not so well proved by the correspondence of the period. Dona Carlota Joaquina's vivacity could make a man forget her ugliness and could hold him captivated. Nor was it surprising that she should have become the subject of court gossip when her later accouchements coincided with a notorious deterioration in her relations with her husband.

Slander was in especially brisk circulation about the time of the Junot's coming to Lisbon. Dona Carlota Joaquina was growing tired of Queluz ; she dreaded gruesome encounters with the mad Queen who was sometimes to be met with in sequestered walks about the palace grounds with her white hair streaming in the wind, attended by some watchful, athletic-looking physicians. She therefore spent much time at her Quinta of Ramalhâo (the house which Beckford had rented from the Street Arriaga da Cunhas on his first visit to Portugal), which she had purchased in 1794. Scandal asserted that the Infanta's retirements at this Quinta were far from innocent ; that they were spent, to speak bluntly, in pastimes reminiscent of Messalina, and that the thickets of her pleasure-grounds concealed orgies in which it was by no means a privilege only of individuals of courtly rank to share. Many of these allegations were doubtless invented at a later date, and sprang from political enmity. Nor can the serious historian substantiate them by solid proof. But in attempting to draw Dona Carlota's portrait, he cannot omit reference to their existence.

Chapter II

THE summoning of the States General by Louis the Sixteenth in 1789 is conveniently regarded by historians as marking the end of the eighteenth century. The changes which came over the face of Europe in the following thirty years were so vast that it is difficult for us in retrospection to imagine that by-gone age when the Queen of France and her court moved like some gorgeous ballet through the galleries and gardens of Versailles. For those changes were not brought about by political convulsions alone. The introduction of steam and machinery—the Industrial Revolution—destroyed the atmosphere of the past century more ruthlessly than the decrees of the National Assembly, modern systems of education, or the armies of Napoleon.

But though the eighteenth century, and all that those words imply, was first shattered in France in 1789, it lingered on for several unquiet years in kingdoms and principalities beyond the French frontiers. In Parma and Tuscany, in Saxony and Spain, statesmen received with incredulity the news contained in the latest despatches from Paris. They learned with horror how the French people, who seemed suddenly to have gone mad, had insulted and imprisoned their King. The courtiers and ecclesiastics who shuddered at these crimes belonged to social systems that centred round Church and throne. These institutions still appeared to them to be in their very essence as permanent as the landscape, and they themselves still wore the powdered wigs and the knee-breeches, the lace ruffles and the buckles, of the *ancien régime*. Such was the costume of the polite, privileged audience that gathered at the Palazzo Sessa in Naples, to admire Sir William Hamilton's latest addition to his collection of busts and bronzes, and to rave over Lady Hamilton's classic poses. It was true that certain signs of an alarming spirit of change were visible all over Europe, even in the carefree *décor* of Naples. Some young men there were who affected an enthusiasm for new-fangled liberal principles, who quoted Rousseau and talked of equality, and who—the outer man being a symbol—sported new fashions in pantaloons and trousers, wore their hair unpowdered, smoked cigars and sprouted whiskers. For the most part these belonged to the professional classes, being students in law or medicine, or budding poets. But among them were to be found certain young sparks of the aristocracy whose liberal ideas and whose passion for Romantic scenery and Gothic architecture outraged their elders. The statesmen and ecclesiastics of countries far removed from Paris did not, however, recognize in these uncouth crazes the omens of a coming cataclysm which was to engulf them all.

During the last decade of the century the kingdom which remained the least troubled by the echoes of terrible happenings in France was certainly Portugal, which was the most remote from the theatre of revolution. Alike during the September massacres, the Terror, and the first triumphs of Bonaparte, Portugal lay wrapped in a trance-like tranquillity. " How often," exclaimed Beckford, lolling in a window of the monastery of Cadafaiz one June evening in 1794, " how often, contrasting my present situation with the horrid disturbed state of every part of the continent did I bless the hour when my steps were first directed to Portugal ! " No wonder that forty years afterwards, in his lonely but still splendid hermitage at Bath, he used to recall the magical " Claude-like " Cintra hills, and that he should delight in preparing for publication those travel-diaries which are still today the best guide-book to Portugal.

They are still the best guide-book because fortunately, in spite of all the changes that Portugal has witnessed since Beckford's day, its countryside has to a great extent remained unaltered. Little industrial development has conglomerated the population in factories or mines. Though modern highroads are nowadays ubiquitous, the traveller has only to step aside to find himself surrounded by an agricultural life of biblical simplicity. The water-wheels and the ox-carts, the white-washed windmills crowning the green hills, the very bonnets and thatch cloaks of the peasants, are of an immemorial pattern, in the verdant and smiling valleys that provide so remarkable a contrast to the arid Spanish plains. The Atlantic still beats on a coastline unspoiled, save in one or two places, by villas and promenades. Between the Douro and the Tagus, busy with the commerce of Oporto and Lisbon, the coast stretches in almost unbroken solitude, studded here and there with picturesque fishing villages in whose vicinity are to be found, perched on the cliffs above the sea, the grass-grown battlements of some ochre-coloured fort, still seeming on guard against Barbary pirates.

But the Portugal that Beckford knew displayed in the structure of its society extraordinary features of which no trace remains today. It was still the Portugal of King John the Fifth, an absolute monarchy with a king whose powers were as despotic in theory as those of an Oriental despot, and supported economically by the wealth derived from its colonies overseas. Its foreign trade was almost exclusively in the hands of foreigners, mostly English, who imported corn and textiles in exchange for colonial produce. Among the Portuguese themselves the spirit of enterprise had died out, and both the filth of the Lisbon streets and the swarms of beggars at the church doors were symptoms of a radical decay. In spite of Pombal's reforms, the power of the Church was still tremendous, and the converts still immobilized vast capital resources. Out of a total population of about three million, three hundred thousand were either in holy orders or indirectly connected with monastic establishments. In Lisbon alone there were no less than a hundred and eighty monasteries. Practically every large building visible anywhere in the countryside was either a church or a convent. And besides the monks, some of whom were efficient agriculturalists, there existed a swarm of friars who lived in casual intimacy with the populace and exercised a tyrannical influence over every action of their lives. What the confessor was to the noble household, the friar was to the Lisbon hovel.

For three centuries the priesthood had kept the people in submission, plunged in what Protestant travellers described as abject superstition. The science of medicine was almost unknown. If Saint Braz or Saint Marcos failed to respond to a votive offering, application was made to remedies worthy of witch-doctors. Crushed snails were put to poultice open sores, and elderly invalids were nourished on viper broth. The aristocracy were hardly superior in learning to the peasantry. Though Queen Maria the First's reign was marked by the foundation of a Royal Academy of Sciences, and though the operatic performances of the countless musicians and singers maintained by the Royal Chapel were unexcelled in Europe, the education of the average Portuguese nobleman was confined to a smattering of fanatical doctrine. Having succeeded in his life object of securing a court pension, he passed his days in indolent vacuity, in promiscuous familiarity with the grooms, underlings and negroes of his huge establishment. There is, indeed, something attractive in the Portuguese tradition, which still survives, of regarding the servants of a household as part of the family. At moments of emotion the marquis was, and is, to be seen receiving a hearty hug from his coachman. Both shared an identical relish for bull-fights, miracles and squibs. Both ate much the same food, and the English traveller Mrs. Marianne Baillie noted that "the courtly whisper of the highest-bred fidalgo, loaded with garlic and oil, differed not at all from the breath of the humblest peasant."

Queen Maria the First's consort Dom Pedro was commonly supposed to have been unable to read and write. Her Minister of Marine could add and subtract, but had never mastered multiplication and division. The Count de San Lourenço used customarily to entertain his guests at dinner with garbled accounts of the part he had played at the Congress of Aix-la-Chapelle, which actually he had never attended. The Marquis of Castelo Melhor, according to the description left to us by the Marquis of Fronteira in his memoirs, whiled away his afternoons tormenting and cajoling in turns the favourite old negress whose duty it was to swat flies round him. The sole passion and pastime of the wealthy Count de Villa Nova was to precede the canopy of the Sacrament in a scarlet mantle, tinkling a silver bell. "He is always in close attendance on the Host," wrote Beckford, "and passes the flower of his days in this singular species of dangle-ment. No lover was ever more jealous of his mistress than this ingenuous youth of his bell. He cannot endure any other person should give it vibration." As for the Count de Villa Verde, a Minister of State, his corpulence and gluttony defy description. After eating six men's dinners he used to subside into a chair and quaff iced water throughout the evening, punctuated by resounding hiccoughs. In fact, in comparison with individuals of our own world, the courtiers of Queluz must appear so odd, and their manners so antiquated, that it is wellnigh impossible for us to form any conception of them, unless we picture a gallery of faces reflected in the depths of a time-corroded, twisted mirror.

Even at the time of Madame Junot's residence in Lisbon, however, the picturesque, crazy edifice of Portuguese society was being undermined. In spite of Portugal's geographic remoteness, and in spite of the fact that both Government and Church did their utmost to suppress new ideas (no Portuguese nobleman was allowed to travel abroad without special permission from the King, which was seldom granted), the theories of the French revolution were beginning to circulate in secret. It is necessary at this stage to say something of the Freemasons.

Freemasonry had been introduced into Portugal as early as 1733. It was inspired by a spirit of free thought and criticism that immediately rendered it suspect to the authorities. But the horror with which it was regarded by the majority of the population as well as by the Government was mainly due to the fact that the masons directed their inquiries towards established religion. Their attitude of mind towards the mysteries of the Church was held to be utterly blasphemous. The secrecy in which their activities were wrapped also heightened the loathing with which they were regarded. We read of masons being imprisoned in 1742, 1762, and 1778. By the latter date there were certainly lodges at Lisbon and Coimbra, and soon afterwards the movement gained impetus in the capital following a mysterious meeting of masons on board the English frigate *Phoenix*.

There is no doubt that certain well-meaning but misguided Englishmen encouraged the Portuguese masons. They were enthralled, no doubt, by the revivalist religious movement that was then sweeping over England. In 1801 we hear of a lodge in Lisbon near the Estrella in the house of a certain Andrew Jacob. The English were ignorant of the real political problems of the country where they lived, and they did not see clearly that an enthusiasm which they themselves, being individualists like all Englishmen, regarded as an effort towards personal salvation, became for foreigners a channel for subversive political doctrine emanating from France. Portuguese officers in the army seem to have been particularly open to conversion.

The Prince Regent's Chief of Police, Pina Manique, was indefatigable in his attempts to suppress Freemasonry. It is significant that in his conversation he bracketed them with the Jacobins. But he met with dubious success. In dark corners, cloaked figures were to be seen exchanging furtive signals and whispering their doubts as to the veracity of the latest miracle attributed to the image of Saint Anthony. The whole system of Church and State was threatened when such articles of faith were questioned. Uneasiness spread. Dreadful rumours reached Pina Manique's ears : the " Marseillaise " had been heard being sung in a café ; Mr. Ratton's workmen were plotting to plant a tree of liberty in the Rocio.

But if threatened from within, Portugal was to a far more dangerous extent threatened by events abroad. The rise of Napoleon's empire soon constituted a direct menace to Portugal's very existence as a nation

The French Emperor, bent upon destroying the only Power that dared challenge his supremacy in Europe, determined to cripple

England's foreign trade. The various states which he had subjugated, or had cajoled into alliance, could be counted upon to comply with his commands. One of these allies was Spain.

It would be beyond the limits of this biography to review in detail the sordid motives, the selfishness and cowardice, which characterized the relations of the Spanish court with Napoleon. The Emperor was actuated throughout by the conviction that a Bourbon in Spain was a potential menace to his throne. He treated with King Charles the Fourth for the time being, only to further his own designs, and subjected to successive humiliations the Spanish monarchy which it was his intention to destroy. King Charles had surrendered the government into the hands of the Queen's lover, Godoy, whose whole policy in regard to France consisted in servile acquiescence. He consented to sign a treaty of alliance with Napoleon in 1796.

It is not difficult to explain the dangerous implications of such a treaty as far as Portugal was concerned. An eternal apprehension existed among the Portuguese that their hated Spanish neighbours might march over the frontier and attempt to revive by conquest the empire of Philip the Second. Moreover, if Spain was now the ally of France, Portugal was the ally of Great Britain, Napoleon's inveterate enemy.

Portugal and Great Britain have been united for six hundred years in an unbroken alliance, which is perhaps the most remarkable political connection known to history. This ancient alliance is based on geographic reasons, and has been cemented by mutual interest and sentiment. Both Britain and Portugal are essentially maritime nations looking to the Atlantic Ocean. Both are the mother-countries of vast empires overseas. Each has rendered services of incalculable value to the other. On nine successive occasions British arms have helped Portugal successfully to resist the invader, while the Portuguese coastline and her Atlantic islands have succoured the British fleet. A numerous and opulent British merchant community resided at Lisbon and Oporto, and, at the end of the eighteenth century, were still in enjoyment of privileges bestowed on them by a succession of treaties. Pombal, whose jealousy had been excited by the English merchants' prosperity, had introduced severe laws that encumbered, but did not permanently injure, their commercial activity. On the accession of Queen Maria the First they had largely reasserted their position.

These facts will suffice to demonstrate the position of extreme delicacy and danger in which Portugal was now placed. The Emperor Napoleon assessed the value of the Portuguese trade to England, and constantly pressed the servile Godoy to embarrass the feeble government at Queluz. For the Portuguese the years 1796 to 1804 were years of uncertainty and anxiety, punctuated by recurring complaints, made in unison by the French and Spanish governments, against Portugal's commerce with Great Britain. In 1801 Godoy even persuaded Charles the Fourth to declare war, and pushed a Spanish army across the frontier. The Spaniards' arms were antiquated and their generals incompetent, but the Portuguese had no equipment and no generals at all. A German princeling, the Duke of Waldeck, was hastily summoned to command the Prince Regent's troops. On arrival in Lisbon he caught cold and expired. His place was taken by the eighty-year-old Duke of Lafoes, a fantastic figure in black velvet boots, his cheeks covered in rouge and patches. This commander did not even acquire the distinction of leading the retreat. A few weeks after war had been declared the futile campaign petered out, and peace was signed at Badajos.

The signatories of this meaningless treaty on behalf of Spain were Godoy and Lucien Bonaparte, who exacted an undertaking that the Portuguese ports were henceforth to be closed to the British. But undoubtedly their main object, which they succeeded in achieving, was to exact a huge ransom simply in return for calling the dogs off their victim. The Portuguese, to buy off their tormentors, raised a loan with Hopes of Amsterdam and Barings of London, on the security of the diamond and tobacco imports from Brazil ; so that Godoy and Lucien Bonaparte returned well satisfied to Madrid. The treaty was meaningless because Napoleon saw no reason why this blackmail-money should not be turned into a regular tribute, and so he refused to ratify the treaty, which the Portuguese therefore had to sign all over again at Madrid after making further promises to close their ports against the English—promises which Portuguese feeling together with British influence would never have permitted to be carried out—and paying the ransom twice over.

But if the Portuguese envoys returned to Lisbon in the belief that French rapacity had been satisfied, they were soon disappointed. If Portugal had consented to buy a treaty of peace, why should she not now be requested to buy a formal treaty of neutrality ?

In March, 1802, the Marshal Lannes was appointed French Ambassador and arrived in Lisbon to sell them one, figuratively, at the pistol point.

It is interesting to remark that whereas Napoleon employed in dealing with defenceless neutral countries the identical cat-and-mouse tactics used at a later age by Herr Hitler, he likewise employed subversive methods which Hitler is erroneously supposed to have invented. The Marshal Lannes was instructed to cultivate in Portugal a political party in favour of French revolutionary doctrines. He set to work to organise a fifth column among the masons. He met with considerable success, and thus at its very inception we find Portugal's " left-wing " acting the part of collaborationists contrary to the spirit of the ancient alliance with Great Britain.

It is difficult nowadays to appreciate the sensation that was caused in foreign capitals at the end of the eighteenth century by the arrival of a French ambassador. He appeared like the inhabitant of some other planet. He was regarded not merely as the representative of a terrifying new military power, but also with the awe, devotion and repugnance which is inspired by the prophet of a new religion. People gazed with astonishment at his equipages and his liveries, examined and themselves eagerly copied the cut of his clothes and the set of his hair, and paraded their sympathies for French principles by means of French cockaded hats and luxuriant whiskers.

To deal with the Marshal Lannes, the Prince Regent, Dom John, sent for Antonio de Araujo, a diplomat of long experience who had served at The Hague, Berlin and Paris, and who now returned from the Portuguese Legation in St. Petersburg to assume control of the Ministry of Foreign Affairs.

Antonio de Araujo was a man of the world, and a subtle negotiator. A single incident will suffice to illustrate the resource of this accomplished man, who played so prominent and at the same time so mysterious a part in the Portuguese drama of 1807. On his return journey from St. Petersburg he stopped in Paris, where Madame de Talleyrand entrusted him with two valuable ornaments to carry to friends of hers across the Pyrenees. One of these was a blue-enamel clock with the hours marked by twelve splendid diamonds, which he was to carry to the Duchess of Ossun. The other was a pearl and diamond collar, for the Marqueza de Oriza. In travelling across Spain, Araujo's coach was set upon by thieves. They flung his terrified secretary into a muddy ditch and demanded of the minister that he should surrender either his money or his life. Araujo never for an instant lost his imperturbable good-humour. He was robbed of his purse but he saved the jewels. The clock he had stuffed into his boot, and he had slipped the necklace into the seat of his breeches.

Araujo was a Francophil, and it must not be supposed that his liking for the French sprang only from his conviction that they were the winning side. He had a genuine taste for French culture, French manners and French bonnets. He was a close friend of both the Junots, who succeeded Lannes. In comparison with the Count of Vila Verde, Madame Junot considered Araujo perfectly Parisian. She said she liked his " little grey-black wicked eye and his delightful wit." He, on his side, did all in his power to render the Junot's stay in Lisbon agreeable. He even did his best, though without success, to waive the tedious but long-established ceremonial dictating that a French Ambassador on his arrival in Lisbon must sit down *alone* with the Chief of the Protocol at a banquet at his Embassy laid for eighty persons. He was more successful in securing, at Junot's request, the removal of Pina Manique, whose indefatigable activity had hitherto ensured the suppression of all books, plays or poems tainted with the dangerous French doctrines. The disgrace of Pina Manique was an important step in the French plan for organising a fifth column.

In fact, Araujo, who had been called upon to cope with French pressure, was a fifth columnist himself. He was soon the acknowledged leader of the French party. His nomination to the Ministry of Foreign Affairs spelt a policy of appeasement, which was bound to lead to disaster. In 1804, a year before the arrival of the Junots, Araujo negotiated and signed a disgraceful treaty which amounted to this : Napoleon promised to leave Portugal in peace in return for a monthly tribute of forty thousand pounds.

In embarking on the policy that Araujo's promotion made inevitable, historians have charged the Portuguese court with cowardice. It would be as sensible to scold a naked man for shivering. Portugal's defences were in ruin, her army was disorganized, and her fleet decayed. Nevertheless, though the French party and Araujo seemed to have the upper hand at Lisbon in their efforts to placate the bully, the Portuguese who had some fight in them, and who were of course immediately styled the English party, since they looked for help in their distress to England, were more numerous. And it is interesting at this point to glance at the personality of the Englishman who was at this time minister in Lisbon.

It may be that Lord Strangford, whose Legation was put in the shade by the clatter and lavish hospitality of the Junots, had little cosmopolitan charm, but he had those solid qualities which allow Britain to continue to flourish like some great oak while mushroom empires rise and crumble. He was short-sighted, and one day in the studio of the Portuguese painter Sequeira he made a solemn bow to an artist's dummy, under the impression that he was saluting Snr. de Araujo. Nevertheless he was a fine man. Byron wrote of him :—

" Hibernian Strangford, with thine eyes of blue
And boasted locks of red or auburn hue."

He had arrived in Lisbon as secretary in 1802, and had distinguished himself by publishing an English edition of Camoês' poems—nowadays it would be regarded as an adroit piece of cultural propaganda. He was appointed Minister-Plenipotentiary in 1806. A year later he found himself faced with a first-rate crisis.

In August, 1807, France and Spain together presented an ultimatum to the Portuguese Government demanding anew that the Portuguese ports should be closed to the English, that English residents in Portugal should be arrested, and their property confiscated. Portugal was ordered, in short, to submit to the Berlin Decrees by which Napoleon had declared the British Isles to be in a state of blockade. In the event of these demands not being complied with, the French Chargé d'Affaires (Junot had left Portugal two years earlier to join the Emperor on the battlefield of Austerlitz) was instructed to ask for his passport on the 1st September, together with the Spanish Ambassador.

The Portuguese cabinet was appalled by this brutal ultimatum. The proposals were preposterous, yet it was evident that Portugal was menaced by an immediate invasion. The prestige of Napoleon's armies struck terror in every breast. Araujo, of course, counselled acquiescence. He seems to have honestly believed that some arrangement was still possible. The English party, on the other hand, under the leadership of the courtier Dom Rodrigo de Sousa Coutinho, realizing that a French invasion was imminent and inevitable, were in favour of the Prince Regent's acting in concordance with the advice of the British Cabinet—of his quitting Portugal and, together with the mad Queen, the Portuguese court and government, setting sail over the Atlantic to Brazil.

Chapter III

WHILE these events were going forward, Dona Carlota Joaquina remained isolated at Ramalhâo. She was resentful at never being consulted and never informed of anything that was going on. But it is hardly surprising that Dom John and his Cabinet should have declined to take her into their confidence when they were aware that she was conducting a secret correspondence with Madrid—that is to say, with her father, who was now Napoleon's ally. Also, she had adopted an attitude of uncompromising hostility not only towards her husband, but towards all his ministers without exception. Her sharp witticisms were carried to their ears. They grew to dislike as much as they distrusted her. So in tacit agreement with the Prince Regent, they adopted the one tactic to which she could find no answer ; they boycotted her—they put her into political Coventry. As a result, her heart turned ever more fixedly towards Spain, while her dislike and contempt of her husband grew until they extended to the whole Portuguese nation. Her thoughts centred round far-off Madrid ; and her only hope of ever finding herself freed from her exasperating situation was that her father might one day be persuaded to intervene on her behalf.

Dom John lay at Mafra in a state of the most painful irresolution. The wonderful project of removing his court to Brazil was not a novel idea. Pombal had seriously entertained it at the time of the Spanish invasion of 1765. Lord Rosslyn and Lord St. Vincent, who had come to Lisbon in 1806 on a special mission to attempt to persuade the Portuguese to put their country in a state of defence had urged the Brazil scheme as the only alternative. But Dom John dreaded the thought of being separated from a landscape that he had known since childhood. Above all, he dreaded the unknown terrors of a sea voyage. The altars of the royal chapel smoked with incense, but the saints he invoked vouchsafed no clear guidance. September came, and the French and Spanish envoys left Lisbon. Araujo's appeals for appeasement grew more insistent, while the agitated courtiers and monks at Mafra were divided into two parties, the one supporting Araujo and the other standing behind Coutinho. By the end of four more weeks no definite decision had yet been taken one way or the other—for surrender or retreat.

When Dona Carlota Joaquina realized the full implications of the international situation, she was acutely alarmed, but she had no thought other than for herself. On the 27th September, she wrote two vaguely worded letters to her parents, imploring them to take her and their unhappy grandchildren under their protection. The letters opened with obsequious expressions of contrition for her past conduct;

evidently her earlier appeal on the score of the Regency had met with a reprimand. Her confidential messenger had hardly ridden away with these letters before Dom John sent for her, and explained to her that it might be necessary for some at least of his family to go to Brazil for safety's sake.

Dona Carlota Joaquina was aghast at this information. She hated the French—she hated everybody who was not Spanish—but she hated *los Ingleses* even more. The mere fact that the voyage to Brazil was being urged by Lord Strangford was sufficient to render it odious. But what was a hundred times more repulsive than the thought of satisfying the English was the prospect of being carried off out of the reach of Madrid, to become a prisoner, she and all her children, in the complete grasp of the Portuguese. She instantly penned another letter to her mother. " Yesterday," she wrote, " after I had written to you, the Prince told me he wanted three of the children to go to Brazil, to serve as a guarantee to the English, and that at any moment it might be necessary for us all to go there. Dear Mother, I cannot willingly fling myself into a well—if I should go, it will mean my ruin, for if they have treated me here as they have done, how will they treat me there, far away from you ? There is only one way of saving me. I implore you, write to the Prince saying you wish me, and the daughters I may choose to accompany me, to go and stay with you, so as to be in safety—quite as safe as if we gave ourselves up to the English. And make it plain you will accept no refusal."

The Spanish National Archives contain a further letter, written to her parents ten days later, telling them to arrange everything for her journey to Madrid, and then to write to the Prince Regent as if the plan were entirely their own idea. " Save your wretched grand-daughters," she ended, " from the claws of the lions ! "

While these missives were speeding on their way, the Portuguese court continued to dispute, to hesitate, to shiver and to do nothing. The Prince Regent himself, vacillating though he was, stood firm on one point ; he refused to submit to the French demand that all Englishmen should be arrested. But during October, Araujo's influence was so much in the ascendant that on the 22nd, a decree was published closing the ports to English ships. On the 5th November, a decree even more humiliating to Portugal's dignity was drawn up, giving satisfaction to the French over the matter of British property, which it declared to be confiscated.

The publication of this second decree was resented in a proper manner by Lord Strangford. He removed the Royal Arms from his Legation, and on the 17th November went on board the flag-ship of a British squadron which, under the command of Sir Sidney Smith, was blockading Lisbon, cruising off Cascais in readiness either to escort the royal family overseas or else if need be to seize the Portuguese men-of-war in the Tagus to prevent them from falling into French hands.

Araujo's miserable concessions were, of course, powerless to prevent the fatal course of events that had already been decided upon by

Napoleon. The partition of Portugal had actually been planned by the French Emperor in concert with Godoy early in the previous year. And on the 27th October, Napoleon signed a treaty with Spain at the Palace of Fontainebleau, for " arranging the future lot of Portugal by a healthy policy and conformably to the interests of France and Spain." Portugal was to be divided into three unequal parts : the small northern province of Entre Minho e Douro was to be given to the young King of Etruria : the largest portion, comprising Estremadoura, Beira and Traz-os-Montes, was reserved for a future arrangement at a general peace, but was to be meanwhile under French control ; the southern provinces of the Algarve and Alemtejo were to be handed over as a kingdom to the infamous Godoy.

Even before the Treaty of Fontainebleau had been signed, Marshal Junot had received orders to hurry the army of the Gironde, numbering twenty-five thousand men, across Spain and into Portugal, to swoop down on Lisbon, to seize the Portuguese fleet at anchor in the Tagus, and to make prisoners of the royal family.

The Marquis of Fronteira has recalled in his memoirs how one afternoon when he was five years old, his father's palace at Bemfica was shaken by a sharp earthquake. Several chandeliers crashed to the ground. The whole household together with the monks of the near-by convent of Saint Anthony, rushed into the little square in front of the house and flung themselves on their knees. The tremor was felt in many parts of Portugal. And the odd circumstance was afterwards discovered that at that very hour Junot was rolling out of the courtyard of the Tuileries in a post-chaise, to put himself at the head of the army of the Gironde.

The invading army pressed forward at impetuous speed. No scene in history, one might think, could provide a more exciting subject for a film than Lisbon during November, 1807. While the Prince Regent still hesitated, Lord Strangford paced the deck of Sir Sidney Smith's ship, fuming with impatience.

On the 22nd November, news reached Lisbon of the approach of the French army. On the 24th, Junot was at Abrantes, not sixty miles from the capital. The Prince Regent, surrounded by agitated courtiers offering conflicting advice, still maintained in effect a perilous immobility. It has been suggested by some historians that he was actually the victim of treachery among his household, and that Araujo was an accomplice of Godoy in holding back from the Regent the intelligence of the French army's approach. Canning affirmed in the House of Commons that there were certainly reasons for believing that treachery had existed. How else explain the secrecy in which the French advance was wrapped, or the fact that the Portuguese army, such as it was, had been ordered to remain on the coast ? And in one of Junot's despatches is to be found the following significant sentence : " Mr. Hermann [a French agent, who was sent forward to Lisbon from Abrantes] was unable to get in contact with either the Prince or with Monsieur d'Araujo. The latter merely left a message for him, to say that all was lost. . . ." The Portuguese historian Antonio Sardinha convinced himself, after examination of all the evidence obtainable, that Araujo was in league with the Portuguese Ambassador at Madrid, the Quisling Count of Ega, to allow the French to occupy the country and seize the royal family. On the other hand, General Gomes Freire, who was in command of the troops on the coast and who was never even informed of the French advance until Lisbon was already in Junot's grasp, remarked in after years that there could never have been any truth in such suggestions, since the whole court was too imbecile to be capable even of treachery.

Dom John's procrastination, so nearly fatal to him, did not spring merely from lack of information purposely withheld. It was rooted also in his typically Portuguese distaste for believing in the reality of the unpalatable truths that Strangford had been telling him for months past. A singular occurrence saved him in the nick of time. He was at Queluz, his agony of mind deepened by the incoherent ravings of the Queen, when a copy of the Paris *Moniteur* of October the 13th, which had somehow found its way into Portugal, was placed in his hands. He read in it Napoleon's proclamation that "the House of Braganza had ceased to reign in Europe."

This thunderbolt opened his eyes at last. The whole court was galvanised into movement. Hastily summoning a Council of State, the Prince made public his intention to leave Portugal. A secret convention, signed previously at Ajuda, provided him with an assurance that the British Government would never acknowledge any dynasty but his own on the Portuguese throne. A decree was published instituting a Provisional Government at Lisbon and explaining that His Royal Highness intended to remove his court to Rio de Janeiro until a general peace.

Meanwhile, Lisbon was in a state of pandemonium unparalleled since the great earthquake. The priests of San Rocque hurried to conceal their far-famed relics. They bricked up the skull of St. Crysanthus of Basle, the thigh-bone of St. Procopius, the arm of St. Josippa, the authenticated skulls of several of the eleven-thousand virgins and (O wonder!) the complete head of St. Gregory Thaumaturgus. Orders had been given for everybody to be on board before the next night but one. More than seven-hundred vehicles carrying the court and their belongings moved into the capital, and the Lisbon quays, blocked with carriages, and piled with furniture, treasure and trunks, presented a scene of indescribable confusion. The books and manuscripts of the royal libraries, the archives of the Foreign Office, the silver plate from the Ajuda palace and the fabulous accoutrements of the Patriarchate, lay sprawling under torrents of rain. Seized by panic, thousands of souls crowded on the river banks. Only fifteen small men-of-war and thirty merchantmen composed the fleet at the disposal of the exiles, and the majority of these ships were not in trim. Preparations had indeed been made two months earlier, in case of emergency, but the stores which had then been laid in had been partly used or plundered, and many of the ships' water casks were now found to be broken.

The Prince Regent was in the first of the royal coaches to arrive at the Sodré quay, accompanied by the Spanish Infante Pedro Carlos, who had for many years resided at the Portuguese court. The mob thronging the quay pressed round him, and he could with difficulty, make his way to the jetty. With tears streaming down his face, he surrendered his hands to the multitude to kiss. The air resounded with piercing lamentations. At last he took his place in the boat which carried him over the Tagus to the *Principe Real* that lay in the stream ready to weigh anchor.

A long caravan of coaches and mule carts lined the waterside. In one of these rode the mad Queen, who for years had been kept hidden from her subjects. " Do not drive so fast ! " she is said to have exclaimed in a fleeting moment of lucidity on the road from Queluz ; " they will think we are running away ! " Her heartrending shrieks of " Ai Jesus ! " heightened the mournful character of the scene. At times her muttering revealed that she was under the impression she was being propelled to the guillotine.

In the last vehicle of the procession came Dona Carlota Joaquina, grim, contemptuous and full of hatred. She rode in a heavy coach shaped like a figure of eight, holding, besides herself, two ladies-in-waiting, her eight small children, and their nurse. Every fibre of her being revolted against this undignified flight and recoiled with horror at the thought of the fate in store for her. But she had been swept away, as it were, by the universal avalanche, and at her heels were the French, the monsters who had cut off the heads of her cousins in Paris. Moreover, she loved her children like a tigress and was determined to stick to them. In the surrounding hubbub she was unmoved. She personally superintended the embarkation of her ladies and her brood at the quay. She sent the little Dom Pedro to join his father and the Queen on board the *Principe Real* while she herself went on board the *Affonso d' Albuquerque* with the other children, including the five-year-old Dom Miguel. As the hours passed, the distress on the quays increased.

" Thousands of men, women and children," wrote Lieutenant O'Neil of H.M.S. *London*, who received the account from a Portuguese nobleman, " were constantly on the beach endeavouring to escape on board. *Many ladies of distinction waded into the water.* . . . At length, the ships became so crowded that with the most painful reluctance the officers were compelled to refuse their admittance. . . . Many of the females who had actually embarked were totally destitute of any change of apparel, and had to undertake a passage of five-thousand miles on board ships whose officers had only three days' notice to prepare for such a voyage : and what infinitely increased their terror was, that they momently expected the French to arrive and seize on them as prisoners."

Besides the court, besides the treasure chests and the state papers, between sixteen and eighteen thousand souls were crowded promiscuously on the ships. On board the *Principe Real* there were no less than 412 persons, besides the crew. Among the noble emigrants was the aged Duke of Cadaval, and the venerable General Forbes, who had held a high command in the Portuguese army for many years. Antonio de Araujo slunk on board the *Medusa* under cover of darkness, fearing to be made a victim of popular indignation.

By the evening of the 27th, the work of embarkation was complete, but the terrors felt by the exiles were by no means ended. For the past twelve days the wind had obstinately continued to blow directly into the harbour. It still showed no signs of veering. The sea beyond the Tagus bar, where Sir Sidney Smith's squadron with Lord Strangford on board loitered, was too rough to allow the Portuguese ships to get out of the river. Meanwhile, Junot's troops were pressing forward towards the capital, and a detachment had made a deflection at Loures on the Lisbon road, with intention to seize Saint Julian's fort and to train its guns on the river mouth. Junot, of course, knew the lie of the land like his own hand.

The anxiety of Lord Strangford and Sir Sidney Smith can be more easily imagined than described. It was a matter not of days but of hours, perhaps of minutes. Were the royal family and the Portuguese government to be caught like rats in a trap ? Were they to fall prisoners to the French, and to witness the pillage of all their treasure ? Or were they to slip through Napoleon's fingers in the nick of time, and carry the crown of Portugal to safety and independence ?

For twenty-six long hours their fate hung in the balance. Providentially, at two o'clock in the morning of Sunday, the 29th November, a fair wind sprang up from the eastward. There is a Portuguese proverb to say that no good comes of a Spanish wind or a Spanish marriage, but in this case the east wind was an exception to the rule. Orders were given to every ship to be ready to weigh anchor at daybreak. At seven o'clock the dawn broke cloudless and serene, and the breeze wafted the fleet directly out of the Tagus. " We had now the heartfelt satisfaction," wrote Lieutenant O'Neil, " to see that our hopes and expectations were realized to the fullest extent : the whole Portuguese fleet arranged itself under the protection of that of His Majesty, whilst firing a reciprocal salute of twenty-one guns. . . . To any heart but a Bonaparte's, the scene was sublimely beautiful, impressing every beholder, except the French army on the hills, with the liveliest emotions of gratitude to Providence."

The combined fleets were still well in sight of the shore when Junot's vanguard straggled into Lisbon. One frigate, indeed, found difficulty in crossing the bar, and lagging behind was still in range of Saint Julian's when the French detachment from Loures entered the fort. The French commanding officer dashed to the battlements, and with his own hand trained a gun on the frigate. But he was too late. The shot was like the roar of a lion that has missed its prey.

In long-after years the Baron Marbot, whose memoirs throw the lustre of heroism over the French Empire, was to record the grievous mistake made by the Emperor in sending raw levies to invade the

Peninsula. When the frightened inhabitants of Lisbon turned out to gaze with curiosity on the representatives of Napoleon's world-famed armies, they were astonished to count in the vanguard not more than fifteen hundred ill-nourished youths, many of them bare-foot, and sick with fatigue. The rest of the army were still strung out along the roads leading from the frontier.

Chapter IV

Dona Carlota Joaquina lay in her cabin in the *Affonso d'Albuquerque* brooding darkly on her misfortunes. She, who felt she possessed the energy and spirit of a man, had been compelled to be a helpless spectator of the humiliating sequence of events of the past ten years. She, who was born and bred a Bourbon and whose soul was steeped in a frantic pride and faith in the divine right of Kings, had watched one royal cousin after another insulted and dethroned. True, she had escaped the fate of Marie Antoinette. She still had her head upon her shoulders. True, the house of Braganza was to continue to reign in Brazil. But she who had found Lisbon petty and provincial in comparison to Madrid felt herself degraded when she thought of reigning at Rio de Janeiro. However limited Lisbon had proved to one of her restless arrogance and ambition, it was at least a European capital. Her pride was wounded to the quick. Her attendants are said to have discerned some trace of emotion on her gloomy and iron features when she thought of the prospect of finding herself a colonial queen.

She was at present in the absolute power of her ponderous, maddeningly placid husband and his garrulous, incompetent ministers, who knew she hated them. They in their turn were in the absolute power of the detestable English, whom she not only looked upon as the traditional enemies of the Bourbons, but as heretics to boot, predestined, each one of them, to Hell's flames. So she was a prisoner twice over, and meanwhile was being called upon to support discomforts more frightful than those of a prison.

The convoy had no sooner gained the open sea than a storm of unprecedented violence broke and raged for four days (even in the sheltered harbour of Lisbon boats were cast up on the steps of Corpo Santo). The ships were scattered and did not join up again until the 5th December. But on the night of the 8th, a new storm began, again dividing the squadrons, so that on the following morning only the *Principe Real*, the *Affonso d'Albuquerque* and the *Urania* were in sight of each other.

The privations suffered by the refugees were dreadful. Many, including the aged Duke of Cadaval, succumbed to their sufferings. Lieutenant O'Neil was eloquent over "a scene of distress which a feeling, generous heart can alone conceive ; females of royal and most dignified birth, nourished in the bosom of rank and affluence ... many of them tottering with the feebleness of age, others too young to lisp their sufferings ... such women, compelled to encounter November colds, and tempests through unknown seas, deprived of all the delicacies and most of the necessities of life, without a change of raiment or even a bed to lie on—constrained to huddle promiscuously on

board shipping totally unprepared for their reception. . . ." The flock
of priests and friars who had scrambled on board in the footsteps of
the court now clung in foam-soaked groups to the heaving deck, with
piercing lamentations imploring the intervention of the saints, clutch-
ing their crucifixes, and in turn invoking and smothering with frantic
kisses reliquaries that framed, it might be, the thumb-nail of Saint
Ursula or sealed a bottled sigh of the venerable Ludmilla.

One is reminded irresistibly of the flight of another royal family,
the Bourbons of Naples, that had taken place only eight years earlier
in not unsimilar circumstances; the frightful storm that beset Nelson's
Vanguard in its passage across the Tyrrhenian Sea ; the prostrate
Queen Maria Carolina surrounded by her weeping children ; King
Ferdinand and his dishevelled courtiers telling their beads between
bouts of sea-sickness ; Sir William Hamilton holding a pistol to his
head, ready to shoot himself if the ship went down that " he might
not hear the guggle-guggle in his throat " ; the Imperial Ambassador
flinging into the angry sea the miniature of his naked mistress, fearful
of entering the presence of his Maker with so profane an article upon
his person ; and Lady Hamilton herself, with her hearty British common-sense in an emergency, bustling from one to another, dabbing
their foreheads with vinegar and emptying their basins. Alas ! the
Portuguese royal family had no Lady Hamilton to minister to them.
The demented Queen, however, seemed to benefit from the sea air.

When the storms had blown themselves out, a monotonous month
passed before the fleet crossed the line. Land was sighted on the 22nd
January, and on the evening of the same day the royal family set foot
at Bahia. By this time, noblemen and lackeys, ladies-in-waiting and
their domestics had been reduced to an indistinguishable herd by dirt
and misery. Dona Carlota Joaquina and her children had been compelled to shave their heads, so verminous were they, and walked on
shore in white muslin caps. Here, and again at Pernambuco, the
squadron lingered for more than four weeks to allow the exhausted
refugees to collect clean clothing, and to recover some composure
and better health.

It was not until the 7th March that the *Principe Real*, with the Prince
Regent's standard fluttering at the main, led the squadron into the
harbour of his new capital.

Rio de Janeiro is one of the wonders of the world. That breath-
taking bay, gemmed with islands and girdled by mountains of a fantastic grandeur, is a sight which, once seen, can never be forgotten.
The seaman who has for days and perhaps for weeks, gazed upon
a monotonous horizon feels a thrill of excitement when at ten leagues
from shore he first catches sight of the immense rock, called the
Sugar-loaf, which points out the entrance to the harbour. As his ship
steers towards this famous landmark, a panorama of mountains covered
with the luxuriant verdure of the tropics emerges above the sparkling
waters, and every moment reveals fresh and astonishing details.
Dwarfed by their colossal background, the modern sky-scrapers
lining the Copacabana beach appear no larger than dominoes. Yet,

in spite of the astonishment which the scene inspires, the visitor to Rio de Janeiro who already knows Lisbon cannot fail to be struck when at closer quarters by certain similarities existing between the two. It is not merely that he treads on the Via Branca the familiar tessellated pavements of the Lisbon streets ; that he hears Portuguese spoken around him, and finds the cafés and the shoe-blacks, the newsboys and the strollers of the Rocio. Both cities are seaports whose alleys and squares have become saturated with the intangible, nostalgic essence of the sea. There can be few better places than Rio de Janeiro or Lisbon for buying a parrot or a marline-spike. Again, though we must admit that Lisbon is far less theatrical, and has none of the exotic splendour of Rio, the beauty of both depends, after all, on a combination of hills and sea. The vast mountain-locked bay which is the harbour of the Brazilian capital may recall at times the expanse of the Tagus viewed from the height of San Vicente. On the deep slopes of the virgin forest that hems in and invades the outskirts of the city there are glimpses of foliage grouped round fantastic columns of rock that may bring to mind Cintra and the gardens of Montserrat. Fancy, indeed, can conjure up the vision of a divine Creator who first experimented on the coast of Portugal in a combination of mountains and sands and harbours, and who then excelled Himself on the other side of the Atlantic, letting His imagination run riot in creating Rio de Janeiro. The two capitals are like mother and daughter ; Rio can be likened to a daughter of exuberant beauty who is a multi-millionairess.

But when Dona Carlota's ship broke the waters of the harbour, she found little promise of the glittering city that exists to-day. Amidst its extravagant surroundings, Rio still wore the aspect of a provincial Portuguese town. Two sun-baked forts guarded the narrow entrance to the bay, looking very much like the forts that are to be seen on the Portuguese coast at Cascais or Peniche. On mountain pinnacles above the town were perched small monasteries. Near the principal quay stood the Viceroy's palace, the customs-house, the cathedral and the mint, grouped round a square open on its fourth side to the sea. Here were steps leading down to the water on much the same model as Lisbon's Black Horse Square.

This place was to provide a background to the various public events of the Brazilian Empire in its early years. Here the crowd gathered, for instance, on the occasion of Dom Pedro's marriage to the Archduchess Leopoldina, and of the baptism of the infant Maria da Gloria, to applaud the rich processions from the palace to the church. And this was the scene also of popular demonstrations and historic political convulsions which will find mention in due course.

From this Palace Square radiated the main streets, of which the most important was the Rua Direita, lined with simple old seventeenth-century façades. Here were situated the chief shops and counting-houses, as well as a few handsome houses occupied by Portuguese merchants. Apart from this street, there were few buildings of more than one storey. But there was a multitude of huts and cabins thatched with palm, with no better flooring than trampled earth.

These last were the dwellings of the negro population. For in a town that numbered about a hundred and fifty thousand souls the vast majority were either the descendants of African slaves, or had themselves been transported across the Atlantic by the slave-traders. Few among these negroes had bought their freedom from their masters, while every month, on the average, two thousand fresh slaves arrived from Angola or Quilumana, from Benguela, Luanda or Cabinda. They performed all the menial labour in the capital, and cultivated the plantations in the vicinity, while many thousands more worked the mines in the hinterland. In some their African blood had become mingled with that of the original natives of Brazil, and there were numerous half-castes. At any rate, in visualizing the various episodes in the history of the Portuguese court at Rio de Janeiro it is necessary to bear in mind that of the populace that cheered beneath the palace windows probably three-quarters were black.

The negroes lived a simple life not very different to the existence of savages, but it must not be supposed that they were unhappy. The voyage across the Atlantic was unspeakably wretched (it has been calculated that one in five perished in the holds of the ships on the way), and the conditions under which they were sold in the slave-market of the Rua Valonga were shameful. But the Portuguese are kind to coloured people, and the missionary spirit which inspired their discoveries put no barriers in the way of their intercourse with natives. The negroes in Brazil were baptized ; they began and ended their days by chanting prayers in common ; they were given plots of land to cultivate for themselves when their day's labour was done ; and a special ground was at their disposal where they might congregate to sing and dance. In the breathless summer nights the suburbs throbbed with the rhythm of drums and the mournful twang of primitive guitars.

They did not have to work on Sundays or saints' days. Having been persuaded to deflect their devotions from whatever savage gods they had been wont to worship in Africa to the painted and bejewelled dolls and images of their masters' altars, they were naïf but fervent Christians. Bands of them loved to accompany the religious processions that on saints' days passed slowly through the streets of the capital, dancing an equivalent to the Black Bottom or the Green Apple in honour of the saint. The feasts of Saint Anthony, Saint John and Saint Paul, when fireworks and crackers make sleep impossible in Lisbon, were held in no less special reverence in Brazil. " Without witnessing it," wrote a British minister in Rio de Janeiro, describing Saint John's Eve, " one could with difficulty form a notion of the quantity of wood and gunpowder wasted on this anniversary."

For the colonial residents, the entire social life of the capital centred round the Churches, whose charming Italianate façades must have appeared incongruous against their background of gum-trees and banana. As there were no newspapers, the Church bells performed the function of announcing births, baptisms, marriages and deaths. The bell was rung nine times to announce the birth of a boy ; seven for a girl. During Holy Week the Portuguese community spent the whole day in the Churches, gossiping, praying and picnicking, or gorging fruit and sweets which the slaves carried to the Church doors in silver baskets.

There were no newspapers, because there were so very few people to read them. Since the expulsion of the Jesuits there had been no system of education in existence. Only Brazilian clerks in merchant houses or government departments could read and write, having learned their letters in one or other of the monasteries.

It is not difficult to imagine how great was the sensation caused in this colonial, half-primitive community by the news of the imminent arrival in their midst of the aged Queen of Portugal, the Prince Regent, the Princess Carlota Joaquina, and all their court. At two o'clock on the afternoon of the 7th March, the roar of cannon, echoing over water and wafted among mountains, announced to the expectant populace that the royal squadron had dropped anchor in front of the Palace Square. Volleys of artillery from the forts and the ships were mingled with the pealing of church bells and the explosion of rockets, to mark, in the words of an enthusiastic eye-witness, " the triumphal arrival of the First Sovereign of Europe to the most fortunate city of the New World."

The Viceroy of Brazil, Dom Marcos de Noronha, went on board the *Principe Real* with a numerous delegation to wait upon the Prince. That night the city was illuminated. The disembarkation took place on the following day. An altar had been erected on the quay, where the cathedral clergy were waiting in their white silk vestments shot with gold, and it was in harmony with Portuguese traditions of five hundred years, so rich in Christian endeavour, that the first act of Dom John in setting foot in his new capital, after mounting the water-steps between a guard of honour formed by Portuguese and British sailors, was to kneel with all his family and kiss the crucifix held out to him by a priest. Then the court formed in procession and made their way to the cathedral to assist at a solemn Te Deum. The Prince Regent, Dona Carlota Joaquina and their family walked in a bunch beneath an awning of gold and crimson silk carried by four notables of the city, followed by the city magistrates and the friars of all the principal convents bearing their processional crosses. They walked on a carpet of flowers scattered in delirious joy by the negroes, to whose wondering gaze Dom John and his marvellously be-gemmed consort must have appeared to be almost divine personages. Certainly the simple blacks could not have felt greater awe had Saint John or Saint Anthony themselves suddenly descended out of the clouds.

The warmth of their reception was indeed most gratifying to the royal party. Even Dona Carlota Joaquina admitted that the adulation surrounding her was entirely satisfactory. But at the same time, she was aware—and what would nowadays be termed the political angle was already uppermost in all her meditations—that the successful voyage to Brazil and the reception with which Dom John had met at Rio de Janeiro was a triumph for the English party whom she hated, and above all a triumph for the English. Dom John recalled the insistent appeals made to him by Lord Rosslyn, Lord Strangford and others to escape before it was too late, and it was clear that his mind was now impressed with a profound sense of gratitude towards the British government. This impression was, of course, increased a hundredfold when he received the news, shortly after his arrival in Brazil, of how the Spanish Royal House had been tricked, dethroned and imprisoned by Napoleon. No illusion was possible as to what his own fate would have been had he refused to follow Lord Strangford's advice. Dona Carlota Joaquina herself was compelled to realize that the English had been in the right, but this fact did not make their triumph any the less bitter to her. All the men she most loathed at court were now in the ascendant. Two days after his disembarkation, Dom John announced the creation of a new Ministry whose three members all belonged to the English party. Dom Rodrigo de Sousa Coutinho was Minister of Foreign Affairs.

When in the following May the Prince Regent did Sir Sidney Smith the honour of dining with him on board the *London* on the occasion of King George's birthday, Dona Carlota Joaquina did not accompany her husband and thus missed what must have been a most successful party. All the guns were removed from the quarter-deck to give space for a banqueting table for a hundred and sixty persons. The cabins were decorated with the English and Portuguese colours ; there was a picture " containing the likeness of all our naval heroes," and the deck was strewn with flags captured from the French, so as to provide occasion for the following little dialogue between Sir Sidney and the Prince Regent when he stepped on board (surely the play must have been arranged beforehand) : " His Highness remarked," says Sir Sidney Smith's biographer, " that the decks were covered with the colours of the enemy. The Admiral answered in the affirmative, and the Prince replied that he was indebted to his faithful ally and his brave subjects who had enabled him thus to trample them under his feet." At the ensuing banquet Dom John gave the toast : " The King of Great Britain, and may he live until time shall be no more." He then addressed the Admiral : " To you," he said, " I and my family owe our liberty, and my mother her crown and dignity." His toast was honoured with a salute from all His Majesty's ships in the bay.

Chapter V

THE joy felt in the breasts of Portugal's ancient allies at the news that the Portuguese court had landed safely in Brazil did not spring solely from their satisfaction at seeing the House of Braganza free from Napoleon's clutches. Hitherto the Brazil trade had always been closed to all nations save the Portuguese themselves, and this rigorously guarded monopoly had been an age-long source of envy to the City of London. When Lord Strangford had promised the protection of Sir Sidney Smith's squadron to escort the royal family across the Atlantic and had signed the convention at Ajuda declaring that the English would recognize no sovereign in Portugal save a Braganza, an engagement had been made that the Brazilian ports should be opened to British trade when the court arrived. The Prince Regent was as good as his word. Not more than a week after setting foot at Bahia he signed a decree abolishing all restrictions on direct trade between his dominions and Great Britain.

The decree caused a boom on the London Exchange. Manufacturers who had been deprived of their European markets by Napoleon were quick to perceive that boundless trading prospects existed in South America. Ships were chartered, freighted and sent off with the first favourable breeze. And not many weeks had passed after the arrival of the Portuguese court at Rio de Janeiro before the quays, where few warehouses yet existed, were piled high with merchandise of every description, the result of optimistic but in many cases imprudent speculation. British manufacturers were ignorant of the local conditions existing in their new market. As a result, hundreds of English cast-iron fire-places were dumped in Rio, where the temperature is like an oven; thousands of ladies' corsets, where such articles are quite insupportable; up-to-date coffins, where custom dictated that corpses should be laid in the earth wrapped only in the habit of a religious order; chandeliers, where there were no candles; skates, where there was no ice; and everything totally unsuited for the Brazilian climate. More cotton goods arrived in a few months than could have been absorbed in twenty years. What need had the half-naked slaves for Paisley shawls and bonnets? The goods were left to rot or to be pilfered, and the remainder were eventually disposed of for sixty or seventy per cent. less than their real value.

One imaginative north-of-England manufacturer sent out a shipload of instruments of his own invention, a kind of combined pick-and-hammer with which he envisaged the eager Brazilians collecting diamonds and gold nuggets on their hillsides.

Many fortunes must have been lost in these mad ventures. After early failures, however, British commerce struck root and flourished. In 1811 there were already sixty-five English business-men established at Rio, and five years later there were more than a hundred. Maria Graham, authoress of " A Journal of a Voyage to Brazil " (in later life when she had become Lady Calcott, authoress of " Little Arthur's History "), noticed at Rio the " numerous English pot-houses whose Union Jacks, Red Lions and Jolly Tars, with their English inscriptions, vie with those of Greenwich and Deptford."

This growing trade was largely due to the invaluable exertions of Lord Strangford, who was now accredited ambassador to the Portuguese court in Brazil. He succeeded in negotiating with Sousa Coutinho an important commercial treaty, signed in January, 1810, granting to English traders many of the privileges formerly enjoyed by the British colony in Portugal. The houses and warehouses of British subjects resident in Portugal's overseas territory were not to be liable to any vexatious visits or searches ; the English were to enjoy the valuable privilege of nominating special magistrates to settle legal disputes in which they might become involved : they were to enjoy religious liberty ; they were to pay on imports not more than fifteen per cent. *ad valorem* in taxes.

The Treaty also made concessions to the Portuguese (the British for instance, consented " to waive the right of creating Factories or incorporated bodies of merchants"). Nevertheless, since British traders and British shipping outnumbered the Portuguese by twenty to one, the working of the treaty was overwhelmingly in England's favour, so that the Portuguese were not slow to complain that the Prince Regent had permitted an emotional sense of gratitude to his friends to influence him to their own disadvantage. There were even some who spitefully observed that to live comfortably in Brazil it was necessary first to arrange to be born in England. Among these wagging tongues, none was more bitter or more spiteful than Dona Carlota Joaquina's.

If the working of the Commercial Treaty gave rise to jealousies among the Brazilians against the English, it must also be noted that the seeds of even deeper jealousies had been sown among the Portuguese themselves since the very first day when Dom John took up residence in his new capital. The Portuguese who were already settled in Rio de Janeiro had lived long enough overseas to acquire a dawning sense of nationality of their own. They felt themselves to be, in fact, not Portuguese but Brazilians. And these colonial residents were irritated and offended by the manner in which they were now expected to make sacrifices in favour of a set of idle counts and marquises, who, having spent half their lives gossiping and card-playing in Lisbon, were apparently determined to continue a similar existence in their new surroundings. Dom John deserved every respect for the sentiments that had inspired him to show favour to the men who had chosen to share his vicissitudes. It was even touching to know that his eyes streamed with tears when he pressed to his heart some companion of his exile whose face recalled old days at Mafra. But when he issued a decree reserving fifty thousand pounds annually from the customs-house receipts at Bahia and Pernambuco to distribute in court pensions, the Brazilians not unnaturally felt offended. They found themselves besides expected to place their own houses at the disposal of the court : a gesture which they were pleased to perform as an act of temporary hospitality when the court first arrived. But they soon discovered that, once their distinguished guests had taken possession of their property, it was exceedingly difficult, and often impossible, to get rid of them. There were actually cases of property owners, who, in order to retrieve even a part of their houses, found themselves compelled to become the tenants of their own guests. The rancour caused by such incidents struck root in Brazil, and was unfortunately to bear fruit in the years to come. It was to find vivid expression sixteen years afterwards in a speech in the Brazilian Assembly, when a deputy burst out : " Who but Lord Cochrane delivered Bahia from the Portuguese, that swarm of drones that threatened to devour the land ?"

This jealousy against the court favourites blinded the Brazilians to the substantial benefits bestowed on them by the court's arrival. Rio de Janeiro ceased to be a colonial settlement and became famous in the world. The Lisbon courtiers transplanted their vices, but also brought their taste and refinement, to their new capital. To cater for a royal family whose passion and talent for music are hereditary, a fine opera house was constructed and opened in 1813. An unwonted luxury and elegance became evident on all sides. Enormous fortunes in jewellery and valuables had been carried from Lisbon. When the Baroness de Bassagnes visited Rio de Janeiro and attended a ball where she met the court ladies, the British Minister wrote in a letter home : " The richness of their diamond ornaments very much astonished her, since upon such occasions it is by no means uncommon for them to wear jewels to the value of four, five or six thousand pounds, and some even as much as thirty or forty thousand."

Who will write a book on the influence of scenery on taste ? Who will trace the subtle unconscious influence exerted on the minds of Chinese artists by the delicate contours of their own landscape ? Who will examine through the ages the influence on different schools of painting of Spanish sierras, Italian skies, and English mists ? It is not fanciful to suppose that the extravagant Brazilian scenery rapidly exerted an effect upon the taste of the new European residents. The dress and manners of the members of Queen Maria's court at Queluz, for the most part so antiquated that they would not have been inappropriate at the levée of Louis the Fifteenth, had not long been transplanted to Brazil before they assumed a gaudier note. Maria Graham, who watched Dom Pedro ride in procession to the Cortes in 1822, noticed among the spectators on the balconies " feathers and diamonds in profusion," and described an exotic vehicle she saw drive past : " A very gay pea-green and silver chariot, very light, with silver ornaments, silver fellies to the wheels and silver where any kind of metal could be used."

The Prince Regent took up his residence in what had formerly been the Viceroy's palace. After so many years of political anxiety, culminating in the terrible Atlantic crossing, he felt now an immense relief. The spirit of revolution and unrest that had made life of late so uncomfortable for the royal houses of Europe had been stimulated, indeed, by the war of independence in North America, but it did not appear to have yet spread to Brazil. Dom John was touched by the obsequious homage of his Brazilian subjects, a homage as sincere and complete as any absolute King could desire. He felt his heart expand among the hot-house scenery and unruffled tranquillity of his new home. The sedative effect of a warm climate on his lymphatic nature was heightened by an unwonted sense of peace and confidence. Ghastly visions of impending invasion or revolution no longer disturbed the long hours of indolent repose that he loved to spend in the Royal Oratory. His new life provided him with all the things that his Braganza heart loved : the stately court ceremonies of an untroubled age ; the interminable sermons as elaborate in phrase and gesture as the baroque ceilings of the churches ; the crowd prostrating themselves in the nave, marking the preacher's discreet allusions to the sanctity and earthly omnipotence of their Prince, whose presence could be glimpsed through clouds of incense in the gilded tribune set close to the altar ; the long masses set to the music of Jomelli or Perez ; the amusing futile existence of the court, with its traditional Portuguese mixture of reverence and familiarity. It was an atmosphere of security and permanence, with no conceited intellectuals to disturb it by discussing the Rights of Man ; or so, at any rate, it seemed to Dom John on first acquaintance. In reality, as will in time become plain, his sense of repose was a fool's paradise.

But Dona Carlota Joaquina did not share her husband's happiness. What pleased him invariably disgusted her. When he was contented she was disgruntled, and *vice versa*. " There has always been," a British diplomat was to write some years later, " a coolness and jealousy between these two Royal Persons." In Portugal, they had taken to living apart : they had made the sea-voyage in different ships. The Princess now installed herself independently in the upper storey of a large oblong building on the Palace Square, part of which was still used as a mint. The ground floor was occupied by her numerous train of servants.

To speak of a " coolness and jealousy " was a mild description of Dona Carlota Joaquina. Sir William a'Court was nearer the truth when he spoke of " that asperity, violence and vindictiveness of character from which so much is to be apprehended." Hatred, as we have already hinted, was beginning to absorb her heart ; hatred first of her husband, on whom as Regent and afterwards as King, she was dependent for every penny of her funds, so hopelessly inadequate for her dreams and schemes ; hatred for his weakness and for his obstinacy, for his stupidity and his shrewdness ; hatred, secondly, for the Portuguese nation among whom she had lived since childhood, yet to whose temperament she had never become reconciled ; hatred, last but not least, of the liberal spirit of the age from whose menace she did not feel herself safe—and in this she showed more discernment than her husband—even in Rio de Janeiro.

For indeed neither the distance of Brazil from Paris nor even the whole Atlantic Ocean was a barrier to the infiltration of modern ideas. The very noblemen and ecclesiastics who most dreaded them carried the liberal infection into the new world. Their very abhorrence of liberal doctrine must have helped to make the Brazilians realize that such doctrine existed. Anxiety brings about the reality of the ills dreaded, just as good things may come from prayer. How often must some fanatical Lisbon friar, thundering from a pulpit in Brazil, have served to advertise the very heterodoxy he denounced and of which his uncultured congregation had hitherto lived in ignorance! During the years following the arrival of the Portuguese court at Rio de Janeiro, revolutionary theories spread underground throughout the colony, just as they had been spreading in Portugal. The monarchy had not been destroyed by revolution ; it had been forced to emigrate by foreign invasion. It had arrived intact on the other side of the Atlantic. But as those characteristics of absolute monarchies which were a target for revolutionary movements in Europe continued to flourish in Rio de Janeiro, the normal process of the subversive movement continued to operate also. The old Portuguese régime could not have survived unchanged in Europe. It had even less prospect of surviving in the American hemisphere, where the opening phrase of the Declaration of Independence of 1776 sounded like a trumpet in men's ears : " We hold these truths to be self-evident, that all men are created equal : that they are endowed by their Creator with certain inalienable rights : that amongst these are Life, Liberty and the pursuit of happiness."

Chapter VI

It is impossible to understand the historic events of the late eighteenth and early nineteenth centuries—impossible likewise to appreciate the part played in Portuguese history by Dona Carlota Joaquina and her two sons—without realizing exactly what the spirit of that age was. How could it come about that multitudes who for generations had lived in docile acceptance of their lot should suddenly be thrown into tumultuous motion ? That monarchies and aristocracies which had for centuries flourished in the unquestioned enjoyment of privilege and power should be suddenly cast down ? These things were possible because a new enthusiasm possessed men's hearts : they felt themselves to be tired of all they had inherited from the past, and they set to work to destroy existing institutions, with the object of building a brave new world of their own. It is difficult for us to recapture in the imagination the delirious fervour felt by these men. " Good was it in that dawn to be alive," wrote Wordsworth, "but to be young was very heaven !" The immense convulsions which took place in Wordsworth's lifetime are witness of the explosive power latent in the new revolutionary doctrines.

Just as two chemicals, each of them, it may be, harmless in isolation, can produce a powerful explosive when brought into contact, so the democratic principles of liberty and equality, intoxicating enough in themselves, were rendered a thousand times more potent by being fused with a new faith in the perfectibility of human nature and the automatic progress of mankind. " The ancient Pagans," Dean Inge has said, " put their Golden Age in the past : we put ours in the future. The Greeks prided themselves on being the degenerate descendants of gods, we on being the very creditable descendants of monkeys." The idea of progress which first took root about the middle of the eigtheenth century spread with a remarkable rapidity, and was destined to enjoy an almost untrammelled vogue for more than a hundred years. Nowadays, when civilization is reeling from the effects of two world wars, we are, perhaps, inclined to be less smugly complacent than our great-great-grandfathers, and to regard the self-confidence of the Victorian age with a somewhat indulgent smile. But in 1800, faith in progress was a passion.

It was laudable, of course, to invoke the idea of progress in carrying out long-needed reforms. But what is important to bear in mind is that men came to believe that progress was automatic ; that it was a universal law of human existence ; that the course of history was necessarily an unending process of improvement. Such a belief cannot be proved, and indeed it is preposterous for anyone to hold it to the point of fanaticism. Yet it was a belief which at the close of the

36

eighteenth century was regarded by all those political thinkers who nowadays would be termed " left-wingers " as *axiomatic*. When, at the same period there occurred by chance a series of remarkable scientific discoveries and inventions, these were pointed to as proofs that Progress was a reality. Who could deny—so thought the passengers on the first railway—that men who travelled at forty miles an hour were superior in happiness to their ancestors who only travelled at ten? And what of Mr. Montgolfier and his balloon? Truly it was a wonderful age!

So it came about that all changes (good or bad, as long as they were changes) were regarded as being so many steps forward towards that goal of human perfection envisaged by the Abbé Fontenelle. Even a leap in the dark was better than no leap at all. Such was the mentality of the period.

Another of the outstanding beliefs of the age was that men could be made happy simply by education. A third, that all human institutions should be judged by the rule-of-thumb standard of utility. Whatever the validity of these tenets, the fact remains that at the close of the eighteenth century the whole civilized world became a battleground between the liberal enthusiasts who believed in them on the one side and the minority representatives of conservative tradition on the other. Kings were confronted by Jacobins; bishops by free-thinkers; and noblemen who for years had wielded a hereditary political power were confronted by radicals demanding a vote.

There was a battle even in the realm of art. Instead of looking for their ideal to the classic age, the moderns now sought it in the Middle Ages. Palladian façades and Corinthian pediments gave way to Gothic mansions, Gothic villas and (even) Gothic railway stations. Instead of following the rules of Racinian drama, poets who believed in untrammelled freedom of expression fascinated their public by descriptions of nights " when the moon is in eclipse and all nature in alarm." The contrast between the new and the old was a marked one even in England. But England, that land of intuitive compromise and slow adaptation as gentle as its climate—and where, moreover, the conquest of fundamental individual liberties had already been achieved in the Reformation and the Civil Wars—did not experience half the violence of the battle as it was waged in foreign, especially in Catholic, countries.

As the daughter, sister, wife and mother of absolute kings, Dona Carlota Joaquina was a living symbol of the old world that now came to be menaced. Her reactions to the manifestations of the liberal spirit that arose around her are easily understandable. It must be remembered that she was by blood a Bourbon, the scion of a branch that reigned at once at Madrid and at Naples, and to appreciate the implications of her heredity (the key to her character and her career) it is necessary to ignore all nineteenth-century moral standards and principles. It is necessary to throw the imagination back into the world which the French Revolution destroyed. Her uncle was King Ferdinand the Fourth of Naples, some portrait of whom is not out of place since it will serve to describe the stock to which Dona Carlota Joaquina belonged.

King Ferdinand is described in Sir Nathaniel Wraxall's memoirs as " tall, muscular, and active in his frame, capable of immense fatigue." He had the naif mentality and the physical excellence that fancy may ascribe to some classic hero in remote times. He was master of no language except Italian, and his ordinary talk was a Neopolitan dialect such as was spoken by the lowest of his subjects, the Lazaroni. All the correspondence which took place between him and his father the King of Spain was carried on in this jargon, while their numerous letters were filled almost entirely with accounts of the variety and quantity of game respectively killed by them. For both sovereigns possessed in the highest degree that inordinate passion for hunting and sport which has always been a distinguishing characteristic of their family.

King Ferdinand spent nearly every day of his life either hunting or shooting in the royal woods, or else, in Wraxall's words, " more laboriously engaged in an open boat, exposed to the rays of a burning sun, harpooning fish in the Bay of Castellamare." The quantity of deer, wild boar and stags slaughtered in the parks of Astruni, Caserta and Caccia Bella was beyond credibility. Sir William Hamilton said that he had often seen a heap composed only of the offal and bowels reaching as high as his head and many feet in circumference. The King himself insisted on dissecting the principal pieces of game. He used to strip himself, and then having put on a flannel apron, knife in hand, distribute haunches and joints among his favoured courtiers. " No carcass-butcher in Smithfield," said Sir William, " can exceed him in anatomical ability."

King Ferdinand was greatly beloved by his people. He liked to challenge the best athletes among them to wrestling matches, and on his fishing expeditions he was customarily accompanied by a chosen and devoted band of fishermen from the islands of Lipari. He enjoyed no less a popularity among his courtiers, whose only serious duty was keeping the sovereign amused on wet days. The amusements in which they indulged on these occasions would have shocked exceedingly the genteel Victorian society of a later age. When King Ferdinand was seventeen, the news arrived in Naples that his bride-to-be, the Arch-Duchess Josepha, had died of the small-pox, and he was informed that it was quite indispensable for him to forgo his usual hunting expedition on this day of mourning. So he set about amusing himself to the best of his ability indoors, and having exhausted the excitements of billiards, leap-frog and wrestling, someone proposed to celebrate the funeral of the deceased Arch-Duchess. The proposal was no sooner made than it was carried unanimously. A comely young lord-in-waiting was chosen to represent the corpse, was dressed to suit the part, and was laid upon an open bier according to Neopolitan custom. Then they pocked his face and hands with chocolate drops, and when all was ready, the funeral procession was put in motion, and proceeded through the principal apartments of the palace, King Ferdinand officiating as chief mourner. " Having heard of the Arch-Duchess' decease," related Sir William Hamilton, " I had gone thither on that day in order to make my condolences privately to His Majesty on the misfortune, and entering at the time, I became an eye-witness of this extraordinary scene, which, in any other country in Europe, would be considered incredible."

Many more anecdotes of a similar character could be told of the Bourbon sovereigns in the setting either of Portici or of Aranjuez. But the above will suffice to show why it was that the liberal historians of a succeeding epoch were wholly incapable of arriving at any adequate understanding of Dona Carlota Joaquina. She belonged by blood and temperament to a vanished age, and historians of the generation that followed would have been unable to draw her portrait in proper perspective even if their vision had not been grotesquely distorted by political animosity. She has been blamed for never having given her sons a liberal education. It has been forgotten that to Dona Carlota Joaquina, the offspring of that line of antique picturesque princes, education in the modern sense of the word was completely meaningless. She saw no intrinsic value in being intellectual. If King Ferdinand the Sixth of Spain had patronized Scarlatti it was simply because it was his pleasure to do so. It happened that her own pleasure was in horses, bullfights, shooting and the coarse excitements of the common people. She was, in fact, one of those royal beings of the eighteenth century whose passions and whose whims knew no bridle save the formal restraint imposed by the elaborate, minute etiquette of their courts.

Liberal historians, who at the same time as being historians were the rabid political enemies of the Queen's party, proclaimed themselves shocked by Dona Carlota's manners, her zest for the stables and her coarse or even obscene language. Perhaps they had never heard tell of how her uncle at Naples customarily took his place in his earth-closet surrounded by his boon companions, or of how the ladies of the Spanish court used to assist at annual fêtes for the castration of bulls. These historians were full of faith in education, sanitation, universal suffrage, free trade and the automatic progress of mankind. They also believed in equality and fraternity, while at the same time they were tortured by a class-consciousness that the Bourbons had never for an instant known. They could understand neither Dona Carlota's affectionate familiarity with her domestics nor her arrogant insistence on her rank.

This arrogance became markedly accentuated after her arrival in Brazil. It sprang partly from an instinct of self-defence in view of her presentiment that the spirit of revolution was seeping into South America from the United States. Secondly, though she had wept at the thought of finding herself a colonial queen, it may be supposed that she was not unmoved by the theatrical beauty of her new capital, which she must have realized was sufficient to put even Naples in the shade. It may be supposed, again, that she had not been unaffected by the acclamations of Emperor with which Dom John had been welcomed on his disembarkation. (Even Dom John himself had been impressed by that shout. Not content to concentrate on developing the wellnigh limitless resources of his Brazilian possessions, he soon became obsessed by plans to extend his huge empire still further by establishing in fact the traditional suzerainty of his crown over those lands which now compose the republic of Uruguay). But neither hostility towards what she regarded as a new spirit of insubordination, nor pride in her new capital, nor even her dawning sense of imperial destiny, is an adequate explanation of the manner of life which Dona Carlota Joaquina adopted in Rio de Janeiro.

Her jewels were now more magnificent than ever. They astonished all beholders. She surmounted her hideous profile by a fantastic arrangement of tropic plumes, not unbecoming to the sovereign of so many Indian tribes. Her palace swarmed with swaggering guards who were known as her corps of cadets, mostly half-castes of a brutal appearance. With these guards as outriders, she from time to time made journeys to and from her country residence at Santa Cruz, a mansion that had formerly been a Jesuit convent, overlooking a vast plain where herds of cattle roamed. On these drives she insisted on everybody she met on the road kneeling as she passed, like the simple peasantry at Ramalhâo. If strangers were on horseback or in carriages they were required to dismount and woe betide any that dared disregard her imperious orders. Her bodyguard would set upon him instantly and chastise him with their whips. Outrageous scenes occurred, which gave rise to indignation among travellers in Brazil. One day, Dona Carlota's cadets assaulted the Netherlands Chargé d'Affaires ; on another, an English seaman, Commodore Bowles, suffered a similar insult, and Lord Strangford very properly insisted upon the responsible guards going on board the Captain's frigate to present their apologies. As for the American Minister, he only saved his skin by drawing a pair of loaded pistols and threatening to blow out the brains of his assailants. As a result of the scandal occasioned by this incident, Dom John imprisoned the guards who had been implicated and published a decree excusing foreigners from paying the homage which Dona Carlota demanded.

The fundamental explanation of her strange style of living is to be found in Dona Carlota Joaquina's fast developing passion for power. If kept at a distance by her husband, at least she was determined to live as an absolute sovereign in the small province of her own domestic establishment, the model in miniature of a system she dreamed of applying to a whole empire. Lastly, she was determined not to be put in the shade by the boycott of the cabinet and court ; she would impose her own will in this small sphere in defiance of her husband, and the day might yet come when her entourage of desperadoes, respecting no authority on earth except hers, might serve as the nucleus of a political party in the State.

Her eldest son, Dom Pedro, lived with his father, but her other son lived with herself. All the Princess's heart that was not absorbed by her ambition or her hatreds was occupied by her passionate affection for this son, Dom Miguel, whose character from an early age displayed every quality in harmony with her own. She took it for granted that

Miguel ought to be encouraged to grow up in a manner befitting a prince, according to her own interpretation of the word. She used sometimes to beat him savagely with her slipper, but she desired the boy to be subject to no will but hers. In the new world that was taking shape such an experiment would have been dangerous for any prince, but for Dom Miguel, in view of his tendencies and temperament, it was bound to be tragic.

There was no trace in him of Dom John's indolence, secretiveness and irresolution. In physique also, except for his dark complexion, he was the very antithesis of his father. He grew up tall and slim, with muscles like whip-cord. No wonder that when people looked at him they sometimes recalled old scandal at Queluz, that declared his true father had been a gardener at Ramalhâo, a very Priapus, whose form, it was whispered, had enflamed the Infanta. From dawn to dusk he was on the run after some fresh mischief. His companions were grooms and cowboys, and he moved in a perpetual tumult. At the age of ten he was to be seen in the miniature uniform of a general, with a star on his coat, leading a mob of urchins amidst dust and commotion down the pavements of Rio de Janeiro, dashing into houses to smash up the crockery or to fling the furniture out of the windows. Sir Sidney Smith rashly presented the boy with a pair of tiny cannon. So grave visitors at Santa Cruz found themselves met on the threshold by a whiff of grapeshot. At sixteen he was to be seen galloping like mad across the suburb of Mata-Carvalos, with a cowboy who was his inseparable companion at his side, knocking off the hats of passers-by with his riding crop.

Hunting and shooting, bull-fights and fireworks, were the habitual pastimes of the youthful Dom Miguel. At the age of sixteen his hand was badly burned by a rocket, an accident which did nothing to suppress his high spirits. He pleased his mother by remarking that his only regret was that he had not got his wound in a battle. Could it be that the Brazilian sun had something to do with it, producing in the boy a kind of permanent condition of fever and precocity? He spent most of his time with a rowdy band of half-caste or Indian farm-hands at Santa Cruz, where in breaking horses, lassoing heifers, and killing bulls he soon excelled the most expert cowboys of the plains.

How his mother adored him! How she loved him when one night he burst into her apartment where her ladies-in-waiting were assembled, dragging with him a young bull that knocked down a ridiculous old Mistress of the Robes and broke the whole place up! What a delirious scene of chaos and excitement!

No wonder the historians of the early Victorian epoch were to raise their hands in horror at the recollection of such escapades! Even Dom Miguel's contemporaries in Rio de Janeiro were shaken when the Prince and his companions feasted one night in the lowest tavern in the codfish market, where their behaviour at last created a riot among the sailors, negroes and prostitutes who frequented it. Dom Miguel was seen extricating himself with a lady of the town on each arm, and finished the night in an orgy with his mother's notorious cadets.

He was a spoilt boy, and he was spoilt by his mother deliberately. The disorder in which he grew up may be gauged from the fact that the Russian ambassador, who at considerable expense had fitted up his Embassy in a house adjoining Dona Carlota's palace, found the noise so intolerable that he packed up his belongings and moved to a distant part of the town.

But Dom Miguel was likewise spoiled by the whole of his mother's household. Even as a child he had a strange power over them. His nurses worshipped the ground he trod on. To supply his toy cannon, gun-powder was stolen for him by the lackeys whose own legs were his favourite target. And just as an actor's power of holding his audience develops with time and success, the charm which Dom Miguel exercised over the common people grew to a degree that was phenomenal. Few could resist his smile, or fail to be fascinated by the easy, graceful nod he gave as he galloped by.

Well, if a new age was dawning in which the people were to be supreme, let the prince be the people's darling.

Chapter VII

WHEN Dona Carlota Joaquina learned of her father the King of Spain's misfortunes as Napoleon's prisoner, her imagination became inflamed with a great project. She herself being the only representative of her illustrious family who was not a captive, it seemed clear to her that she was by right the Regent of the Spanish American Empire. She therefore opened a correspondence with the leading citizens of Buenos Aires, Montevideo, Santiago and Lima. She circulated a manifesto, inviting American Spaniards to place themselves under " the immediate protection and government . . . of the Infanta Don Carlota Joaquina de Bourbon, and to acclaim her as our Sovereign Regent. . . ."

In the very inception of her plan, she found an unexpected ally. Admiral Sir Sidney Smith, after having escorted the royal family to Brazil, had resumed the post he had formerly occupied as Commander of the British squadron in those waters. He was a general favourite at the Portuguese court, and as a reward for his services, the Prince Regent presented him with a country estate. Dona Carlota was not behindhand in her expressions of gratitude. There was an exchange of ceremonial visits between them. She gave the Admiral a diamond ring and a jewel-encrusted sword, picked up in a pawn-shop, but splendid. Sir Sidney, indeed, earned a double distinction : he was the only man whom Carlota liked who was also liked by Dom John, and he was the only Englishman she ever liked in her life. He, for his part, was charmed by the Princess, whose frankly expressed admiration was probably not feigned, for Sir Sidney was a fine man ; he had already in the course of his career made a conquest of royalty, his name having been linked with a certain much-discussed sofa in the Blackheath villa of Queen Caroline.

It was Sir Sidney who at this juncture found a secretary for Dona Carlota Joaquina in the person of a resourceful Spanish adventurer named José Prezas. This dubious individual was a renegade from Buenos Aires who had attached himself to the English expeditionary force which landed there in 1806. Afterwards he had become secretary and interpreter to Sir Sidney. Passing now into the service of the Princess, for four years, from 1808 to 1812, he conducted her correspondence.

For a time, fortune appeared to smile on her. Though her appeals addressed to far-away Peru and Chile remained unanswered, her prospects seemed bright in Buenos Aires. The rivalry between this colony on the south and Montevideo on the north of the Plate River provided an opening for intrigue hardly less favourable than the internal political feuds that were distracting both. On the 21st March, 1808, Dona Carlota Joaquina wrote a letter to the *Cabildo*, or governing council of Buenos Aires, suggesting that she should come and place herself at the head of the colony " to defend it " (the idea was hers) " against attacks from the

43

French." Meanwhile, Prezas addressed letters to certain prominent citizens of Buenos Aires, such as Belgrano, Saavedra and the Pêna brothers, urging the Princess's suit.

Dom John's cabinet nursed plans of their own in regard to the Spanish colonies of the River Plate. They aspired to place them under the protection of Brazil as a step towards ultimate annexation. So while Dona Carlota opened her correspondence with the *Cabildo*, Sousa Coutinho, lately created Count of Linhares, sent off an envoy called Xavier Curado to open direct negotiations with the Viceroy of Buenos Aires. This Viceroy, by name Linniers, was of French extraction. He had been chiefly responsible for the defeat of the English expeditionary force, which under General Whitelock was repelled from Buenos Aires in 1807.

While the *Cabildo* returned answer to Dona Carlota Joaquina, that they did not fear a French attack, and were well enough armed to meet any emergency, Linniers sent word that he refused to receive Curado, who was therefore forced to land at Montevideo. Here he received a good welcome from the Spanish Governor, Elio, and from the local authorities who, living in fear of an incursion from their neighbours across the Plate River, considered that the friendship of the Portuguese government at Rio de Janeiro might stand them in good stead. That Curado was all too eager to promise assistance to Montevideo was proved by the protraction of his visit, a circumstance that excited the resentment of the Argentines to a high degree. (We may here legitimately give the name of Argentines to the people of Buenos Aires, where the ambition to achieve independence was already awake.) Towards the end of 1808, Linniers published a manifesto protesting against Curado's presence in Montevideo.

Dona Carlota Joaquina was ill informed as to the state of public opinion in both these Spanish colonies. She realized neither the progress that had been made in separatist sentiment nor the suspicion with which any manœuvre originating in Rio—whether hers or anybody else's—was looked upon in Buenos Aires. In reality the Argentine's desire for independence was accompanied by a constant fear of aggression on the part of the Portuguese—and they could not forget that Dona Carlota, however much she insisted on being first and foremost a Spanish Bourbon, was married to the heir of the Portuguese throne. The Princess did not fully realize the implications of these facts. Her imagination was intoxicated by the thought of the moment when she should place her foot on Spanish soil, to be tumultuously welcomed by a populace devoted—so she fancied—to the Spanish crown.

In this opening phase of her negotiations, the main obstacle in her path, apart from the incomprehensible lack of enthusiasm shown by Linniers, was her husband's cabinet. The Count of Linhares was daring to put forward a rival candidate to the regency of the Spanish empire in the person of Don Pedro Carlos, the Spanish princeling who had for years resided at Queluz and had accompanied the court into exile. He was a simple-minded, ricketty youth who hung about the corridors of Dom John's palace, teased and pampered in turn by courtiers with an hour to waste. That Linhares should dare put forward this puppet to dispute her claims naturally enraged Dona Carlota Joaquina, who, in August, published and circulated a manifesto urging her own superior, indisputable rights.

Shortly afterwards, however, we find the court party and the Princess in temporary agreement. It occurred to Dom John that he would have nothing to lose, and might have much to gain, if his consort became Regent in Buenos Aires. In the minds of both the idea existed that Spain and Portugal might never recover from the confusion and prostration resulting from the Peninsula having become one of the chief battlegrounds where England was fighting Napoleon. Should this apprehension be realized, might there not come into being two new imperial crowns in the new world, to shine with a marvellous lustre on the brow of a new line of Bourbon-Braganza monarchs? Certainly, Dom John was already contemplating with equanimity the idea of remaining perpetually in Rio de Janeiro. The recollection of the disturbed state of Europe was a nightmare to him.

There were other considerations to recommend Dona Carlota's scheme to Dom John. It would mean that she would sail away to Buenos Aires, taking with her, it was to be hoped, her ruffian guards, and so leave him in peace. How happy a cure to the interminable pin-pricks which she caused him! There would be an end to her incessant requests for money, an end to the disturbances caused by her disorderly household and to the ceaseless anonymous letters telling him of her depravity. There would be an end to the wounds to his sensitive pride inflicted by her stinging witticisms at his expense, invariably carried to his ear by some busy, idle courtier flitting between her household and his own. And even if Dona Carlota did not succeed at Buenos Aires, his ministers seemed agreed that her claims to the regency there would strengthen his own comparatively modest claims to the Uruguayan territory to the north. It will be observed from all this that Linniers' suspicions of Portuguese intentions were not unfounded.

So Dom John gave permission to her to sail, and Sir Sidney Smith came forward with the offer of a ship to take her off. Saavedra wrote to the Princess to say she had only to show herself to be acclaimed. Saturnino Pena, who had lately arrived in Rio as Linniers' envoy, was outwardly enthusiastic.

Dona Carlota's dreams appeared to be taking shape, when she met with a cruel rebuff. A Spanish frigate, named the *Prueva*, put into Rio de Janeiro on its way to England, carrying General Huidobro, the Viceroy's friend and emissary, with despatches for the British Government. Dona Carlota imperiously summoned the General and the ship's captain to an audience, confident that once in the presence of Dona Carlota Joaquina de Bourbon, they could not fail to swear devotion to her cause. She received them with antique ceremony, as became the Regent of the Spanish Empire. She let it be known that it was her wish and pleasure to go on board the *Prueva*, that the ship should reverse its course, and carry her to the River Plate. To her amazement, humiliation and fury, the General and the ship's captain both flatly refused to accede to her request.

This frightful disappointment did not extinguish her hopes, but it caused them to be temporarily deflected in their object. In November, 1808, we find her addressing a despatch to Jovellanos, who at that time was the chief of a provisional Spanish Government at Seville. She offered him her services as Regent of Spain.

Seville or Buenos Aires—the one was as good as the other. Either would afford her the opportunity she longed for to exercise political power, to use her truly masculine talents, and to give proof of that genius for statecraft which she was convinced she possessed. The weeks passed in an agony of suspense, but brought no answer from Jovellanos. So her ambitions became focused once more on Buenos Aires.

She wrote to Dom John, intimating her renewed resolution to set sail thither. She was exasperated and astounded to receive in reply a letter refusing permission to her to go on the grounds that the Portuguese government could take no step in this matter without the concurrence of the British. The Seville plan had Dom John's approval: he had even consented to instructions being sent to the young Pedro de Sousa Holstein (afterwards celebrated as the Count, Marquis and Duke of Palmella) to go as plenipotentiary to Seville to press for the recognition of Dona Carlota's rights to the Spanish throne in the event of her brother's death : secondly, to secure recognition of Dona Carlota as Regent of Spain for the time being. But the Buenos Aires plan he was no longer disposed to sanction.

The fact is that Lord Strangford had now joined in the complicated conflict of interests which was being waged at Dom John's court, and that for the British government a number of independent republics in South America offered a more satisfactory prospect for British trade than either the establishment of two powerful and perhaps confederated empires or the continued subservience of the Spanish colonies to Spain. Nevertheless, Lord Strangford's influence was not the sole, though it was the most insistent, reason why Dom John had changed his mind. At the bottom of his heart he feared Dona Carlota Joaquina, and knew that she despised and hated him. When his ministers hinted that were she to find herself reigning in Buenos Aires not a month would pass before she would be organizing an army to march against Montevideo and Brazil itself, Dom John shivered. Terrible as his wife was in proximity, would she not be a hundred times more terrible, because more dangerous, in Buenos Aires ? All things considered, he became convinced at last that she was less of a positive and potential nuisance where she was.

Once having made up his mind (not without suffering the throes of mental anguish which were habitual to him when faced with taking a decision), Dom John embarked on the only policy which is ever adopted by a timid person towards an impetuous and pestilential enemy when both are equally stubborn at heart—a policy of evasion, invisibility and temporization. For nearly four years a strange drama was enacted at Rio de Janeiro ; a play that might be considered a comedy had there been passions less ugly than downright fear and hatred between the players. Dom John and the Princess hardly ever met. Yet when communications passed between them they were in the form of letters couched in terms of the most lavish endearment. Dom John lived at his palace of San Christovâo or in his island summer-house in the bay. Dona Carlota lived on her estate at Santa Cruz, at her town residence above the old mint, or in her delightful villas at Larangeiras and Rio Comprido, bowered in jacaranda and flowering aloes. Two distinct entourages composed the two royal households. The Prince Regent's most trusted counsellor was still Lobato, who shaved him. His chief minister was still Linhares, for whom Dona Carlota had a small repertory of venomous nick-names. She called him the Whipping-top, Old Fusspots, or Old Pot-pourri. Then there was the Marquis of Angeja, whom she styled Old Blockhead. Last, but not least, there was Lord Strangford, whose influence was in the ascendant until 1812.

On the side of the Princess was José Prezas, stuffing his ears against the almost incessant uproar in the servants' quarters and continually scribbling his inflammatory epistles to political malcontents in various parts of South America ; and there was Sir Sidney Smith, who no doubt found Dona Carlota's colourful establishment a welcome relief to life on board. The Admiral's only objection was to the education which she was giving Dom Miguel, an education so very different to that of an English Public School. He once remarked to Prezas, " If this boy is brought up properly, he has the makings of a hero. Otherwise he will turn into a tiger. . ."

A new actor was introduced on to the scene in February, 1809, when the Marquis of Casa Irujo arrived as envoy from the Seville Junta, with instructions to prevent Dona Carlota Joaquina going to any Spanish colony whatever, on the grounds that her presence would encourage the already existing separatist movements. Casa Irujo shared to the full the Princess's distrust of Lord Strangford, regarding him as primarily responsible for all the misfortunes that the Spanish empire was suffering, and it might be well argued that he would have been wiser to have made an ally out of Dona Carlota. But no : both the Spanish and the British envoys were equally hostile to her pretensions.

From the date of Casa Irujo's arrival the skein of intrigue becomes almost inextricably involved. The satellites whom Prezas had persuaded to act as the Princess's agents in Buenos Aires deceived her in secret, some remaining all the time hand in glove with Linniers, Dona Carlota's inveterate enemy ; others corresponding with Linhares at Rio and thus revealing the course of the negotiations to the Prince Regent's party. None was loyal to her with the exception of Prezas and the gallant admiral, and the latter, having very understandably caused considerable vexation to Lord Strangford by his indiscreet enthusiasm for Dona Carlota's cause, was recalled by the Admiralty in 1809. " That he had been over zealous," wrote his biographer, " was more than rumoured— it was publicly affirmed."

In May of the following year, the situation in Buenos Aires took a further turn unfavourable to the Princess. A revolutionary movement broke out, resulting in the formation of a practically independent provisional government. The Viceroy Cisneros, whom the Seville Junta had sent out to replace Linniers, was compelled to resign. Almost immediately afterwards the long-standing feud between Buenos Aires and Montevideo flared into open hostilities. The allegiance of both to Spain now hung by a thread. Rio de Janeiro swarmed with Argentine agents bargaining for foreign support in favour of an independent Argentine Republic. Casa Irujo endeavoured to secure their expulsion, but Lord Strangford protected them. In August, Casa Irujo wrote to his government that Montevideo was without adequate means of self-defence against the Argentines and that both colonies were as good as lost.

Confronted by this crisis, Dona Carlota and Casa Irujo at last buried the hatchet. Sending for the Spanish minister, she informed him that she had decided to sacrifice her jewels to provide arms for the defenders of Montevideo. Circumstances, she said, had made her aware at last that the Argentines were a pack of rebels ; but let Montevideo at least be saved at all cost for the Spanish crown. With that talent for dramatizing a situation which she shared with many famous men of action, she declared she intended to retain only a single gem, a brooch which she could not bring herself to part with since it framed a miniature of her beloved husband. Her magnanimous offer was accepted with emotion by Casa Irujo, who described the gesture as " worthy of Isabella, the glory of Spanish Queens."

Not content with this contribution, Dona Carlota wrote to Elio in Montevideo offering to go there at once " to animate the people." But having once been snubbed by Linniers, she was now snubbed by Elio. He sent word that her presence was not necessary. She wrote back to him in indignation, to say his refusal of her offer could not damp her ardour : " You will never," she wrote, " break my heart."

The sale of her jewels having realized fifty-three thousand pesetas, Casa Irujo and Dona Carlota spent part of this money on purchasing a small printing-press. It was put on board ship in the greatest secrecy for fear of Lord Strangford's intervention, and sent to Montevideo, where the governor, Elio, still loyal to the Spanish cause, was thereby enabled to organize some propaganda to combat the activities of innumerable rebels who were printing pamphlets in favour of republicanism and independence.

In the autumn of 1811, the Argentines were blockading the port of Montevideo, and Portuguese troops stationed in the south of Brazil marched to the aid of the beleaguered city. Dom John had, of course, his own designs in wishing to establish a protectorate. The issue of the war was a request for an armistice by Buenos Aires, whereupon Lord Strangford showed unsurpassed dexterity in getting himself appointed arbiter in the dispute. On the 11th October, an agreement was signed by the representatives of Portugal, Spain, Buenos Aires and Montevideo. The two colonies were declared, contrary to their sentiments, and traditions, to be bound by a defensive alliance, and the Portuguese troops were instructed to retire.

This treaty paved the way to the severance of the last slender ties that still attached the colonies to Spain. Dona Carlota was furious with Elio for having signed it ; furious with Casa Irujo ; more furious than ever with Lord Strangford. Though it may be argued that from the beginning she had been fighting a losing battle and that the eventual independence of the Spanish American possessions was inevitable, it must be admitted that she had shown more foresight as well as more spirit than the Spanish junta in Seville or the later-formed Council of Regency at Cadiz. The Spaniards might have done better to have trusted her and to have supported her cause. As it was, the Princess's hopes grew fainter as the months passed, and by the beginning of 1812, they were almost extinct. In March of that year Dom John insisted upon the dismissal of Prezas. In this matter also, Lord Strangford's influence was paramount.

Dona Carlota's grandiose plans had come to nothing because they had been confronted by a combination of insuperable obstacles. The suspicions of the British cabinet, the immemorial antipathy between Portuguese and Spaniards, the jealousy felt by the Argentines on account of Dom John's interference in Montevideo, the growing spirit of independence which caused Linniers and the Seville junta to be both suspicious of Dona Carlota but for opposite reasons—these are the real causes of her failure. In spite of her phenomenal vitality, the task she had set herself was impossible of achievement. Above all, it must be remembered of what huge dimensions was the chess-board on which she was manipulating her pieces. A letter might take three weeks to reach the Plate River : to reach Cadiz it might take three months.

Her hopes regarding Spain were doomed to a similar disappointment. Though Dom John, Linhares—everybody at Rio—was eager to abet and to see the last of her, and though the successive chiefs of the provisional Spanish governments during the Peninsular War—Jovellanos, Florida Blanca, the Marquis d'Astorgo—received her despatches by almost every Spanish ship that crossed the Atlantic, carrying her offers of services and statements of her claims to the Spanish Regency, yet the belated replies she received were invariably evasive. Spain was infected by the spirit of the age. Who was Carlota Joaquina ? A Princess whom a few remembered as a child of ten, leaving Madrid to marry a Portuguese Prince. She had become allied to a Royal House which had been driven by the French invasion far from European shores. The little that was known of her character consisted mostly of gossip that reminded men only too forcibly of her mother, the hated Maria Louisa.

Lastly, in analysing the reasons for her lack of success, we must bear in mind the curious but important fact that persons outside Spain, *even Spaniards themselves*, are incapable of assessing political forces inside Spain, and consequently always do the wrong thing.

Palmella at Seville actually succeeded in securing recognition of Dona Carlota Joaquina's eventual claims to the throne in the event of her brother's death, but this was a mere gesture of courtesy on the part of the Spaniards. No one in Seville was particularly anxious either to welcome Dona Carlota or to satisfy her numerous requests to be appointed arbiter in the Buenos Aires-Montevideo quarrel. In the summer of 1812, Palmella was transferred to London. He himself had never regarded the Princess's claims to the Spanish regency as practical, but at this time she chose to regard him as a personal supporter and his removal was a severe blow to her. In June of that year, news reached Rio de Janeiro that the Cadiz Council of Regency had adopted a Constitution, which was equivalent to hoisting the liberal flag.

Chapter VIII

THE news that the Spanish had adopted a Constitution shocked Dom John profoundly. Chamberlayn, who was Consul-General and Chargé d'Affaires in Rio de Janeiro after Lord Strangford's departure, noted " the sort of horror, notorious to everyone, with which he hears or utters the name of Constitution." Thus Dom John felt more than ever grateful that fate should have removed him far from the theatre of so much unrest, and the last thing in the world that he would have chosen to do was to return to Portugal.

When the soil of Portugal was at last liberated by the victories of the Peninsular War, the government at Lisbon was placed in the hands of a Council of Regency presided over by the Cardinal Patriarch. The Council consisted of nobodies who spent their time squabbling with Lord Beresford, who had been put in command of the Portuguese army and who was the real ruler of the country. It is not surprising that after eight years of war, suffering from the effects of first Junot's and then Massena's invasion, the nation was in a state of disorganisation and exhaustion from which it would have needed years of peace and ordered government to rescue her. The British government, therefore, in the hope of seeing normal trade relations with the Peninsula re-established—impatient, also, of Dom John's meddling in the affairs of the River Plate colonies—now suggested to the Prince Regent the expediency of his returning to his European kingdom. Frequent appeals in the same sense were also addressed to him by the Lisbon Council of Regency.

Dom John, however, not only preferred his present situation, but he regarded with loathing the inconveniences and perils of another sea voyage. He lived in particular dread of thunderstorms, and customarily insisted on retiring with his ministers into a grotto whenever there was a clap of thunder. Lord Strangford fell out of favour during the last two years of his mission for having pressed the Prince Regent somewhat too tenaciously to return to his former capital. Dom John, in short, refused to budge. Ward, the British Chargé d'Affaires at Lisbon, wrote in a despatch the year after Waterloo : " His Majesty's return is considered an object of remote contemplation."

The mad old Queen died in March, 1816, and Dom John became King John the Sixth. He was now heavier in build, much given to humming and hawing when anything occurred to vex him ; not in good health, suffering from a kind of hereditary scurvy that covered his legs in scales and pimples. Nevertheless, the first three years after his succession were to prove the most agreeable for him personally of all his agitated reign. Queen Carlota Joaquina, though she maintained contact with the Portuguese commander of the troops that still lingered in Montevideo, had had her powers for intrigue effectively crippled by the dismissal of Prezas. Don Pedro and Dom Miguel, who were both destined to cause him so much pain in later years, were engrossed in a succession of hectic love affairs. The King enjoyed pursuing his own obscure, tortuous, imaginative schemes for the territorial expansion of his empire, and was well content to confirm Lord Beresford's command in Portugal.

The Count of Linhares died in 1810, and was succeeded as Prime Minister by the Marquis of Aguiar, who on his death at a ripe old age was succeeded at the close of 1816 by none other than Antonio Araujo, now styled Count de Barca, who had played so prominent a part in the years previous to the court's migration. Though his pro-French policy had been proved a failure, and he had been forced to retire from active participation in government, he had never been removed by the King from the Council of State, and after ten years employing his active mind in the solitude of his vast library—translating Dryden's odes and Gray's " Elegy "—he once again became the principal figure at the King's side. But by this time he was as old and frail as his predecessor had been. " It is in fact somewhat surprising," wrote Chamberlayn, " how the government has gone on even till this time in the hands of two such infirm ministers. . . . Every branch of the administration is reported to be in almost irretrievable confusion." The Count de Barca undertook, in spite of his feebleness, responsibility for more portfolios than one. He devoted Monday to the department of Foreign Affairs and the Ministry of War ; Tuesday to that of the Interior ; Wednesday to that of the Treasury ; Thursday to transacting business with the King ; Friday to the Department of Marine ; Saturday to general conferences ; and Sunday to the affairs of the Household.

The employment of faithful old public servants until they drop in their tracks is a tradition in Portuguese public life. For several months towards the close of his life the Count de Barca, who continued to transact almost the entire business of the country, is said to have signed papers only with the aid of one, and later two, persons. And it may be added that when the Count de Barca expired and Chamberlayn went to see his successor *ad interim*, Bezarra, he found him in bed, unable to write, crippled with the gout, and trembling with the palsy.

The years 1816 and 1817 were marked by two outstanding events. In February of the former year a decree created Brazil a Kingdom, and united it to Portugal under the appellation of the " United Kingdoms of Portugal, Brazil and the Algarve." The decree flattered Brazilian sentiment, and if the recognition of two distinct though united crowns paved the way to their eventual separation, for the time being this aspect of the business passed unnoticed.

The latter year saw the arrival in Vienna of the Marquis of Marialva, with a suite whose magnificence evoked an Arabian tale, to ask the hand of the Arch-Duchess Leopoldina on behalf of Dom Pedro, Prince of Brazil. The miniature which the Marquis presented to the bride, a miniature of Dom Pedro set in a frame of diamonds of the finest water, caused a sensation at the Austrian court. The marriage took place by proxy on the 13th May. Then the bride, accompanied by a marvellous train of ladies-in-waiting, physicians, servants and musicians, set out for Leghorn to meet the Portuguese squadron that was to escort her to Rio de Janeiro.

She arrived at her destination on the 5th November, her baggage swelled by numerous cages containing parrots and macaws purchased in Madeira. Dom Pedro, tearing himself from the arms of the French opera dancer Naome Thierry, whom he had lodged in a chalet in the grounds of his father's residence at San Christoval, went to the ship to meet his bride. They were wafted to the quayside in a gilded barge, and thence proceeded to the royal chapel in procession. Every balcony was hung with carpets and shawls; the streets were strewn with flowers. In the forefront of the cortège moved a squadron of cavalry, followed by grooms of the palace leading two horses carrying the scarlet damask stools to be used at the ceremony. Then came mace-bearers, musicians, a coach containing the counsellors-of-state, and then lords-in-waiting and ushers, all riding in rich coaches and berlines, escorted by lackeys walking bare-headed. Lastly came Dom Pedro and his bride, in a state coach drawn by eight horses caparisoned in scarlet and gold.

Dona Carlota Joaquina made one of her rare public appearances to attend Dom Pedro's wedding, gorgeously decked out with plumes of birds-of-paradise.

All day long the cheers of the loyal populace resounded in the Palace Square, whither the cortége moved after the church ceremony to attend a state banquet in the royal palace. And at night, when the entire city was illuminated, the procession again formed, and made its way under elaborate triumphal arches erected for the occasion, the liveries flashing in the savage light of innumerable torches, to the quay of the Royal Arsenal, where a fleet of gondolas sparkling with candles waited to transport the Prince and Princess by river to San Christoval.

When one remembers the setting of these festivities, the extravagant mountains looming in the background, the tropic climate, the brilliant sunshine by day and the velvet warmth of the air by night, it will be realized that the Rio de Janeiro of King John the Sixth must have been a place of almost magic beauty.

And yet the ceremonies of Dom Pedro's marriage were eclipsed in magnificence by other masterpieces of state pageantry in the following year. There was, for instance, the Princess Leopoldina's birthday, celebrated by bull-fights and fireworks at San Christoval, and a gala performance at the Opera, where the ballet-master Lacombe presented a troop of two hundred dancers dressed as Indians. (The Indian, with his barbaric headdress of jewels and plumes, was fast becoming a kind of new national symbol for Brazil.) Then there was the great firework display to celebrate the anniversary of the decree creating Brazil a Kingdom, when a huge set-piece blazing on the mountainside portrayed an allegorical figure laying aside an Indian's feathered cape and head-plumes to assume a royal diadem and cloak. The House of Braganza has always patronized fireworks no less generously than music, and at Rio de Janeiro were to be seen fireworks that would have satisfied the standards even of King John the Fifth.

The apotheosis of the reign was Dom John's " acclamation " in February, 1818. For the ancient ceremony at which the monarch was acclaimed by his subjects, a huge gallery was constructed at one corner of the Palace Square, decorated with eighteen arcades, surmounted by a riot of allegorical plaster statuary, and containing various tribunes reserved for the royal family, the diplomatic corps, and the court. The ceilings displayed paintings " representing " (writes the historian Oliveira Lima) " the virtues of a King who was ascending the throne of his ancestors far from the ancient seat of his monarchy, but at the heart of a new empire which he himself had called into being." On the water-side the Municipality had constructed a " Temple of Minerva," designed by a talented French émigré. A statue of the goddess was to be seen in an attitude of benevolent protection, her hand extended over an effigy of the King. At the entrance, in bas-relief, were Poetry, History and Fame, paying tribute to the monarch (somewhat confused, perhaps, by the proximity of the Principal Rivers of the Four Parts of the Globe, presenting cornucopiæ symbolic of commercial opulence). Nearby was a triumphal arch in painted scenery, erected at the expense of the Royal Board of Trade, crowned with another busy group of mythical or allegorical beings, and framing transparencies representing Dom John's patronage of the Arts and Commerce. In the middle of the square rose an imitation red granite obelisk of striking elegance of design.

A glittering assembly of knights-at-arms, heralds, guards, lords-in-waiting, bishops and grandees attended Dom John at his acclamation. Dom Pedro acted as Constable ; the Marquis of Bellas commanded the gentlemen-at-arms ; the Marquis of Castello Melhor, groom of the bed-chamber, presented the cushion when the King knelt. At night the populace flooded the Sant'Anna gardens, where the royal family and the court took their seats in a pavilion, to admire a hundred and two illuminated obelisks grouped round an artificial lake, and to applaud a two-hour spectacle consisting of cavalry manœuvres, dances, recitations and patriotic hymns.

But even the every-day life of Rio de Janeiro at this period was like some gorgeous, perpetual ballet. The magnificence of King John the Fifth—a magnificence at once slovenly and splendid—was revived under the tropic Brazilian sky with an exuberance, an extravagant wealth of picturesque detail, which even the Lisbon Patriarchate never equalled. The *Miserere* of Pergoletti was sung in Holy Week in the royal chapel with a perfection comparable to the performances of the Sistine Chapel. At the Opera House the orchestra was hardly less accomplished. The scenery and dresses were sumptuous, while the eye wandered from Monsieur Lacombe's cosmopolitan corps-de-ballet (there were French girls and Spanish, and a famous mulatress) to the fabulous display of beauty and diamonds in the boxes.

At his favourite country retreat of San Christoval the King, according to the ancient traditions of the Braganzas, received the homage of his subjects—rich and poor, white and coloured—every evening, except on Sundays and saints' days, from eight to nine o'clock. A band of music played below the palace windows (on a flight of steps identical to those at Syon House, presented to Dom John, for some reason unknown to the historian, by the Duke of Northumberland). On foot, on horseback or in cabriolets, the inhabitants of the capital jostled each other in the cool of the evening on the road to San Christoval. The King was never happier than on these occasions. His prodigious Braganza memory for faces and anecdote enabled him to recognize and remember every one of the multi-coloured crowd passing before his throne. His goodness of heart expanded in countless small acts of benevolence.

Yet it was not necessary to go to the Royal Chapel, the Opera House or the court to watch an unending spectacle of colour and amusement which was to be enjoyed in every alley and corner of the Brazilian capital. Here were the begging friars in green or blue or scarlet tunics, with their large crimson offertory bags embroidered with an image of the Virgin in heavy silver ; here might be seen the baptism of some young negro, his estatic god-mother arrayed with barbaric splendour ; or the funeral of a black baby, in an open coffin as richly decorated as a wedding-cake, exposing to view the tiny black corpse fitted with doves' wings ; or, perhaps, the dramatic funeral of some slave who had been a great lord in Quilumana or Cabinda, the body transported to the grave in a net-work hammock, attended by the solemn representatives of a dozen African tribes, preceded by a gigantic nigger letting off squibs and rockets, and followed by a long train of grief-stricken blacks, some venting their sorrow in wild, obscene gestures, others raising their voices in piercing lament to the accompaniment of drums and tom-toms.

On the days of the great religious processions all Rio de Janeiro was *en fête*. On the 28th January, the image of Saint Sebastian was carried through the streets dressed in the rich robes of the Order of Christ. On Ash-Wednesday Saint Anthony was borne in a procession whose pomp contrasted forcibly with the poverty of the Franciscan Convent where the image customarily reposed. The figure stood upon clouds of gold and silver wire, studded with countless painted-plaster cherubs, attended by angels with puffed skirts like ballerinas. A jumble of other saints figured in the cortège, dolls representing the negro Saint Benedict, a King, a Queen, a Pope complete with his Sacred College ; King Louis of France wearing his three carnations and a crown of thorns, but represented returning from the crusades in a court-costume of the eighteenth-century, with a powdered wig like a character in Molière and a magician's star-spangled cloak. And to complete the picture, we must recall the hundred rich banners and palanquins of scarlet and gold flashing in the sun, the thousands of candles carried by the faithful ; and the profusion of tropical flowers trampled in the dust and commotion of the streets.

For the whole city, rich and poor alike, these feast-days were public holidays. The respected members of the Municipal Council in their robes, bishops in their mitres and gold-shot vestments, grandees in knee-breeches, glittering with stars and ribbons, rubbed shoulders with the half-naked slaves that crowded in from the neighbouring plantations to see the fun.

The procession of the *Corpo de Deus* in June was the most famous. It was a carnival in itself. Its principal feature was the armed figure of Saint George on horse-back, glittering with diamonds lent for the occasion by the Duke of Cadaval, escorted by outriders and picadors in the royal liveries, preceded by negro musicians half-choked by the gunpowder from ten thousand rockets, squibs and bombs.

But of all the religious solemnities that punctuated the year, surely the strangest mixture of the mystic with the profane must have been that ceremony on the second Friday in Lent when the women of Rio de Janeiro went in a body to the cathedral to kiss the feet of the Saviour. Old and young, countesses, shop-girls, female slaves and prostitutes, all decked in their best, prostrated themselves before the Symbol of Sacrifice, and at night, returning from the church in procession, moved in promiscuous confusion down the illuminated streets, escorted by courtiers and grave senators carrying lanterns on long staffs, and attended by the King's liveried guard.

In reading the yellowing letters and despatches of the period, such are some of the episodes that form the scintillating backcloth to the Brazilian stage, in front of which the principal actors of the period stand out in vivid relief ; the indolent, good-natured, uncouth figure of the King, sprinkled with stale snuff ; the dwarfish beplumed Queen, her heart smouldering with hatred and frustrated lust for power ; Prince Pedro with the frame of a ring-master and as swarthy as a gypsy, brandishing an immense stock-whip all day long in the royal park, breaking-in the horses of the royal stables ; Dom Miguel hardly distinguishable in his dress from a cowboy, soaked in perspiration (as the traveller Henderson surprised him at San Christoval), with a long goad, driving a new plough behind a treble team of oxen ; the King's second minister, the Count de Arcos, naïvely inquiring of the French chargé d'affaires ; " Expliquez-moi, s'il vous plait, ce que c'est que la guerre du Rio de la Plata, dont la politique et le bût sont aussi enigmatiques pour moi que les mouvements du Général Lecor ; " the eccentric Russian ambassador, de Balk Polef, who according to Chamberlayn constantly and openly designated the Count de Barca by the appellation of " Conde de la Limonade," and whose improprieties ultimately caused the King to apply to St. Petersburg for his recall ; the Austrian envoy, Count Eltz, whose pecuniary distress alternated with Balk Polef as the favourite subject of gossip among the diplomatic corps ; and, last but not least, the Nuncio, the aged Cardinal Callepi, the kindest, the wittiest and the most polished of diplomatic deans, who, having been left behind in Lisbon when the French entered the city, managed to escape at night attended by a single servant, both disguised as fishermen, and to get on board a British frigate beyond the bar.

Then, besides princes and ministers and statesmen, other less worldly personalities find mention in these despatches : the British merchants with their flair for securing all the best sites for their villas on the beaches at Flamengo and Botafolga ; the two rival English clergymen, Mr. Crane and Mr. Hoste, whose struggle to get possession of the pulpit of the English Church split the English community into two opposing camps ; passing travellers, such as a Mr. William Effingham Laurence who arrived in a small cutter, with mechanics and agricultural instruments on board, on his way to form an establishment at Van Diemen's Land. " This gentleman during his stay," wrote Chamberlayn, " was exceedingly desirous of contributing his mite towards the liberty and happiness of Brazil, for which purpose he had provided himself with some of Mr. Jeremy Bentham's constitutions which he presented to various people." And lastly there was King Tamehameha of the Sandwich Islands with his queen and a suite of ten, on their way to England to pay their respects at Windsor. " The King," wrote the British Minister, " seems to be about 27 years of age, and the Queen to be some years younger. She is above six feet high."

It may be added, that apart from the intrinsic interest of their subject matter, the diplomatic despatches of this period preserved in His Majesty's Record Office deserve reading for their very style. The English language has never become crystallized like the French (the memoirs of the Count de Castellane are essentially in the style of Saint Simon). No one, therefore, would wish to argue that the form of Chamberlayn's or Sir Edward Thornton's correspondence should serve as a model for His Majesty's ambassadors and ministers today. But they are admirable in themselves—admirable because the English language in Sir Edward's day happened to have produced a vehicle of expression which in lucidity and exactness has perhaps never been excelled at any other period. Their phrases are chiselled like lapidary inscriptions, while in feeling as well as in style they call to mind those epitaphs decorated with their marble urns and their weeping willows that, in the aisles of our English churches, are so evocative of the sensibility and fine feeling of a vanished age !

" His Majesty's faithful and loyal Subjects in this Part of the World," wrote Thornton to the Foreign Secretary (Lord Castlereagh) on receipt of the news of George the Third's death, " had been prepared for the confirmation of this melancholy Intelligence by the Report of a Merchant Vessel, which had spoken His Majesty's Sloop *Brazen* off the Cape Verde Islands ; and I should not be doing Justice to them all, if I did not assure Your Lordship that it was received with Feelings not unworthy of that Veneration and enthusiastic Attachment which had never ceased to adorn and to console His Majesty's long, glorious, and eventful Reign."

Chamberlayn's pen was hardly less polished than Thornton's. The last paragraph of his despatch describing Count Eltz's pecuniary troubles is as consciously balanced as a sonnet : " In Fact," he wrote, " the very retired Manner in which Count Eltz has lived, and the total Absence of that Pomp and the generous Style of Living suitable, and customary, amongst Ministers of His Excellency's exalted Character, have been the general Topick of Conversation, in which even his own Suite have joined ; and they disguise neither their Dissatisfaction nor their Disappointment at the Effect necessarily produced on the Opinion of the Publick by the very parsimonious Scale of Establishment adopted by the first Austrian Ambassador that has been seen in Brazil."

Chapter IX

THE theatrical beauty of Rio de Janeiro meant little to Dona Carlota Joaquina. Political power was what she thirsted for, and what there now appeared to be no hope of her ever attaining as long as the court remained in Brazil. Her last attempt to establish influence in Spain was made in 1811 : She wrote to the Cadiz Cortes in June of that year congratulating them upon the adoption of their " good and wise Constitution "! And there is also extant an unctuous letter which she addressed about the same time to a Father José Ramires, a secretary of the Seville Junta, in which she affirmed that she hoped to live to see the end of all despotism, " a system so contrary to the interests of peoples and of sovereigns themselves, that only by ignorance can they employ it."

These letters are most damaging evidence against the Queen's character. She, the heiress of the Bourbons, the symbol and flag—as she later became—of the Absolutist cause, conveys these congratulations to a Cortes ! To meet the charge of hypocrisy that must inevitably be made against her, it can only be suggested that at this time of her life she simply did not understand what the Spanish Cortes stood for. But these letters show above all how her political opinions were based on personalities and not on principles. She detested her husband : she was aware at the same time that he feared and loathed Constitutions. Automatically the spirit of opposition tempted her to espouse the Constitutional cause. Later on, it was to be Dom John's tolerance of a Constitution which was to prompt her to raise the standard of absolutism, a cause which she was naturally fitted to support by her temperament and family traditions : but it was accident that dictated her choice of that side. It happened, as we shall see, to be the side holding out the best prospects for the gratification of her two principal ambitions— the humiliation of her husband, and the acquirement of the supreme influence in the state.

The replies which she received to her letters to Seville were aloof and curt, and the correspondence petered out. After all the strain and excitement of the past four years, her disappointment now brought about a nervous reaction that took toll of her health. Following a slight heart attack, she retired into seclusion at Santa Cruz. Fate had decreed that for ten years she should remain in the political wilderness. If she was rescued from her impotence and given the opportunity to play a hand at last, it was only as a result of a long sequence of events that occurred both in Portugal and in Brazil. It is necessary, therefore, in order to understand the significance of her name in Portuguese history, to leave Queen Carlota Joaquina for the time being sulking in the hybiscus groves of her villa, and to examine those historical happenings which not only brought about the return of the royal family to Portugal, but provided the Queen with her long-awaited chance after she had returned.

In March, 1817, news reached Rio de Janeiro that a rebellion had broken out among the troops stationed at the coastal town of Pernambuco. This revolt had not been caused primarily by any effervescence of liberal idealism. It was simply the result of mal-administration combined with anti-Portuguese feeling. But it was lent a liberal and republican complexion by a handful of political agitators who exploited the general unrest for their own ends ; they proclaimed the formation of a government and the independence of the Republic of Pernambuco. The ill-starred Republic lasted just ten weeks. The populace in Rio rallied in support of the King. He was given a delirious reception at the Opera House : and seven thousand volunteers offered to take up arms for the unity of Brazil. By the end of April General Luiz de Rego was ready to march on Pernambuco from Bahia : the infant Republic became demoralized at the news of his advance, the population fled in panic into the jungle, and on the 23rd May the government troops occupied the port almost without bloodshed.

The extinction of the revolt provided an excuse for fireworks and illuminations in Rio de Janeiro, but seemed at the time to have no more important political sequel than general rejoicing. Nevertheless, this rebellion has historical significance because of the repercussions which it caused on the other side of the Atlantic, in Portugal.

The population of Portugal felt a growing resentment at the prolonged absence of their King and court. They knew that King John not only wished to stay where he was, but did all in his power to prevent his courtiers from returning to Lisbon. Seeing that the metropolis of the Portuguese empire had been moved to Rio de Janeiro, the Portuguese were indignant at the thought that Portugal was to become, if Dom John persisted in his present attitude of mind, a mere colony of Brazil. They were jealous of the power wielded by Lord Beresford as Commander-in-Chief of the Army—he was a brave and competent soldier, but in political matters he was heavy-handed and short-sighted—while Portuguese soldiers coveted the places still being occupied by British officers. Above all, the Portuguese were resentful at seeing the royal revenues exported across the sea. All these sentiments in combination, reinforced by the economic distress which was the result of the late wars, created a hot-house for masonic revolutionary intrigues that were now linked with international secret societies at Paris, Madrid and Naples.

The Lisbon conspiracy of May, 1817, which was directly encouraged by the news of the rising in Pernambuco, is associated with the name of General Gomes Freire, the same who had been in command of the Portuguese troops on the coast when Junot's army invaded Portugal. This man is an object of particular odium to modern Portuguese nationalists because he is regarded as representing an internationalized type perverted by foreign ideologies. Subsequent to the invasion of Portugal, he accepted joint command with the Marquis of Alorna of the

Portuguese Legion which was sent to France to fight under Napoleon's orders. After Waterloo, he returned to Lisbon, and being a mason was shortly afterwards elected Portuguese Grand Master.

He soon began to parley with masons at Madrid with a view to overthrowing the Regency at Lisbon, expelling Beresford, and setting up some kind of liberal Peninsula Federation in conjunction with Spain. No scheme could have been devised to create a greater menace to Portugal's independence. The Spaniards, who were irritated by Dom John's occupation of Montevideo, dreamed of annexing Portugal as compensation; and, observing the state of neglect into which the country had fallen during the court's absence, imagined that their task would be easy.

They had not, however, reckoned with Beresford, who on the 24th May informed the Regency at Lisbon of the indubitable evidence of a conspiracy that had come to his hands. The Lisbon garrison was called to arms : Gomes Freire was arrested, together with sixteen other officers who were implicated. They were taken to Saint Julian's Fort, tried by drum-head court-martial, and shot.

The conspiracy was thus nipped in the bud, but Beresford felt increasingly uneasy. He knew that his severity had offended the populace and that he had lost his popularity with the army, whose wages he was unable to pay because there was no money in the Regency's exchequer. So in September he sent an emissary to the King with despatches urging the return of at least one member of the royal family " as the only means of quieting Portugal or even of saving her."

Dom John, however, turned a deaf ear. His whole attention was absorbed by the news coming in from the Plate River. That very August he had returned a refusal to a request from the Spanish government to evacuate Montevideo, and in September he sent another two thousand men to reinforce General Lecor who, at the head of the Portuguese troops (all the best regiments who had distinguished themselves in the Peninsular War and whose removal from Lisbon was another cause of discontent), had been holding Montevideo for the past year against the Uruguayan patriot Artegas. Considering Dom John's usual indolence and good-nature, his obstinacy over this question of Montevideo is astonishing.

Lord Castlereagh was alive to the difficulties inherent in the proposal that the Portuguese royal family should return to Lisbon. He supposed that the Brazilians would themselves resent such a step. But, as he remarked to Palmella in June, 1817, the continued absence of the Braganzas " reduced to a state of paralysis one of the members of the European republic." He urged that the King should at least send to Europe his eldest son Dom Pedro. But to this plan also Dom John was obstinately opposed. He would take nobody's advice in the matter, yet he had no proposal to make on his own. For three years the British Minister Sir Edward Thornton argued with the Count de Barca without making the smallest headway.

By the spring of 1820 Beresford considered the situation so desperate that he decided to make a personal attempt to influence Dom John, and in May he arrived in Rio de Janeiro. He told the King frankly that a revolution would break out in Lisbon unless something was done. He asked for a seat on the Council of Regency. Lastly he urged for the payment of the arrears in wages due to the Portuguese army.

But Dom John was still unable to make up his mind. " Delay," wrote Thornton, " is the radical fault of this government—I ought, perhaps, to say absolute in action." Rumours of political disturbances in Spain increased the King's timidity, and at the same time piled fuel on the smouldering fires of unrest in both Lisbon and Rio de Janeiro. " The increasing interest in new events," wrote Thornton, " as well as the ill-judged anxiety of this government to prevent their Circulation . . . are all calculated to give new Force and Vivacity to these Conversations and Sentiments." Dom John's pusillanimity is illustrated by the fact that, although he was fighting against any suggestion that he should move, he was one day overheard remarking placidly to his crony Lobato that " perhaps he might see himself in Lisbon when he least expected it."

His words were prophetic. The situation both in Brazil and in Portugal was in reality more critical than even Thornton or Beresford knew. If the long-impending explosion took place first in Portugal, it was merely because a spark to touch the powder happened to blow over the frontier from Spain.

It will be remembered that the Spanish Cortes summoned by the Seville Junta in 1812 had adopted a Constitution. This Constitution had been based on the French Constitution of 1791, from which it had borrowed all the most enthusiastic and most unworkable provisions, rejecting altogether the traditional system of government in Spain. When, in 1813, Napoleon restored the crown to King Ferdinand the Seventh, the Cortes exacted a conditional promise of respect for this Constitution, but it was so odious to the nation that Ferdinand soon repudiated it without exciting a murmur of protest.

But Ferdinand had not been a month in Madrid before Spain was once more burdened with all the paraphernalia of her traditional misrule. The Inquisition was restored, the innumerable religious communities were reinstated in their wealth and power, and a relentless persecution was begun against all that savoured of French fashions or liberalism. Even the most reactionary European powers viewed the excesses of the Spanish government with alarm, which was increased by the obviously precarious condition of the country's affairs. Trade had been ruined ; commerce overseas had been destroyed by the revolt of the South American colonies ; armies of brigands scoured the highroads, while the soldiers, ragged and starving, joined the beggars at the monastery gates.

The general distress soon caused the repudiated Constitution to become a rallying cry to the discontented. When in January, 1820, mutiny broke out among the troops at Cadiz, Colonel Riego at the head of a battalion raised the standard of revolt and proclaimed the Constitution of 1812. One province after another rose against the government : rioting broke out in Madrid, and in March King

Ferdinand was compelled to " sware to " the Constitution once again and to summon a new Cortes.

The news of this revolution across the frontier spread like wild-fire among the political clubs in Portugal. The masons, who remembered the prompt suppression of the Gomes Freire plot, realized that with Beresford absent at Rio de Janeiro their hour had surely struck. It was not the masons, however, who made the first open move ; discontent, as we have observed, was universal, and the revolution of 1820 was at its outset a truly national movement. Its first instrument was the army, jealous of the British command and angry at the non-payment of its wages. It was only when the torrent had been loosed that the masons pushed their boats into the stream.

A certain Colonel Sepulveda was in command of an infantry regiment quartered at Oporto. On the 24th August he and a Colonel of Artillery named Sebastiâo Cabreira ordered their troops on parade and called for cheers for " the Constitution." No single soldier on the barrack square could have understood what exactly a Constitution meant : it is extremely doubtful whether the colonels themselves knew. But the regiments answered with a roar, the explosion of five years of pent-up discontent. The whole of Oporto—the clergy, the nobility, the people and the army—came out in support of Sepulveda.

The following proclamation was then issued by a Military Council : " Soldiers ! Our patience is at an end, our country reduced to slavery, your own consideration lost, our sacrifices made in vain, a Portuguese soldier on the eve of being reduced to ask alms. Comrades ! Let us make a provisional government, which may call upon a Cortes *to organize a Constitution, the want of which is the origin of all our evils* ! " In response to this appeal the various regiments stationed in the northern provinces proclaimed their adherence to the constitutional cause, and marched into Oporto.

Colonel Sepulveda and Colonel Cabreira combined with various members of revolutionary clubs to form a " Provisional Council of the Supreme Government," to which the troops and the city authorities swore obedience. The first act of this Council was to dismiss all British officers holding commands in the Oporto district.

At Lisbon the members of the Regency gathered in perturbation at the palace of the Cardinal Patriarch at Junqueira. But little was to be hoped for from a body of men the chief of whom, in Ward's words, was " little better than an old woman," the second of whom was bedridden, and the other two, " however good and estimable men, by no means possessing that energy of character which the present crisis demands." The only decision they took was to send for Palmella, who happened to be lodged close-by in the palace of the Marquis of Marialva, having recently relinquished his appointment as minister in London. Palmella had been appointed a Minister of State, and was on his way to Rio de Janeiro to add his voice to Lord Beresford's appeals to the King either to return to Portugal himself or to send the Prince Royal. He now waited in Lisbon to see what turn the events at Oporto were going to take.

Summoned to the Regency, Palmella persuaded them to call a Council of State, and proposed that they should summon a Cortes of their own accord without delay, in which proposal he was warmly seconded by his relative, the Marquis of Castello Melhor. But just as the question was being put to the vote, the meeting was thrown into confusion by the Marquis being struck by a fit of apoplexy.

Meanwhile terrifying news was filtering into Lisbon : the Oporto regiments were marching on the capital and had already occupied Coimbra half-way ; the Coimbra garrison had gone over to the Constitutionalists ; the entire country was rising.

The Cardinal Patriarch was in no manner fitted to deal with the crisis. Being a dwarf hardly four feet high, he was lost in the crowd of ecclesiastics that now swarmed in alarm through the corridors of his palace. The three hundred and forty prelates, canons, chaplains and confessors of the Patriarchal Church, and the deacons of his Sacred College (attired, according to the special privilege granted to King John the Fifth by the Pope, in robes identical to those of the Vatican), and the Patriarch's servants (all dressed like the Pope's chamberlains), and a countless number of sacrists, acolytes and monks, fluttered helplessly round him. The confusion was certainly not lessened by the influx of most of the Castello Melhor family, come to nurse the stricken marquis, who was too ill to be moved. The Cardinal Patriarch, however, rather enjoyed the airless sick-room, and one day arrived at the bedside accompanied by the bishops of his Patriarchate, to inform the invalid in the strictest confidence (there must have been at least fifty persons present) that efficacious measures had been taken to confound the advancing rebel army ; he had excommunicated them ! Then, forgetting in the anxiety of the moment what little geography he ever knew, he informed his entourage that there was no danger, since the rebel army had no means of crossing the Tagus (whose course does not, in fact, run between Coimbra and Lisbon). Moreover, he declared, a miracle had been vouchsafed ! Every fountain had dried up all the way between Redinha and Leiria, and so Colonel Sepulveda's regiment had died of thirst.

The Regency did not, however, rely upon miracles to save the situation. The Count of Barbaçena, who had lately arrived from Rio de Janeiro, was promoted general and ordered to march northwards with an infantry division and two regiments of cavalry.

It might be supposed that a civil war was inevitable. But on the 15th September the flames of revolt made their appearance on the very threshold of the Regency. On that day the Lisbon garrison and all the troops remaining in the capital threw in their lot with the constitutionalists at Coimbra. Two regiments commanded by the Count of Redinha and the Count of Penafiel marched in good order to the Rocio Square. The Mayor of Lisbon was forced to appear on a balcony, to declare the Regency deposed and to announce the formation of a new interim government of Lisbon.

The Oporto army halted in Alcobaça. And with them halted the motley group of clerks, lawyers and half-pay colonels, who, uninvited, had proclaimed themselves to be active members of the Oporto government. With the capital in revolution at their backs, the regiments of the Count of Barbaçena would have been helpless even if the majority of his general staff had not been already secretly in league with the insurgents. They went over *en masse* to the other side. And on 11th October the united constitutionalists made a solemn entry into Lisbon. The chief members of the Oporto junta rode in brilliant state coaches, while the others were packed into the string of broken-down caleches covered in dust, in which they had made the long journey from the north.

The personages in the cortège who attracted the greatest public attention were, of course, the two colonels, Sepulveda and Cabreira. The former was a smart and serious young officer, and it is significant that his staff was largely composed of officers who ten years later fought and died for Dom Miguel. It was not enthusiasm for liberal doctrine, but simply disgust with the wretched condition of their country, that had brought them out. As for Colonel Cabreira, who was an old man, it was obvious that he belonged to the old régime rather than the new. The skirts of his coat touched his ankles ; his epaulettes were of different sizes, and his gigantic lop-sided hat was plumed with a black horse's tail. His sword was so long that it dragged on the ground behind him ; and so he had fixed on the tip of the sheath a small wheel that left a little furrow where he passed. Over his uniform he had put on an antique breast-plate. He imagined himself to be another Holy Constable and believed that his march on Lisbon was a victory as historic as Aljubarrota. He had collected around him a general staff of more than a hundred persons of every description and degree of eccentricity.

The Oporto revolution was certainly an epoch-making event, though not in the sense that poor old Cabreira imagined. The traditional, centuries-old Portuguese monarchy—the absolute royal power tempered by the sovereign's paternal care—was shattered for ever in August, 1820, by the cries of *Viva a Constitucâo !* Gone for ever was the old unity, the simple faith and loyalty centring round church and throne. But above all else the revolution was a manifestation of the new spirit of the age demanding expression. For the past quarter of a century it had been infiltrating the economically-weakened structure of Portuguese society. It was now potent enough to constitute a challenge to inherited institutions and, in conflict with them, to produce a series of explosions. The Old and the New Spirit stood face to face, and it was the conflict between them which was ultimately to provide Dona Carlota Joaquina with the chance she longed for to re-enter the political arena.

Chapter X

DOM JOHN was continuing his customary existence at Rio de Janeiro, going backwards and forwards from San Christoval over the blue water to his summer-house on the Island of the Governador. The island was shaped like a ship, and it was the only ship that the King ever wished to tread again. He who always regarded the peacefulness of his Brazilian capital as its first recommendation and who was lulled into a sense of divine security by its balmy and enervating sunshine never dreamed that there in Rio de Janeiro also an underground unrest was threatening his throne just as an obscure disease can be at work in the blood without its victim being aware of it.

For the past two years two inflammatory newspapers, the *Correio Brazilense* and the *Portuguez*, had been circulating in Brazil. King John, having no experience of the power of the press, was unconscious of the dangerous influence they wielded. Palmella, who was a man of the nineteenth century and who knew moreover how closely linked were the subversive movements in Brazil and in Portugal, had secured a promise from Lord Castlereagh that copies of these newspapers should not be carried to Lisbon in British ships.

Dom John, however, was so truly loved by his Brazilian subjects that the political agitators at Rio de Janeiro might not have succeeded in making serious trouble had it not been that they were encouraged by events in Portugal and that, just as the masons in Portugal were able to exploit political discontent and economic difficulties for their own ends, so in Brazil the agitators were astute enough to exploit the jealousy felt by the Brazilians towards the Portuguese.

Some more troops that had lately arrived from Lisbon under the command of the Marquis of Angeja were not sent to reinforce General Lecor, but were placed as garrison in Rio de Janeiro. The bitterest hatred soon sprang up between these Portuguese and the Brazilian regiments lately returned from Pernambuco. All ranks in the Brazilian army above that of captain were reserved by an ill-judged decree for Portuguese officers. There were frequent brawls at night in the ill-lit streets of the capital, and the jealousy between the Brazilians and the Portuguese grew to such proportions that a review of troops had to be postponed for fear that the " Heroes of Pernambuco " and the " Heroes of Talavera " should kick each other in the ranks. Another cause of resentment against the government was that Dom John was prepared to take into consideration the urgent demands being made by Great Britain for the abolition of the slave trade.

The King was still humming and hawing over Lord Beresford's most unpleasant and worrying report of affairs in Portugal when, on the 17th October, the frigate *La Créole* arrived in the bay with despatches giving an account of the Constitutionalist movement at Oporto (news of subsequent developments in Lisbon did not reach him until nearly a month later). The ship also carried mail, so the information was all over the capital in less than twenty-four hours.

Thornton on going to San Christoval found the poor King very much alarmed. He pointed out to Dom John, however, that his absence from Lisbon at this juncture might prove an advantage. " I observed," wrote Thornton, " that the Distance of His Majesty from the Scene left him at complete liberty with regard to the deliberations of the Cortes which they might present for his Acceptance : that his Sanction could not be extorted by the tumultuary Demands of a mutinous Army, as in Spain, or with the Bayonet at his throat (the King interrupting me with this expression) as with the King of Naples."

Dom John sensibly asked for written opinions from two ministers, Villanova and the Count de Arcos, and eleven of his courtiers, as to the best course of action for him to pursue. Eight of these advised sending Dom Pedro to Lisbon without delay. Then the King shut himself up alone and composed a despatch which was sent on board a ship in the harbour, and the ship was kept under guard all night before sailing.

The King's instructions to the Regency were in harmony with the traditional paternal clemency of the Portuguese monarchy. He sent his royal pardon to the Oporto rebels ; he sanctioned the summoning of the Cortes, merely expressing his regret that an appeal had not been first made to the crown. Lastly, he asked to receive a statement of the nation's complaints and promised either to return himself to Lisbon, or to send the Prince Royal Dom Pedro in his place.

It is of no use to point out the much more energetic measures which Dom John ought to have taken to deal with the situation ; to say that he ought to have sent Dom Pedro to Lisbon on the first ship leaving Rio de Janeiro. Had he been capable of such foresight or energy, he would have done so directly he received the news of the revolution in Spain. It is equally useless to reproach him for not forming a strong cabinet to decide upon a firm line of policy. The necessary talent did not exist among his courtiers, who, like the King himself, mentally as well as geographically, were remote from Europe.

It seemed at times as if the King deliberately shut his eyes and ears to the political problems confronting him. When the French Chargé d'Affaires attempted to discuss the question of Constitutionalism objectively, Dom John declined to continue the conversation. It was something altogether too horrible to admit of discussion. If he had been incapable of taking any decision when Junot's army was advancing on Lisbon, until compelled by the desperate turn of events to do something at the very last moment, how could it be expected that now that he was thirteen years older, after thirteen years spent in a tropical climate, he should give proof of any greater capacity for making up his mind ? The only thing he could think of was to instruct his police to suppress all news from Portugal, as if he believed that the fools' paradise in which he had been living so pleasantly could be preserved artificially. Of course the police found their task impossible. The whole town knew as much, and more, than he did. And unpleasant portents of coming trouble now made their appearance in the very heart of his capital. As if in response to a long-awaited signal, a torrent of pamphlets ridiculing the monarchy issued from secret printing-presses. The *Correio Portuguez* was now openly insulting. But no police action was taken over this dangerous propaganda. The King just did nothing and hoped for the best. He was an optimist like the Cardinal Patriarch at Lisbon, and perhaps, like him, was waiting for a miracle. Lord Beresford, at any rate, was now on his way back to Portugal. Would not discipline at Oporto be re-established when he arrived with money for the army ?

The frightful news of the spread of the revolution to Lisbon arrived in Rio on the 12th November, not long after Beresford's departure. It threw Dom John into a fresh agony of mind worse than the first. And the more distressed he became, the more impossible was it for him to make any move one way or the other. The British Government, fearful of the consequences that might ensue upon the possible intervention of other European powers in the affairs of the Peninsula, put their hopes in the influence that Palmella, who had at last started for Rio de Janeiro, might be able to exert over the King. Thornton was no less anxious than Lord Castlereagh to see Palmella arrive. " I take the Liberty of observing to your Lordship," he wrote on the 18th November, " that since the Count of Palmella is called to take no part in the new System of Government at Lisbon . . . his Presence becomes more and more essential here. The two Ministers who divide the Government of this country, Mr. de Vilanova and the Conde de Arcos, are in decided Hostility to each other, and, as far as I can learn and as seems to be the case, propose Systems of Action diametrically opposite to each other. . . . Between these two opposite Impulsions, the King, whose very Character is Irresolution and Uncertainity, will I fear take no Steady or Quick Decision, or perhaps none but under the Impulsion of some new and violent Emergency, for which any Decision may perhaps be too late. So much is this the case, that I have the best Ground to believe that His Majesty has never given the Slightest Intimation to the Prince Royal of an Intention to send His Royal Highness to Portugal, the latter having learnt it from Communications of Persons more immediately about the King."

Another circumstance (the despatch went on) added to the King's customary irresolution. The news of the Emperor of Austria's interference in Italy, to protect Milan and Tuscany from the revolutionary contagion which had broken out in Naples, led the King to believe in exactly that possibility which was most feared by Lord Castlereagh—that the European powers, bound in an alliance against revolution under the inspiration of Metternich, might be prepared somehow to put his house in order on his behalf.

Thornton closed his despatch by a reference to the effect that the news from Europe was having on public opinion in Brazil. " Whatever that Effect may be," he added, " it is unquestionably increased by the injudicious Conduct of the Administration, which endeavours to suppress in a Manner almost ridiculous the Circulation of Intelligence which is secretly known to everyone." There were already current rumours of fresh discontent at Pernambuco and Bahia. The only thing that everyone could agree upon was, that for the time being they had better simply wait for Palmella.

Palmella ! The name already cast a spell. Who was this still-youthful statesman (he was thirty-nine) whose prestige caused everyone concerned with Portugal's destinies to turn to him in the hour of impending storm ? It will be convenient to say something of his biography previous to this date, even at the cost of making a considerable digression, not only because Palmella is one of the most remarkable figures in Portuguese history, but also because he played an almost continuous role in the events of Dona Carlota Joaquina's life subsequent to the date of his arrival in Brazil.

From time to time during her history Portugal has produced a diplomat of European reputation—some striking personality whose distinction and charm cause him to be welcome everywhere, and who, acquiring through a long career of public service an unrivalled knowledge of the European stage, becomes at last an epitome of the age he lives in. Such a phenomenon was da Cunha at the Congress of Utrecht. Another was the celebrated Marquis of Soveral, who was so bright an ornament to the court of Edward the Seventh. Another was Palmella.

Considering the adventures and vicissitudes of his career, it is interesting that the lives of both Palmella's father and grandfather were coloured by tragedy and romance. His grandfather was Dom Manuel de Sousa, one of the unfortunate noblemen who were the victims of the Marquis of Pombal. Suspected by the all-powerful minister of complicity in the Tavora plot, he was arrested at his country-house at Calhariz and thrown into a dungeon of the Junqueira prison. Here he languished until his death. His wife, who was the eldest daughter of the reigning Duke of Holstein, was reduced to penury. His two eldest sons, Philip and Frederick, were arrested at the same time as their father, and these two unhappy youths, whose supposed guilt was never investigated by any tribunal, spent respectively eighteen and fifteen years incarcerated in a prison at St. Ubes'. Only one son, Dom Alexandre de Sousa e Holstein, the youngest of the family, escaped Pombal's claws by flying to Malta.

Some years later Dom Alexander learned by accident of the death at Turin of the rich Marquis of Isnardi, Count de Sanfré, who had died without leaving an heir. Remembering that his grandfather, the Duke of Holstein, had been married to this marquis's aunt, he went to Turin and succeeded in establishing his claim to a half of the Sanfré estates. Finding himself established in considerable affluence, he sent for his mother to join him.

This Dom Alexander, who was the only member of his family who left issue, was the father of Dom Pedro, afterwards Count, Marquis and Duke of Palmella. The story of his marriage to Palmella's mother is a romance in itself.

When a little boy, he had done lessons with his English tutor, Mr. Billingham, in company with a girl of his own age named Dona Isabela Juliana de Sousa Coutinho. The two children had fallen in love. Dona Isabela was an heiress, and after Dom Alexander's flight to Malta, the crafty Pombal decided she must marry his own second son, the Count de Redinha. Isabela, who was thirteen years old, refused to obey. For twelve months she was cajoled, scolded, put on bread and water, admonished and bullied by a pack of aunts, cousins and family confessors who wished to curry Pombal's favour. She remained adamant. At last, shortly after her fourteenth birthday, she was literally dragged to the altar, and though no vow could be extracted from her tight-shut lips " married " to the young Count by force. But the marriage was never consummated. For three whole years she refused to speak when spoken to, and declined to accept the slightest caress from her husband. When we remember the circumstances in which a Portuguese wife lived in those days, kept in isolation from the outside world and surrounded by the womenfolk of her hiusband's family, with no single other soul to speak to save a family confessor in league with her enemies, the indomitable obstinacy of this little girl appears almost incredible.

After three years she won her battle. The terrible minister whose word was law in Portugal and whose rivals he had caused to be tortured to death or condemned to living burial in the Junqueira dungeons was flouted by this child in her 'teens. He could do nothing with her. The marriage was dissolved. Isabela was placed in confinement in the Santa Joanna Convent, whose abbess was Pombal's sister. She spent two years in this convent, and six more in a convent at Evora. Then King Joseph died, Pombal was disgraced, Isabela was released, and her lover Dom Alexandre came back from Turin to fetch his bride. Pedro, the future Duke of Palmella, was the only son of the marriage. He was born in Turin in 1781.

He was born under a lucky star. His parents were both " personalities." It is recorded that Frederick the Great, when he first set eyes on Dom Pedro's mother, exclaimed " Voilà une femme que je voudrais connaitre." From her Pedro inherited his dogged tenacity and his keen brain. From his father, whose diplomatic career began in 1786 with his nomination as Minister in Copenhagen, he inherited his perfect manners, his partiality for public affairs, his love of society, and the luxurious refinement of his taste.

From his earliest years he breathed the air of the great world. From Copenhagen his father went as minister to Berlin. A year later he was transferred to Rome, but instructed to pause in Vienna on his journey to express the congratulations of Queen Maria the First to the Emperor Leopold on his accession. Thus the earliest recollections of Dom Pedro, who with his three sisters travelled with his parents, must have been of coaches and hostelries, and of all those odds and ends collected by experienced travellers to lessen the discomfort and boredom of long journeys—the foot-muffs, the smelling-salts, and the flasks of eau-de-Cologne. To move easily from one end of Europe to another became a second nature to him, and from the constant stream of guests frequenting his parents' salon he must have imbibed unconsciously a natural interest in international affairs, and willy-nilly must have grown familiar with the restless, absorbingly exciting atmosphere of his age.

He was eleven years old when his mother died in Geneva. He spent three years with his sisters in Switzerland in the charge of their admirable Swiss tutor, Monsieur Monod.

Geneva at that time swarmed with distinguished exiles. Palmella wrote in after years : " I remember the anxiety with which news from Paris was received. The revolutionary enthusiasm which had spread through all France seemed to excite a kind of delirium, not only in cities, but in country villages also, where all believed themselves to be freed from a yoke that had oppressed them for centuries." And when in 1794 Monsieur Monod received instructions to bring his charges to Portugal, the day of departure was made memorable by the arrival that morning of newspapers reporting the fall of Robespierre.

Wherever the boy went, Fortune seemed determined to throw in his path the most eminent or fascinating figures of his day. The children having been forced to travel through the Low Countries, which were being overrun by the French armies, and to take a ship crowded with refugees to England, one of their fellow-passengers was the witty Count de Rivarol, who in his efforts to save the French monarchy had given to Louis the Sixteenth wise advice similar to that which Palmella was afterwards to give Dom John of Portugal. (It was Rivaral who to describe Condorcet had coined the phrase : " Il écrit avec de l'opium sur des feuilles de plomb.") And when a ship was at last found to carry the children to Lisbon, it was the *Rainha de Portugal*, under the command of the Marquis of Niza (the same that served with distinction under Nelson), and he made the children welcome in his cabin.

Pedro was fourteen years old when in the year 1795 he first set foot in his native country. He passed the next six years there, and afterwards wrote in his journal that he had misspent them. In fact, though he probably learned something from that strange genius, the poet Bocage, whose company he shared on many a night excursion, and from the beautiful and ill-fated Condessa de Oyenhausen—the last scion of the Tavoras—whose house was a *salon*, there is no doubt that these six years were chiefly devoted to sowing his wild oats. He sowed them with gusto, following the example set by all the boys of his age and rank, in a sort of continuous carnival of dissipation. But if in after years Palmella regarded this period of his life with few feelings of satisfaction it is arguable that even in giving him these six years of pleasure and idleness Fortune had kept him under her wing. He had been able to observe and know his country under the old régime. Secondly, if he had begun with his wild oats at fourteen, circumstances had at any rate prevented him from imitating all the other young men of fashion in Lisbon who began at eleven or twelve. Lastly, for one of his abnormally precocious intelligence, these years of physical excitement were probably a healthy holiday. His real education for the part he was destined to play in the world began when he was twenty, when as honorary attaché he accompanied his father who had been appointed ambassador in Rome.

The brilliance and variety of life in Rome at the close of the eighteenth century have often been described. The fugitive celebrities of captive Europe jostled each other in the Corso. And few houses where cosmopolitan society gathered were more prominent than the Embassy of His Most Faithful Majesty, which still shone with the lustre of King John the Fifth's fabulous tributes to St. Peter's. Young Pedro met everyone of mark, and, what is a proof of his good-nature and good-looks, he charmed everyone, and bored no one. In the *salon* of the Countess of Albany at Florence, or exploring the antiquities of Rome under the guidance of the Abbé Fea, he was liked by all. It is evident that he must have combined to a superlative degree the tact of a man of the world (even the great Lord Chesterfield would have acknowledged him a paragon), with that delicacy of feeling—that *sensibilité* of late eighteenth-century literature—which was the delight of his contemporaries in intercourse as well as in books.

And now Fortune held in store for him a connection more brilliant than any his youth had so far known. It was as if the Goddess had for once removed the blindfold from her eyes, had solemnly considered what outstanding and famous personality was worthy of her darling, and had then chosen the most famous woman in Europe to fall in love with him. In 1804, when his father died and Pedro found himself Chargé d'Affaires of the Portuguese Embassy, Rome was electrified by the news of Madame de Stael's arrival in the Eternal City. She, too, had lately lost her father, and was, moreover, in the throes of a second sorrow. There had been a crisis in her emotional life. After terrible scenes, agonizing quarrels, heart-rending reproaches, she had broken her liaison with Benjamin Constant. Now she arrived in Rome, wearing the double halo of Napoleon's oppression and Goethe's homage, and surrounded by a band of devoted admirers whose names were a part of history. She saw Pedro. She was instantly struck by " his mourning and his sad look."

The authoress of *L'influence des passions sur le bonheur des individus et des nations* was the very incarnation of the spirit of her epoch. In her the newly discovered capacities of the human heart for romantic emotion found a voice. Indeed, Madame de Stael was one of the two immortals—Chateaubriand was the other—who acted as chief ushers to the Romantic Age. Her vitality, her almost masculine intellect, her passionate friendships, her superb gifts of self-expression, her " ten years exile " and her fame—all combined to render her irresistible.

The affair lasted just two months. It was conducted with as much impetuosity, and was arranged with as much wealth of romantic *décor*, as Madame de Stael could manage—which is saying a great deal. It was in harmony with the spirit of the age that it should not last longer. " I am one whose faith is, that love and friendship with ardent natures are like those trees of the torrid zone which yield fruit but once, and then die ! " so wrote another Romantic, Edward Trelawny. At the end of two months Madame de Stael resigned herself to leaving Pedro, who had with a discretion admirable in one so young kept his head throughout, defending himself against her clear though perhaps unexpressed desire to marry him by affirming that he was engaged to somebody else.

She wrote him a last note before leaving Rome : " The days pass and I see so little of you ; to-day at dinner, to-morrow at Frascati, I will have no chance of speaking to you from my heart." It was arranged that they should pay a last visit to the Colosseum by moonlight.

During the months that followed their first separation, she addressed him a series of magnificent letters. In one of them she spoke of their last farewells among the ruins of Rome. " My whole soul," she wrote, " was imbued with regret, tenderness, admiration. United by the same love of beauty, we were contemporaries treading the débris of the centuries. In heaven my father pardoned me a happiness so mixed with tears . . . "

Of course, Madame de Stael knew well " how useful," in Wilde's words, " passion is for publication," and that " a broken heart will run to several editions." And so after the sad parting she wrote a five-hundred page romance entitled *Corinne*, describing her heroine's infatuation for a perfectly Byronic hero, Oswald, in the romantic Roman setting. And, as she divulged to Pedro, Oswald was really himself.

For Pedro, apart from the stimulating influence of Madame de Stael's personality, the affair was chiefly important because it brought him into contact with Madame de Stael's brilliant circle. In Rome, and afterwards at Coppet where he paid a two months' visit, he not only met distinguished travellers such as the Prince Augustus of Prussia and Madame de Recamier with her train of lovers, but also conversed with intellectuals such as Benjamin Constant and Sismondi.

A new ambassador having been appointed to the Portuguese Embassy at Rome, Pedro started on a leisurely and roundabout journey home. After going to see his old tutor at Geneva, he stayed for seven months at the Portuguese Legation in Paris.

It was the most dazzling period of Napoleon's Empire, that is to say, between the battles of Austerlitz and Jena. Revolutionary frenzy had given place to the thirst for military glory. Napoleon's new nobility were spending their newly acquired fortunes with parvenu profligacy. All contributed to give Paris a splendour more like a dream than reality. The place was so crowded with crowned heads begging for favours that, when Pedro went to the court theatre at Saint Cloud, a page who was to announce him at the door of one of the boxes inquired of him, " What are you Prince of ? "

From Paris he went to Madrid—a journey enlivened by falling in with the lovely Duchess of Mouchy-Noailles, herself on her way to Spain to keep her fantastic rendezvous with Chateaubriand in the Alhambra (she very nearly accompanied Pedro to Lisbon instead). And in Madrid he had opportunity to observe a decadence and decay similar to what he had known in Portugal : " The same ignorance, servile ambition and degradation," he wrote in his diary, " with the difference in our favour that the character of our prince deserved more consideration and inspired more respect than did that of Charles the Fourth." And so home, where he arrived in time to witness the French invasion and the flight of the royal family to Brazil.

His luck still held : he still gave evidence of his remarkable knack of making himself of service to eminent men. Serving with distinction in the Portuguese army in the second Peninsular campaign, he became interpreter to Wellington. He was in Oporto with his regiment when he received despatches from the Regency at Lisbon acquainting him with his appointment as minister to the Spanish Junta at Seville.

The ostensible object of his mission was to conclude a treaty of alliance and commerce with Spain ; the real object was to secure the return of the little province of Olivença that had been surrendered to Spain by the Treaty of Basle. He was also instructed, as we have seen, to press for the recognition of Dona Carlota Joaquina's rights to the throne of Spain in the event of her brother's death, and for the recognition of her as Regent for the time being. He succeeded in the majority of his aims, and his success earned him the title of Count of Palmella and a fulsome letter of congratulations from Dona Carlota Joaquina ; it seems an ironic document when one recalls the deadly hatred she later bore him.

In 1812 he was appointed Minister in London, and spent the next seven years at the Portuguese Legation in South Audley Street, punctuated by frequent visits to Paris, where he acted as Portuguese plenipotentiary at the conferences called to attempt to find a solution to the Spanish-Portuguese dispute over Montevideo. These years were also interrupted, in 1815, by his appointment as envoy to the Congress of Vienna.

Had he needed to expand still further his acquaintanceship among European statesmen, the Congress of Vienna was surely a perfect opportunity. There were assembled in the Austrian capital, besides the Imperial family, the Emperor and Empress of Russia, the Kings of Denmark, Bavaria and Wurtembourg, and nearly all the German princes. The plenipotentiaries included Hardenberg for Prussia, Nesselrode for Russia, Castlereagh and Bathurst for England, Talleyrand for France, and, last but not least, the Austrian Chancellor Prince Metternich. There were also present more than ninety envoys of sovereign, and fifty-three envoys of " mediatized " princes. There was Cardinal Gonsalvi, the Pope's minister of state ; Count Bernsdorf, minister to the King of Denmark ; and the Marquis of Saint Marsan, minister to the King of Sardinia. By the end of a month Palmella's address book must have closely resembled the Almanach de Gotha.

With all these men he held his own in the general scramble, and it is a proof of his ability that Portugal was represented—and represented by him—at the congress-table of the eight powers.

After it was all over he went back to London, where, almost needless to say, his growing reputation and his social gifts had won him an established position in the *salon* of the greatest of all political hostesses —the Princess de Lieven, and the friendship of the famous Lady Holland.

No wonder that Palmella's arrival in Rio de Janeiro in 1821 raised the hopes of the British government, in accordance with whose advice he had now been summoned to take over the portfolio of Minister for Foreign Affairs. He was regarded as the only man capable of guiding his country through a crisis that all realized was imminent. All prayed for the safety of the ship that was carrying him across the Atlantic.

Chapter XI

In politics Palmella was neither a fanatic revolutionary nor a bigoted conservative ; he was a moderate liberal. And he was such both by temperament and by conviction. He was a convinced enemy of radical innovations and political experiments. He was an admirer of the political system that existed in England. He believed in gradual progress, in peaceful transformation, and in evolution. He believed in grafting improvements slowly on to the solid trunk of inherited institutions. At the same time he was a firm monarchist. But realizing, from his knowledge of Europe, that liberal doctrine had come to stay, he desired to arrange a compromise by which the continuity of Portuguese life might be preserved. He would have liked, therefore, to see the monarchy place itself at the head of the liberal movement, and thus dominate it. He was aware, in the words of his biographer, " that the time had come for the Portuguese monarchy either to be given a new lease of life by liberal inspiration, or else to suffer the fate of a worn-out institution."

If any man could have saved the situation, it was he. He was cool-headed and clear-sighted, and he possessed superlative powers of negotiation. Unfortunately, his task was doomed to failure from the outset because he had no collaborators. He stood alone. Fresh from the *salon* of the Princess de Lieven, he found current opinion in Rio de Janeiro so barbarously violent, or else so hopelessly out of date, that when he spoke to his compatriots he could hardly make himself understood. The revolutionary party were in a permanent state of excitement. The new doctrines had gone to their heads like wine. They were incapable of seeing any danger in the application of principles whose infallibility seemed to them to be self-evident. As for the reactionaries, their views were distorted by sheer ignorance. And so it was inevitable that Palmella should come to be hated by both sides equally. He wished to preserve things that the revolutionaries wished to destroy ; and he wished to abolish things which the reactionaries regarded as sacred. Soon liberals and reactionaries shared no single sentiment in common, except their detestation of the Count of Palmella. Even his manners and his clothes, his boots from St. James's Street and his Lock hat, his eau-de-Cologne and his Bond Street linen, struck a foreign, superior, hostile note. After a suitable period, he went to pay his respects to the Queen, and the result was as if two persons from two widely distant centuries had been confronted with each other. Dona Carlota Joaquina had not yet chosen her side in the coming battle—indeed, if she had any partiality at this time, it was towards the liberals who were causing the King such evident anxiety— but she saw at once that Palmella was not the personal supporter that she had imagined him to be. He, on his side, was aghast at her complete lack of comprehension of the political problems of the age, her vindictive enmity against certain personalities, her widely inaccurate statements based on the most dubious gossip. Whatever passed between them, it is certain that from that day onwards their dislike was mutual.

Meanwhile the political situation was going from bad to worse. Most of the " Brazilian " party wanted the King to remain where he was and to send the Prince Royal to face the Cortes in Lisbon. They considered that this arrangement would involve less danger of Brazil being once more reduced to the status of a Portuguese colony. The " Portuguese " party, on the other hand, wishing to keep the places they enjoyed at the expense of the Brazilians, plotted to keep Dom Pedro in Rio since they believed—with how little reason will be seen in due course—that the Prince was devoted to their interests.

The King continued to procrastinate, in a state of dreadful dejection. He was like a paralysed man seated on a time-bomb. Palmella could do nothing with him. Dom John actually resented his interference, dreaded being compelled to listen to his hateful, unanswerable arguments. He made use of his other Minister, Vilanova, as a kind of buffer to keep Palmella at arm's length. Vilanova was all too effective in the part assigned to him. " He is the most inept man I ever knew," wrote Palmella in despair, " and the most abject flatterer." But the King chose to rely on him entirely : " Tell me what I must say to the Count " was the invariable formula scribbled in the royal handwriting on the memoranda that Vilanova sent him.

In January, however, Palmella and Thornton did succeed in exacting a definite promise from the King that the Crown Prince should be sent to Lisbon. But their troubles were not yet over. Animated by distrust of his son, and labouring under his chronic incapacity to take action, King John postponed from day to day, and from week to week, the task of breaking the news to the Prince. " Until now," he wrote in the margin of one of Vilanova's reports, " I have not yet spoken to my son. I want you to tell me if you are still of the same mind. Tell me what I ought to say to him, and if he replies, what I ought to say then." He told Palmella and Thornton that the Prince was being difficult, because he did not wish to leave the Princess Leopoldina, who was going to have a baby.

On the 17th February there was alarming news. The troops had revolted at Bahia. A revolutionary committee had published a manifesto requesting the King to approve the Constitution being elaborated by the Lisbon Cortes. Thornton was seriously alarmed. He urged the King to send the Prince off without an instant's delay. When the King hummed and hawed, Thornton said roundly that " it was time for His Majesty to exercize his Royal Authority if there was any intention of saving the Monarchy." Partly in response to Thornton's remonstrances, but mostly as a result of the dreadful news from Bahia, the King at last issued a decree informing the public that he was resolved to send Dom Pedro to Lisbon, " to consult with the Cortes concerning the drawing up of a Constitution," and promising " to adopt such parts of it as might be found applicable to existing circumstances and the peculiar situation of Brazil." This was on the 21st February. It was the last decree that Dom John of Portugal signed as an absolute King.

The long-expected explosion took place on the 26th, and the hand that set the match to the powder was Prince Pedro's. It might almost be supposed that some psychological or emotional disturbance had lately taken place in the Prince's breast, for until 1821 he had taken no part whatsoever in public affairs and had shown no inclination to do so. One of the results of the separation between Dom John and Dona Carlota was that their children received little or no education. They were allowed to run wild, and though attached to his father's establishment—Dona Carlota never showed much affection towards him—Dom Pedro had hitherto been distinguished for nothing except the same athletic excellence as the youthful Dom Miguel. His superb horsemanship is his first quality that arrests attention. In his passion for open-air exercise which was sufficient to tire several ordinary men, he was a true scion of the Bourbons. He drove with skill teams of six and eight horses. Thirty-six bad falls and a frightful carriage accident in the Rua de Lavradio did not affect his preference for the most fiery and unmanageable mounts. He broke all records across country, leaving his escort scattered over the landscape behind him. His prowess astounded even the cowboys of Rio Grande, who were described by Garibaldi as the finest horsemen in the world.

He was a scion of the Bourbons also in his exuberant sensuality, abnormally developed by the climate of Brazil. At the age of sixteen he scoured the slums of the city by night, wrapped in a voluminous cloak, in search of adventure. He was irresistible to the French seamstresses in the Rua do Ouvidor; and his tastes were by no means fastidious. He was a Bourbon, too, in his occasional brutal insensibility. The death of the Princess Leopoldina, who adored him, was certainly hastened by the cruelty with which he insisted on introducing his notorious mistress the Marqueza dos Santos into the palace. His behaviour towards his father on the day we are about to describe was as unfeeling as the conduct of Louis the Fifteenth.

At the same time his character derived much from the Braganzas. He had a genuine talent for music. As Emperor of Brazil he himself composed the Brazilian national anthem, picking the tune out on the piano that Maria Graham saw at San Christoval, strewn with stock-whips and pistols. Moreover, though he was capable of behaving ruthlessly, his character was tinged with that excessive Portuguese sentimentality which finds such potent expression in the *fado*, the ballad sung to the accompaniment of guitars in the Lisbon slums. When his father returned to Portugal, Dom Pedro on one occasion wrote to him swearing that under no circumstances would he consent to Brazil becoming severed from the mother country, and he wrote his oath (which he so shortly afterwards revoked) in his own blood. When he heard that the opera dancer Naomi Thierry was to be sent away by ship to preclude her from disturbing his nuptial happiness with the Princess Leopoldina he fell in a swoon on the ground. Naomi gave birth to a daughter at Pernambuco. This baby died before she was six months old. The corpse was embalmed and brought to Rio, whereupon Dom Pedro refused to consent to its being buried. He kept the tiny coffin in his own study, where it remained until 1831, when the Regency government of Brazil arranged for it to be interred. Lastly, in his physical make-up Dom Pedro was a Braganza rather than a Bourbon. In his portraits he bears a distinct resemblance to his father. The " early Victorian " set of his hair and whiskers does not detract from the strong marks of heredity in the heavy jowl and under lip. Above all, it was from the Braganzas that he inherited that tendency to apoplexy, which, combined with Dona Carlota's sensuality and dynamic physical energy, is perhaps the key to his strange personality and the explanation of his early death, at the age of thirty-six, in the same room at Queluz where he had been born.

At dawn on the morning of that memorable 26th February, the townspeople of Rio de Janeiro were wakened by an unusual hubbub in the streets. Looking out, they saw Prince Pedro and Prince Miguel on horseback, both in uniform, leading the Portuguese garrison to the square in front of the Town Hall. They were seen to enter the building, where the municipal council were apparently waiting to receive them. Half an hour later Dom Pedro appeared on the balcony and read aloud, punctuated by resounding cheers from the troops, a " royal proclamation," ante-dated the 24th, promising the royal consent to " the Constitution as it should be formed by the Cortes of Lisbon." He then, with flashing eyes, announced that he would ride out to the palace and return with the King's signature.

Off he galloped, and an hour later back he came flourishing the document. Again he came out on the balcony and was greeted by cheers of " Long live the King, our Religion, and our Constitution." Some shouts were heard naming the Prince, but Dom Pedro himself led a fresh storm of cheering for the King.

When this noisy scene came to an end, the Prince re-entered the Town Hall, and instructed a secretary to draw up the form of oath to be taken to observe the Constitution and also to prepare a list of new ministers to be submitted to the people for their approbation. Then the Prince proceeded to take the oath on behalf of his father. Dom Miguel, the new ministers, and all those present, took the oath afterwards.

Intoxicated by the applause that greeted yet another appearance on the balcony, Dom Pedro now announced his intention of riding out once again to San Christoval to bring his father into the capital. He leaped into the saddle, dashed off through the dust like a meteor, triumphant shouts meeting him at every corner. At San Christoval Dom John was lying in bed nursing a sore leg, trembling with apprehension at having allowed his son to persuade him to sign that appalling Royal Proclamation. The Prince compelled the poor old man to dress, pinned on his ribbons and orders, thrust a sceptre into his shaking hand, and hurried him downstairs. The whole royal family were collected at the door, obeying Dom Pedro in a bewildered manner. Carriages were sent for ; a procession formed. At the head of it, on horseback, rode the Prince, followed by Dom John almost speechless with fright, hunched up in a corner of his state-coach. Behind came two carriages containing the Queen and the Infantas.

King John's long calvary had begun. It began with that—to him—appalling scene in the Town Hall square, when the delirious negroes dragged his horses out of the shafts and pulled their beloved sovereign away to his town palace. There his tottering footsteps were forced to a central window in the main façade, where, according to Thornton, " he uttered in a faint and inaudible voice that he approved of what His Royal Highness had done in his name." His words were repeated to the crowd by the gesticulating Dom Pedro ; and there was more deafening cheering, and the guns were fired off by the harbour forts, and hundreds of rockets, reminiscent of happier days. In the evening the King was taken to the Opera, where there was a gala performance, and there all the cheering for himself and for the Constitution was repeated all over again. " It may be questioned," wrote Maria Graham's busy pen, " whether that night there existed in his wide dominions one heart less at ease than his own."

For Dom John, indeed, the events of the 26th February were a dreadful, an irremediable blow. On that day he ceased to be an absolute King. He became a symbol of monarchy merely, like a crown, or any other inanimate thing. He became what he henceforth continued to be, an object almost as little in command over his own movements as his own throne itself. And it is really a proof of his political acumen that he should have gauged so accurately the implications of the revolution. The enthusiastic town councillors who swore to the Constitution (a Constitution which, in fact, was non-existent, since it had not yet been drawn up) were inebriated by the clap-trap phraseology of the day. That a Constitution—any Constitution—was a panacea for all the ills that men and states are heir to, was for them an article of faith. The long-awaited millennium had dawned, and Rio de Janeiro shone with what the pamphleteers termed the " aurora of liberty." They hardly looked any closer at the practical results of their actions than the happy ubiquitous negroes who at Rio de Janeiro were always so ready to provide a picturesque chorus to the central figures in any pageant. But for Dom John the revolution was a disaster that changed him for ever : a disaster reflected in his face, in his very tread. When the French Chargé d'Affaires saw him on the 27th he wrote : " Without doubt it is the first time that I approached His Majesty without finding an expression of benevolence. I saw only the very manifest effects of what he had just undergone."

The effect of the revolution on Dona Carlota Joaquina was very different. Those cheers in the Town Hall square had woken her, one might say, from ten years of intolerable ennui. As in the case of children, who are more inclined to enjoy a treat if it is preceded by weeks of monotony, she never forgot that day. She had never in her life before had such fun, heard so many squibs exploding and been in the middle of such an exultant mob. In addition, she gloated over anything that caused her husband pain and made his heavy under-lip tremble. She ostentatiously congratulated Dom Pedro—in front of his unhappy father—on the part he had played in the day's events. Miguel congratulated him too, dreaming perhaps of a day when he himself would be the central figure of another such glorious, uproarious scene.

Indeed, Dom Pedro was the hero of the hour, not only to his mother and brother, but to the whole town, and amidst the storms of cheering that met him wherever he went there were already to be heard a few shrill cries hailing him as Protector of Brazil. That he had played a leading part in organizing the upheaval there is not the smallest doubt. The King in after years told the Count de Subserra that it was so, and his misfortunes must have been made bitterer by the know-ledge. The clock-work precision with which the programme of the 26th was carried out (Dom Pedro was back in the square with his father before eleven o'clock) is a proof that everything had been minutely pre-arranged. But mystery surrounds the plot. Palmella's version of the story was, that the Prince had got himself advised and surrounded by dubious people. Thornton believed that these included the King's minister, the Count of Arcos, and two scheming mason-priests named Goaz and Macamboa. But whoever may have guided Dom Pedro's hand, it is an astonishing thing that this twenty-three year-old prince, whose standard of education would hardly have done credit to a child of ten and whose life had hitherto been spent riding and love-making should have suddenly developed political ambitions and without the smallest experience should have given proof of considerable capacity in performing the role assigned to him.

Not the least important result of the revolution was that Dom John made up his mind to go to Portugal. " The King," wrote Thornton, " now wishes to return to Lisbon, in the weak hope of alleviating his Misfortunes by changing the scene of them." It is probable that no experience less cruel than what he had just suffered could have caused him to come to a decision. He had no illusions as to the atmosphere existing in Europe ; he had followed the course of events during the past months with a sort of horrible fascination. The unrest in Spain ; the assassination of the Duc de Berri ; the liberal plots in Prussia and Russia that even Metternich, the presiding genius of the forces of order and authority, had been powerless to stamp out ; the excited state of public opinion everywhere, inflamed by a plethora of radical newspapers and tracts—all combined to create a prospect as ghastly as a nightmare. Was not his own European kingdom in a condition of chronic unrest, its destinies at the mercy of an assembly of persons whose very physiognomy was an insult, with their buttoned coats and black stocks, as dismal as a flight of crows ?

Dom John reminded himself, however, that his return was recom-mended by the British, and, irritable as he felt at their interference, it was at least a consolation to him to remember that it was the British who in 1807 had insisted on his going to Brazil. He had resisted their arguments until the last moment, yet in the end they had been proved to be in the right. Was it not possible that they were in the right now and that Lisbon would not be so bad after all ?

On the 7th March his intention to set sail was made public. Dom Pedro was to remain behind as Regent of Brazil, and the King was to be accompanied to Europe by such Brazilian deputies to the Lisbon Cortes as should be elected by the time of his departure, which was fixed for the end of April.

The last weeks of Dom John's residence in Rio de Janeiro—a scene where he had been so happy and where he was widely loved—was embittered by the rising hatred between the Brazilians and the Portuguese. An excited protest meeting of the Brazilian party took place in the Corn Exchange, demanding that the King should remain. The Portuguese party rushed the building and in the ensuing riot several lives were lost. Party passion deprived the royal family's departure of all dignity or cordiality. They who had arrived amidst such wonderful expressions of loyalty and affection went on board the *Dom João VI* in a manner that was almost furtive. Nearly everybody was feeling heavy-hearted. Those who were to sail were saying farewell to a scene which for fourteen years had been their home, while as regards the prospects lying ahead of them many must have shared the gloomy forebodings of their King. The Brazilians who remained behind were no less dejected. They hoped that the presence of Brazilian deputies at Lisbon would induce the Cortes to consider Brazil on an equal footing with Portugal, and that they might be permitted to retain their own law-courts. But little confidence was placed in the Regency government that was to rule at Rio de Janeiro. It was at present composed exclusively of those Portuguese elements who were primarily responsible for the revolution that had caused the court's going away.

There was only one person who was really happy—Carlota Joaquina. " At last ! " she exclaimed, " at last we are going to a place fit for ladies and gentlemen to live in!" She hated Rio because it was identified in her mind with the defeats she had suffered at the hands of Dom John, his ministers and Lord Strangford. The climate did not suit her, and she had nothing to employ her mind. Her darling Dom Miguel was no longer a boy : his pranks no longer relieved the tedium of her household. She listened with pride to tales of his horsemanship—as jockeys there was little to choose between the one brother and the other—but she longed to see him play a part in the world more brilliant than that of a cowboy. As she stepped on board the ship she took off her shoes in front of everybody, and banged them on the gunwale. " There ! " she exclaimed with theatrical glee, " I have knocked the last dust of Brazil from my feet ! "

She not only welcomed the idea of leaving Brazil, but she was positively pleased at the thought of returning to Portugal. In the first place, Portugal was next door to Spain, the land which still exercised a magnetic attraction over her heart. In the second place, though she was but vaguely informed as to the political condition of Portugal, in her opinion the mere fact that Dom John dreaded going there augured well. Instinctively she drew conclusions from his nervousness and depression. What suited him had never suited her, and *vice versa*. She felt a presentiment, filling her heart with joy, that she was going to like the atmosphere in Lisbon : that in the political game being played there she was going to have a chance to hold a hand. Her energies were as restless as ever. Age had lined her face with evil wrinkles : she was more hideous than Cinderella's ugly sisters. But her strength was unimpaired and her longing for power was now mingled with an equal lust for revenge. Lastly, she felt instinctively that in Miguel she possessed an ideal tool for her purpose. He was the very incarnation of her own spirit ; and even if age were to cripple her at last, she believed that she could project herself into her son and live to see the dying fires of her own passions burn brightly in him.

On the 26th April, 1821, the royal squadron, counting in all fourteen sail, weighed anchor in the bay. The townspeople on the hills watched it dwindle into the distance, bearing over the horizon the good old King, the gnome Queen, and the cowboy prince. There were four thousand courtiers and hangers-on besides.

"The King carries with him," wrote Thornton, "many elements of future Discord and Unhappiness. It remains to be seen, what is left behind."

"What the sea brought," wrote Oliveira Lima, "the sea carried away." The Braganzas were going back to their ancient throne, and the dead went with the living. A few days before the embarkation the body of Queen Maria the First had been conveyed on board the *Dom João VI* with a last flourish of the pageantry associated with Dom John's Brazilian reign. The coffin was placed in a cabin fitted as a chapel. The dead Queen was to be brought home to the capital where she had ascended the throne in all the lustre of hope, to be laid to rest in the Estrella Church, the lasting monument of her piety and her innocent remorse.

Chapter XII

In fact the political situation at Lisbon was already exactly what suited Dona Carlota Joaquina ; that is to say, it was a maelstrom of party feuds. It is not necessary to record the names of the numerous mushroom political figures that made fitful appearances on the public stage following the 1820 revolution. The eccentric old General Cabreira did not remain long in the limelight. After winning the popularity of the populace by his extraordinary devotion to the shrine of the Holy Constable at the Carmo Convent—he laid his sword upon the altar and made frequent visits to embrace alternately the tomb and the old Prior—he spent one glorious day at the head of some disgruntled troops and all the ragamuffins of Lisbon in a crazy attempt to overthrow the provisional government : then, overcome by the weight of years, sank into obscurity. The part played by Colonel Sepulveda, his fellow-hero, lasted longer. He became military governor of the capital.

It is important to bear in mind, in examining the liberal movement in Portugal no less than in Brazil, that from the first the Liberal party was itself divided into two rival sections, the moderates and the progressives, who hated each other quite as intensely as they both hated the conservatives. This explains why later on they were constantly arresting each other and sending each other into exile. In Lisbon, in 1820, however, they did at least agree unanimously on one thing : that when Lord Beresford should return from his mission to Brazil, the revival of his influence should not be tolerated. So having learned of the revolution only when his ship dropped anchor in the Tagus, the Marshal found himself refused permission to go on shore. Of all the crowd that once had carried their servile pleas to the antechamber of his headquarters, only one soul—a Portuguese woman who had loved him—came on board. He sailed a few days later for England.

Over every other subject the hostile parties squabbled among themselves. The ideal of the progressives—who nowadays would be termed the Left—was the unworkable Constitution of Cadiz whereby the crown's authority was reduced to a merely suspensive veto. These men's ascendancy in the ranks of the provisional government was sufficient to ensure that the system of election for the coming Cortes should be based on " Spanish " principles. There was to be a single chamber from which Ministers were to be excluded. One deputy was to be elected for each thirty thousand of the population and he was to be elected by electors chosen by groups of six hundred voters. There were to be 1,444 electors and a hundred deputies in all. The important thing about this scheme in the eyes of the " Left " was, that it was a system ideally suited to the manipulations of the masonic societies.

The Cortes met at the Necessidades Convent in January, 1821. An ecclesiastic styled the Bishop of Bahia was elected president, and Fernando Thomaz, the ablest and busiest head in the revolutionary government, was elected Secretary.

As it turned out, the moderates—country gentlemen for the most part—were the strongest party in the Chamber. But wisdom in debate was not to be expected when a pernicious system permitted the existence of a gallery packed by the political clubs with irresponsible extremists.

" The Cortes," wrote the British Charge d'Affaires in April, " are going to work, cutting up rights and property in all directions and they have made themselves hosts of enemies on all sides. They seem entirely led by about ten individuals, of no consideration in society." These individuals, of course, were the deputies commanding the unruly applause of the masons in the gallery, who hissed, stamped their feet, and shouted down their opponents. Ward, however, was bound to be critical of the Cortes because it proceeded to clap an import duty of thirty per cent. on English cloths in defiance of the 1810 treaty. " The speeches made by many members upon this subject," wrote Ward, " were very violent, and so foolishly so, that they appear like the debates of Bedlamites rather than of statesmen. Yet the individuals who spoke were amongst the leading characters in that assembly."

The more serious proceedings of the Cortes were often suspended for hours, while some complacent orator, burning with enthusiasm for democratic principles, treated the assembly to a harangue on the Rights of Man. We find mention in Ward's despatches, of a certain Doctor Oliveira, who pleaded with vibrant eloquence at interminable length to be permitted to place in the assembly room a bust of Benjamin Constant that he had brought from Paris in a packing case.

An example of the oratory expended on more practical subjects is to be seen in the speech delivered by the deputy Borges Carneiro advocating the abolition of the censorship : "In vain," he cried, with his eyes flitting to the gallery, " in vain do Despotism and Superstition—those two monsters that have for so long oppressed the human race and who have burdened them with more ills than all the other curses of humanity combined—in vain, I say, do these monsters attempt to compel the generous Portuguese nation to suffer the censorship's chains and to prevent the establishment of a free press, the only firm rock upon which those monsters are shipwrecked, the unique and inexpugnable bastion of the liberty of Peoples ! We have sworn to maintain the religion of our ancestors, but not to maintain the superstitions and impositions of Jesuits and other scheming ecclesiastics. We have sworn to maintain the throne of the Braganzas, but not the bloated power of courtiers, that horde of bloodthirsty wolves that surrounds the throne."

It is not surprising that the Lisbon government, which was itself largely moderate in complexion, should have been gradually pushed towards extreme measures by the pressure exerted by these hot-heads who were at once the mouthpieces and the puppets of the masonic societies. In April, they ordered the exile of the Cardinal Patriarch, who, though he had instructed his clergy to submit themselves to the new liberal order, had declined to swear to two articles of the Constitution, the first imposing a censorship on religious publications and the second omitting to declare that the Catholic religion should be the only recognized form of worship in Portugal. The Cardinal went to Busaco, and later found his way to Bayonne. He was the first victim of that anti-clerical feeling which was so pronounced among the liberal and masonic organizations of the period.

There was much excitement in the Cortes when the news arrived that the King had given his consent to the institution of the constitutional régime. One deputy proposed that Dom John should be granted the new title of Father of his Country ; whereupon another argued in reply that " he should be given no title at all until he had proved he deserved it." The royal missive was criticized because it " approved and sanctioned " the Constitution that the Cortes were to elaborate. It was declared that the King had no right to " approve " ; he could only " accept " it or " swear to it."

In May, when the Cortes learned the news of the King's imminent return, there were heated debates as to how the Monarch should be received. It was decided that the King should be required to repair immediately to the Cortes to swear to the Constitution in a formal manner ; that the members of the government should accompany him thither, but should afterwards retire to " make known their orders to the King." It was also decided that no accommodation should be prepared in the assembly room for the royal suite. Then there was the question of what clothes should be worn on the occasion. One deputy proposed that they should all be costumed " in a serious style, in cloth of Portuguese manufacture." In reply to a question, the President ruled that a " serious style " meant black silk in summer, and black cloth in winter. But at this, a deputy rose to his feet and in a well-balanced speech of three hours, declared he could not agree to silk, because it always gave him a cold in the head.

The above is sufficient to indicate the atmosphere of hostility and insubordination which awaited poor Dom John in Lisbon, though the masses, as we shall see, had remained quite unaffected by modern ideas and were devoted to the old King. But to appreciate the cruelty of the insults to which he was to find himself exposed it is necessary to remember that, when he had left Portugal fourteen years before, he had left it as an absolute king, at the approach of whose carriage every one of his subjects who happened to be on the roadside would kneel down, and in whose presence none of his courtiers, however bent with age and honours, would have remained seated. Marianne Baillie, in her charming book " Lisbon in the Years 1821, 1822 and 1823," has recorded that Portuguese ladies who had been admitted to the honour of an audience with Dona Carlota Joaquina (who, of course, kept up all the old customs even after her return) used to go straight home to bed, exhausted by the fatigue of having to remain immobile for two hours or more on their knees.

On the 3rd July, 1821, at eleven o'clock in the morning, salvoes of artillery informed the eager populace that the *Dom João VI* had cast anchor in the Tagus. It has been remarked that Lisbon, with its seven hills overlooking the grand expanse of the river, has a theatrical quality which, though it cannot compare with Rio de Janeiro, provides a splendid setting for historic events. Even Mrs. Baillie, who complained bitterly of Lisbon's smells, mosquitoes, flies, bed-bugs, beggars and dogs, admitted that " the distant effect of Lisbon, when beheld from the mouth of the harbour, is superb in the extreme." Moreover, no place in all Portugal is so rich in historical memories as this river front. The cliffs which command a view of Lisbon in panorama from the southern side show well-nigh the same silhouette to-day as when they were crowned by the camp of the English crusaders who helped Dom Affonso Henriques capture the Lisbon citadel from the Moors. The same cliffs saw Vasco da Gama sail to open the Cape route to the Indies, and Cabral to discover the continent of South America.

All eyes on that July morning in 1821 were turned towards the Tagus. Mrs. Baillie, peering through her telescope in the window of her properly-ventilated English guest-house on the heights of Buenos Aires, could perceive the *Dom João VI* so clearly as to be able to discern all that passed on board. " She is surrounded," she wrote, " by small boats, crowded with people, among whom we plainly distinguish the King's rowers, dressed in scarlet, with gilt plates on the front of their caps ; the river, and its far distant shores, resound with the roar of various royal salutes, poured from the brazen throats of every gun on board the numerous ships of all nations now in the harbour : the English frigate, the *Liffey*, is covered with innumerable flags of the gayest variety of colour, and the crew are attired in their gala costume ; they are swarming amid the rigging, as well as upon deck, like clustering bees, and I can perceive some of the officers fearlessly stationed at the same giddy height."

All were happy, save the Cortes, the clubs and the government. Tortured by the inferiority complex common in the breasts of revolutionaries, they now caused to be published orders which amounted to deliberate and spiteful insults to the King. It was announced that he was not to be permitted to land until the following day and only after he should have signified his acquiescence with all the measures so far adopted by the Cortes ; that only a certain number of his suite should be permitted to disembark with him ; that anyone who cheered for other than " our religion," " the Cortes," " the Constitution " or the " Constitutional King," should be arrested for threatening a breach of the peace ; and that until the King had formally sanctioned the Constitution, he should not be permitted to make any change in the commands of the armed forces. It was furthermore announced that on the most futile pretexts, the King's cronies, the Count de Paraty and Lobato, should be exiled to the provinces. " And as a crowning absurdity," wrote the Marquess of Fronteira, " the Count de Palmella, the most illustrious of the Portuguese nobility, who had represented his country with such distinction at the Congress of Vienna, who already at that time was regarded throughout Europe as being in favour of Constitutionalism, and who was on board one of the ships in the squadron, was intimated that he must take up residence in the village of Borba, in the Alemtejo." It is obvious that an attack on the nobility, which still enjoyed great prestige in Portugal, was one of the main planks of the programme cherished by the secret societies. These clubs were in permanent session throughout the day.

The King and Queen, the four Princesses, Dom Miguel and all the court, had put on their best dresses, their diamonds, their ribbons and orders, in the belief that they were to go on shore at once. Instead, they found themselves obliged to receive the visit of the Lisbon government and a deputation of the Cortes.

It must have been a strange and unforgettable scene. The Braganzas seemed to have returned not merely from another continent, but from another age. Here were many of the more elderly courtiers in knee-breeches and powdered hair. Here was a court all complete, chamberlains with keys, ushers with white wands. Here was the Princess Maria Benedicta—the widowed consort of the Prince of Brazil who had died of the smallpox in 1788—looking, in her black robe sewn with jet and diamonds, "just like a picture," as Hyde de Neuville described her, "that had stepped out of its frame." Here, in short, was an assembly of personages who palpably belonged to a long-past day, before so many gracious and graceful heads had rolled under the guillotine.

Dominating the assembly was the King himself, "in a uniform more thickly embroidered with gold," wrote Fronteira, who had gone on board as Sepulveda's aide-de-camp, "than any I had ever seen; decorated with numerous orders, both Portuguese and foreign, with a plumed hat, leaning on a gold-headed cane, and from time to time taking a few steps to and fro." It is a tribute to his bearing, that when the deputation of the Cortes came on board, though they had solemnly agreed among themselves not even to kiss the King's hand, yet when they found themselves confronted by royalty in the burning gloom of the ship's awning, they could not resist showing their respect by falling on both knees.

Another visitor on board the *Dom João VI* was Captain Duncan of the *Liffey*, who arrived to find the Cortes deputation crowding the deck and who has thus described the scene ; " I went alongside where were five or six large boats placed directly in the way and put there, I believe, as a barrier to keep me off. I, however, soon overcame that, and got on deck which was crowded with people in full dress and looking as if they could eat me. . . . The first words the King said were ' I trust England and Portugal are as good friends as ever,' and this he repeated several times while I was with him . . . he also said a good deal about his attachment to the English, but it was very difficult to understand him, for he speaks very indistinctly from the want of his teeth and he makes a sort of grunting noise between each word. The latter appears, however, a way he has of expressing satisfaction, for to each of my answers he *grunted* more or less according to the degree it seemed to please him. . . . On my return to the quarter-deck my appearance seemed to have the appearance of shutting every mouth, for there was a dead silence. . . . I never saw anything apparently more dirty or worse arranged than the ship seemed to be for a King's accommodation." An interesting feature of this account is the evidence it contains that at this juncture in its history, the Portuguese Liberal Party (who, it may be recalled, had already turned out Beresford and antagonized Ward) could certainly not be described as being pro-British.

Dom John went on shore the next day at noon. Ward wrote that his deportment was " apathetic, with some signs of trepidation." The Cortes had taken the absurd measure of lining the streets with troops, as if the King was so unpopular as to be in danger of an attempt on his life. This measure was in flagrant contradiction to the traditions of the Portuguese monarchy, according to which the monarch moves in trustful contact with his subjects. Another thing disgraceful in Portuguese history is that the troops had been instructed to suppress any cheering for the King. The loyal enthusiasm of the townspeople, however, made these instructions a dead letter. The whole town had been illuminated on the previous evening, and in the morning the streets where Dom John was to pass were filled by crowds giving spontaneous " Vivas ! " They quite drowned the few shouts raised by the Masons of :—" Long live Liberty ! " and " Death to the Courtiers ! "

The old King was accompanied in his coach by Dom Miguel. The populace were instantly fascinated by the Prince's frame of a trapezist and his eye like Satan's.

It was five o'clock before Dom John, having first attended a Te Deum in the cathedral, arrived at the Cortes. Here he ascended the dais and placed himself on the throne—not without difficulty, for he was tired and his legs were hurting—and swore to preserve the Catholic religion and to observe the bases of the Constitution. Then the President of the Assembly made a dignified and entirely loyal speech, followed by loud cheers for the " Constitutional King " from all the chamber and most of the gallery ; only a few low mumbles were to be heard from the emissaries of the secret societies.

The King went to Queluz that night. Though at the beginning of the long programme of ceremonies, he had worn, according to Mrs. Baillie, a " wild and distrustful expression " and had gone through the part assigned to him with " mechanical formality," yet on the whole it had all been less trying than he had expected. Perhaps he did not realize that he had in fact scored a personal success. His placid kindly look, combined with his indefinable dignity, had disarmed the more violent of the Liberals. The moderates were now sanguine, and not without reason, that Dom John would be prepared to act as Constitutional King according to the new rules, and collaborate with them.

The conduct of the Queen on this and on the previous day is of the highest significance. On the 3rd July, Fronteira saw her on board

DOM JOHN THE FIFTH

from a water-colour at Queluz

the *Dom João VI* fluttering her fan and " gesticulating with vivacity," in affable conversation with the radical Borges Carneiro. She was discussing with him in a loud voice, in earshot of the King, the events of Dom John's reign. There is other evidence besides this statement by Fronteira to prove that she received the Cortes deputation with a show of confidence ; and we may therefore presume that up to the time of her arrival in the Tagus she had either not yet made up her mind which side to back, or else was inclined in advance to back the liberals. But the reception on board the *Dom João VI* was the last occasion on which she ever showed the liberals any affability whatsoever. In fact, from that day onwards she advertised her hostility to them. It seems certain, therefore, that at some time during the course of the 3rd she suddenly saw her way clearly, and plumped wholeheartedly for the reactionary cause.

Three primary considerations doubtless combined to dictate this important decision. In the first place, she looked hard at the members of the deputation and she came to the conclusion that they were odious. She saw in them a group of pretentious, conceited, grotesquely-dressed lower-middle-class men, with no knowledge of the etiquette of a court and not the smallest respect for the lineage of a Bourbon. She saw a group of men, none of whom would be of more use in a bull-ring than a clown, and some of whom were actually smoking nauseating cigars. Her personal dislike for the deputation deserves to be remembered, because her political loyalties were based, as has already been mentioned, on her prejudices for and against individual personalities.

In the second place, there is no doubt that she was utterly outraged by the Cortes' refusal to allow the royal family to land at once, and by their dictation of terms to the King. So this was what a Constitutional Monarchy meant ! She had not formerly understood what the words signified, but now the truth was brought home to her. It was a system under which a monarch was publicly insulted with impunity ! It was legalized treason. In her view there was only one answer to such insolence. The deputies ought to be arrested in a body, hanged, drawn, and quartered.

But Dom John, to her amazement, submitted to the whole of the proceedings. He neither ordered the arrest of the deputation nor commanded the ship's guns to be trained on the Necessidades. He weakly agreed to everything. Watching him nodding and stammering civilities to these revolutionaries, her blood boiled. Never had she loathed and despised him more than she did at that instant. And her indignation was further inflamed by observing that the deputies were impressed by Dom John. She saw the future in a flash. Instead of the liberal party plotting the King's ruin, launching an attack upon him in which she would have eagerly joined, she saw them actually in coalition. Her perverse spirit of opposition would have been sufficient to throw her into the opposite camp even if her personal antipathies had not been roused. This was the third cause of the decision she took that day.

But if she so swiftly recognized who were her enemies, with almost equal swiftness she recognized who were her potential supporters. The Cortes might lay down the law to the King, and the officers of the Lisbon garrison might be in league with the rebels, but she had only to cast her eyes over the bulwarks of the *Dom João VI* as it lay in the Tagus to find an altogether different attitude of mind. On the barges gliding down-stream, fishermen were kneeling bare-headed, their eyes moist with tears, cheering for their beloved King. On the quays, too, the multitude were on their knees, offering up thanks to the saints for his safe return. Against the cloudless sky a thousand pin-points of light wreathed in white puffs of smoke showed where the happy crowd were exploding rockets in honour of the day. The echo of distant explosions drifted over the water. The fact was patent to her that, however dangerously liberal ideas had rotted the so-called educated classes, it was only the superficial crust of the nation that was affected. The masses were unchanged in heart.

When at last she was able to go on shore, she drove straight to Queluz. A few days later another deputation from the Cortes came to pay their respects to her. She declined to receive them. She sent word by the Marquis of Valada that she was too ill to appear. From a window of the palace, through a crack in the shutters, she watched the deputies driving disappointed away.

Chapter XIII

PORTUGAL at the time of the court's return, may be compared to a plant into which a new sap—the sap of nineteenth-century ideas—had been injected at the top (that is to say, among the educated and professional classes), but in whose roots and trunk the old eighteenth-century sap was still vital. The poorer people, as Dona Carlota Joaquina had been quick to observe, were still the ignorant peasantry of a past age, submissive to the paternal authority of their King, living in superstitious awe of the Church and her miracles, and swayed by the fanatical friars.

There is another reason why the step forward in the progress of nations that Portugal was commonly supposed to have taken by adopting a constitutional system was more theoretic than real. Manners and customs had not been more than superficially affected by the presence of first the French and then the English army. Though gentlemen now wore side-whiskers and smoked cigars like their contemporaries in London and Paris, their mentality still belonged basically to an older day. And it must be recalled that Portugal's geographic isolation had always preserved among the Portuguese antique, almost Oriental habits and customs. These considerations must be borne in mind in examining the miserable failure of the first short-lived constitutional experiment.

The external appearance of the capital had undergone little change during the fourteen years of the court's exile, and still wore the peculiar features that had amused or exasperated Beckford. The condition of the streets was, to say the least of it, primitive. Fisher-girls, monks and Galician porters were to be seen treading bare-foot through heaps of decaying garbage. Pigs, cats, goats and poultry mingled together at the street doors, in a ubiquitious odour of garlic, rancid oil and fried sardines. Scavenging was still left to the hordes of half-famished dogs—" of every imaginable breed," wrote the horrified Mrs. Baillie, " lank, lean, filthy and voracious "—that howled about the town all night. When the torrential autumn rains broke, streams of dirty water rushed down the precipitous alleys, sometimes carrying away a donkey or a struggling pig. Such features of everyday life must have provided a curious contrast to the elaborate toilettes displayed by the occupants of the old-fashioned cabriolets and four-wheelers rumbling over the cobbles. These, if they were ladies, were to be seen in full dress, sparkling with diamonds, though at high noon.

To loll upon a balcony apparently indifferent to the pestilential odours rising from below, was still the favourite occupation of Portuguese females. At times these indolent spectators might be seen to shows signs of animation, when they exchanged signals with friends, employing the swift mysterious language of the fingers. This form of dialogue had been developed to a high art, especially between lovers. At sunset, the ladies retired to their apartments, to pass the evening and half the night seated cross-legged on the floor surrounded by their maids, in the listless ennui of an Oriental harem.

No aspect of Portuguese life caused greater astonishment to travellers than the manner in which the dead were buried. To begin with, the entire family of a dying person down to his remote cousins crowded the death-chamber, while the street door was left open to invite the intrusion of passing strangers. Beggars and children often penetrated to stare upon the last agonies of the sufferer. If the deceased was a man of rank, he was carried with great pomp to the grave by night, attended by many persons carrying lighted torches, tapers and silver crucifixes. But on reaching the grave-side, which was almost invariably inside a church, the corpse was simply taken out of the coffin and thrown into the hole. If on the other hand the family could not afford a funeral, the corpse was generally taken to the cathedral and left on the steps. But as the ceremony was only performed in return for a fee, it sometimes happened that a dead body was to be seen lying on its back in the open streets with a little cup or pan placed upon the breast for the reception of voluntary subscriptions.

Some months after the court's return took place the funeral of Queen Maria the First, whose body, after being shifted several times from one convent to another, was finally carried to the Estrella. The ceremonies, which lasted for three days, were conducted according to the traditions of remote times. The grand procession bearing the coffin to the church took place on the first night, the King and the royal family passing in their state carriages; after them coming all the nobles on horseback, in black cloaks and wide-brimmed hats with long black streamers, their stars and orders flashing in the light of torches, each fidalgo being attended by two of his servants on foot, one on each side of the horse. Then followed an army of bishops, priests and monks; then the different regiments, horse and foot, each with its separate band of music playing a wild funeral lament.

Two of the young Princesses were appointed to preside over the ceremonies at the Estrella, and four ladies-in-waiting performed the high office of tire-women to the corpse. It had been brought over from Brazil enclosed in three coffins, the inner one of lead, where it had been laid surrounded by aromatic herbs and gums, but not embalmed, a process which the House of Braganza adopted only towards their males. As Queen Maria had been dead for six years, it is recorded that the horrible effluvia that issued from the coffin when opened was such as to overpower all the persons present. One of the Princesses fainted twice, and was too ill to reappear, but her sister stood it out, while her ladies raised the body and completely reclothed it in a black robe, a cap, gloves, shoes and stockings, and adorned it with four splendid orders upon the breast. It is recorded that not only was the body entire, but the limbs were flexible; the face only had changed to a dreadful black colour.

The corpse was exposed in the Estrella for two days, watched all night by a guard of honour, while the nobility came successively to pay their last homages and to kiss the limp gloved hand.

Such accounts indicate that Portugal in 1821 was far from being modern in comparison to England or France. It must be added that murders were by no means rare. Mrs. Baillie wrote in October of that year : " A few weeks since, an assassination of an officer took place in the streets of Lisbon . . . and is talked of as rather an uncommon occurrence *at this time of the year*, for it is chiefly during the dark nights of winter that such occurrences are frequent."

To finish the picture of Portugal in 1821, it must be added that the convents and monasteries still flourished, and that religious processions took place on fixed days throughout the year. Those of Good Friday, Easter and Ascension Day were as sumptuous in Lisbon as in Rio de Janeiro, the King and all the highest state functionaries taking part in them. On Good Friday, when the image of Nosso Senhor dos Passos was taken from the Graça convent to San Rocque, Protestant strangers used to be amazed by the group of penitents who, dressed in sackcloth with hoods over their faces, crawled on their hands and knees under the image, through mud, all the distance between the two convents. English onlookers used to be hardly less astonished by the procession of San Bento which took place during Lent. A group of half-naked penitents walked in front of a float on which were to be seen three men representing Abraham, Isaac and the Angel. At every pause made to rest the stand-bearers, Isaac lay down on the altar, Abraham lifted his knife to strike, and the Angel at the same moment mercifully jerked it back by means of a piece of tape attached to Abraham's wrist. The penitents in the procession flogged themselves with their disciplines, but in doing so they generally managed to give a whack at the bystanders, and all was hilarity and confusion.

Before turning to the activities of the Cortes—or, as it should be more properly termed, the Constituent Assembly, for its chief task was to draw up that Constitution which the King had sworn to respect (in Lisbon as he had done in Rio) before it was in being—it will be convenient to say something more of the King and Queen.

It was not to be expected that Dom John would be able to tolerate living in proximity to Dona Carlota Joaquina at Queluz. The discomfort of the long journey from Brazil during which they had been boxed up on the same ship must have been an experience he had no inclination to prolong. Doubtless he would have liked to have retired into a sort of permanent religious retreat at Mafra, but the doings of the Cortes made necessary the choice of some residence nearer to Lisbon. The vast pile of the Ajuda Palace was still unfinished. The apartments which had formerly been reserved for the royal family on Black Horse Square had been converted into government offices. And so Dom John removed his household to the seventeenth-century convent of Bemposta where the widowed Queen Catharine of Braganza had ended her life in a halo of sanctity and superb prestige.

Bemposta is situated in that part of Lisbon lying to the east of the deep valley at the centre of the capital. Its long façade is broken by the front of the old convent church, which is decorated in the interior with a richness becoming a royal chapel. The escutcheons of England and Portugal, put up in Queen Catharine's day, are still to be seen over one of the entrances.

Here the King installed himself with two of his daughters, and in the midst of a changing and hostile world set himself to recreate as far as possible the atmosphere of the court of the Braganzas. Modern Portuguese historians, who regard Dom Miguel's short and turbulent reign—not without justice—as an expression of the Portuguese national spirit, are inclined to overlook the contribution made by Dom John towards re-establishing continuity in the nation's life, so rudely broken by the French invasion. For instance, shortly after his installation at Bemposta Dom John held a hand-kissing or *beija mão* in the old style. It began at eight o'clock in the morning and lasted until long after sunset. The King sat on a throne with his legs protected by a little gilt railing, for he suffered to an increasing extent from the Braganza gout. Only once during the course of the day did he retire to munch a sandwich. And all day long his faithful subjects, rich and poor, filed in front of the throne. Intermixed with great ecclesiastical dignitaries, treading on the heels of grandees of the realm, came clerks, cobblers and all the populace. The young Marquis of Fronteira, who that day was in waiting, was all but overcome by fatigue. He had to remain standing throughout, and could find no other refreshment in the corridors than a cup of water too foul to drink. But he recalled with astonishment in after years the extraordinary gift which the old King displayed for remembering faces. Of a poor old woman whom he had not set eyes on for fifteen years, he enquired kindly if she were still living in the same small house he had once given her.

The Queen remained at Queluz with a few favourite cronies. It became known that she had become excessively devout. She lived in the utmost retirement, never went into public, and seldom received visitors. According to the accounts of horsemen who sometimes drew rein on the hills round Queluz and caught sight of her at a distance walking in the palace grounds, her dress usually consisted of a shabby déshabillé, an old soiled gown of the cheapest printed cotton and a filthy cotton cap surmounted by a man's black beaver hat. But the most remarkable part of her costume was a pair of enormous pockets descending from the waist nearly to the knee, stuffed with a varied collection of rotting religious relics.

Her behaviour was certainly eccentric and not a little eerie. There was something witch-like about her. A sentinel on guard once mistook her for some down-at-heel elderly servant. When the weather was hot she liked to find a cool grove in the garden and, lifting her skirts, to sit with her legs plunged in one of the fountains. Sometimes, as she brooded thus in the falling dusk, she would take up her guitar and pick out the ghostly notes of some old gypsy tune.

But Dona Carlota's seeming indifference to what was going on beyond her palace walls was a feint. She was biding her time. Meanwhile, she watched the King's actions in the capital as a spider watches a fly. The spider's web—the labyrinthine paths of constitutional government being spun by a people utterly inexperienced in democracy—was not of her making, but it would serve her turn. Dom John disliked the whole constitutional experiment quite as much as she did. But he was really doing his best to play his part and to act fairly towards the Cortes ; while the Queen, who dreamed of his ruin, sat at Queluz and watched.

The keenest enjoyment that existence afforded her at present was provided by the visits to Queluz of Dom Miguel. If it were not so inappropriate to apply the " immortal bard's " lines to such a mother and son, one might say that he was " his mother's glass," and that she in him " called up the lovely April of her prime." She adored him and, moreover, her ascendancy over him was absolute, almost as if she had bound him in a spell. Dona Carlota realized that she, herself, could never be popular. She was a Spanish Princess, and the people disliked her besides for her cruelty towards the old King. The epithets customarily employed to describe her in the fish-market are not printable. Not that she troubled to analyse the reasons for her unpopularity : she registered it as a fact. But Dom Miguel, on the other hand, had been a success from the beginning.

Dom Miguel's physical appearance at the time he returned to Lisbon with his parents calls for some mention. It was impossible not to remark him in a crowd. He had high colouring, with luxuriant black hair and magnificent eyes. His nose was aquiline ; the bone-structure of his face sharply chiselled. There was not the slightest resemblance to the Braganza type in his jaws and lips. His lips were firm and finely cut, his chin well formed. Lastly, he had neither the heavy shape of the Braganzas nor their tendency to scrofula and apoplexy. He had the proportions of antique statuary, such as are derived from a rustic diet, arduous labour, and love. He was what would nowadays be termed a " dynamic " personality, and, like most dynamic personalities, there was something in his physiognomy which repelled as well as fascinated. He struck many observers as crafty. The French Ambassador remarked that Dom Miguel seldom looked a man fairly in the face, and that there was an " indefinable cat-like quality in his gait."

These sinister traits, however, were not apparent to the populace, who saw in him the ideal incarnation of a Prince. And the manner of life he assumed on his arrival in Lisbon raised his popularity to the pitch of frenzy.

He at once realized what aspects of Portuguese life would afford him the most fun. To help round up the young bulls on the Ribatejo plains ; to join the mounted cow-boys with their long lances driving the cattle to be branded ; above all, to fight in the bull-ring—these were fitting pastimes for the Prince who at San Christoval had been equalled in horsemanship by none save his brother. The virile, vivid life of the Portuguese peasantry fascinated him—not the peasantry of Cintra who water their pumpkins in an almost suburban rusticity, nor yet the prosperous yeomen of the north with their maize-fields and vineyards, but the folk of the wide sun-burnt spaces to the south of the Tagus who look as if they had been born in the saddle and whose faces are tanned to almost as deep a brown.

Here is the portrait drawn of him by the Portuguese historian, Oliveira Martins : " Plebeian in his way of life, passionate, coarse-grained, fanatical and brave, the Infante was adored by the people. . . . He dressed like a bull-fighter, with a green cloth jacket, black breeches, high-heeled top-boots, silver spurs and a broad-brimmed blue riding hat. . . . He loved to show the peasant boys how to plough, driving a furrow through the hardest soil. He could tighten the girth of a horse with his teeth. He could lift in his teeth a full sack of corn off the ground and swing it over his shoulder with one hand. In the company of his boon companions, the grooms José Verissimo and Sedovem, he loved to gallop at breakneck speed from Queluz to Lisbon with his whip held between his knee and the saddle. His escort could never keep pace with him. . . . He doted on bull-fights, horses and shooting. He liked the company of muleteers, picadors, fat friars and buxom wenches browned by the sun and smelling of hay. . . . He was, indeed, a demagogue of an antique age, straying in a hostile century. With all the passion of the Portuguese temperament . . . he brought to Portugal the atmosphere of Naples, at a time when both Kingdoms were keeping pace in their decline into a picturesque decadence."

The allusion to Naples is striking. In studying Dom Miguel's character it is as impossible to forget his blood relationship to King Ferdinand the Fourth of Naples, as it is to forget that Dona Carlota Joaquina was King Ferdinand's niece and the daughter of Maria Louisa of Parma.

His zest for the open air, for sunshine, sweat, dust, noise, blood and sand, was inexhaustible. In Lisbon, he loved the guitar-players, the *fado* singers, the pungent flavour of the dark cut-throat alleys on sum-mer nights when the air is pervaded by the brackish breath of the river. He delighted in night escapades, and in the exciting, ridiculous chaos of tavern brawls. As the Portuguese say, he was *fadista*, and he soon became the idol of all the fado-singing elements in the capital.

But at the same time, there is no doubt that the Queen encouraged him in the amusements he had chosen. Sometimes he stayed at Queluz for several days on end, and how did his mother let him lighten the hours that might have hung heavily on his hands ? He arranged ambushes to surprise travellers on the road from Cintra to Lisbon. Some respectable citizen (perhaps a Constitutionalist), returning with his family from an excursion to the Victor Hotel, would find himself suddenly assaulted by masked highwaymen. Before he had time to realize his predicament he would see his coachman hurled from the box and writhing under the whips of the Prince's hirelings ; he might even have his own head cut open. He would be fortunate if his car-riage were not wrecked and his horses wounded.

Thus under his mother's guidance, Dom Miguel grew to be regarded as the very personification of the " good " old days before education, or sanitation, or universal suffrage were thought of.

Chapter XIV

WHILE the Queen bided her time and the Prince swaggered in the bull-ring, the Cortes continued their debates, aided or impeded by the irresponsible nominees of the political clubs in the gallery. Though what was called the " basis " of the Constitution had been published in the previous March, the debates on the subject of the complete Constitutional Code went on throughout 1821, and lasted well into the next summer. With the country in an unsettled state, such procrastination was bound to have serious consequences. Moreover, it soon became clear to unbiased minds that the Cortes were bent on producing a Constitution which, inspired by the most abstract ideologies of the French revolution, was bound to prove unworkable.

The inexperience of the Cortes was demonstrated above all by their conduct in regard to the now desperately critical problem of Brazil.

Since Dom John's departure a movement in favour of Brazilian independence had been spreading with irresistible impetus. " The minds of the people," wrote H.M. Minister in Rio de Janeiro, " are much indisposed towards the Portuguese, but as yet few instances of violence against their persons such as are common at Pernambuco have taken place. Every day produces additional evidence of the progress of the spirit of independence, and it is impossible not to feel convinced that separation from Portugal is at no great distance."

Prince Pedro, who, it will be remembered, had led the February *coup d'état* as head of the Portuguese party, saw which way the wind was veering. He now turned his back upon the Portuguese and placed himself at the head of the Brazilians. He was to be seen surrounded exclusively by Brazilian officers at the Opera. Moreover, he ordered most of the Portuguese troops to leave Rio, and treated with marked coolness the Portuguese gentlemen who had been left by the King to act as his counsellors.

According to the arrangement by which Brazilian deputies were to come to Lisbon, the first of these senators—those from Pernambuco—arrived in August. They were followed by the deputies from Rio de Janeiro in September.

These Brazilians had put themselves to considerable trouble and expense to make the long voyage. They certainly expected that, once arrived at their destination, their advice would be weighed, or at least listened to. But the *exaltados* of the Cortes, puffed up with self-conceit and egged on by the gallery, treated them like inferior colonials. Tempers soon grew frayed over the question of sending a further batch of Portuguese troops to Rio de Janeiro. The Brazilians pointed out that such troops were not needed and would not be welcomed : they reminded the Cortes that dissension had first been sown between England and her American colonies by a similar dispute. But the Portuguese paid no heed to their warnings. The motion was carried. When the troops actually arrived at the other side of the Atlantic, Dom Pedro refused to allow them to land. But this news only reached Portugal many months afterwards. The jealousy of Brazil which had been one of the motives behind the 1820 liberal revolution was only too evident in the contemptuous and even insulting speeches made in the assembly.

Another bone of contention was whether or no the Portuguese still occupying Montevideo should be withdrawn in deference to the wishes of the Argentine ; a third, whether Dom Pedro should or should not, remain in Brazil. The Cortes were already suspicious of the Prince's intentions, and they insisted that he should return to Portugal. " This recall of the Prince from the Brazils," wrote Ward from Lisbon in September, 1821, " was finally carried. It was, in addition, proposed that he should be sent to travel, and this gave room to much discussion. Some opposed it because he could not speak French, others because he ought to stay at home and study the Constitutional system, and one, especially, objected to his visiting England, because he would there see the abominable spectacle of a House of Lords. In the end, it was resolved he should be sent abroad because it was dangerous for him to remain either in Portugal or Brazil." It was decided that Dom Pedro should travel to Spain, France and England, attended by a suite to be specially selected for their sound liberal principles.

If the overbearing speeches of the Portuguese deputies mortified their Brazilian colleagues, they also exasperated Dom Pedro when he came to hear of them. The *exaltado* Fernandez Tomaz affirmed that the Cortes " had no need to indicate their opinions to the Prince ; they had merely to convey to him their orders."

In February, 1822, further Brazilian deputies arrived from the province of San Paulo. They attempted to offer advice on the Constitutional Code in so far as it applied to Brazil. But whenever they lifted their voices they were shouted down by the gallery. In vain they pointed out that whereas Brazil wished to remain united to the mother country, the union could only succeed under conditions guaranteeing the rights of both ; that the Brazilians would consider utterly intolerable the proposal that their courts of law should be removed to Lisbon so that all litigation, so notoriously slow in Portugal, would be subjected to the further delay necessitated by the voyage to and fro. Fernandez Tomaz lost his temper and cried : " If the peoples of Brazil really wish to cut themselves loose let them do it and let us make an end to it."

On this ignorant and conceited man, and on his fellow *exaltado* Borges Cameiro, rests a large measure of responsibility for the dismemberment of the Portuguese Empire. He was a typical product of his age, socially self-conscious, bitterly jealous of the established order of society, self-opinionated, and vain. A contemporary engraving portrays him seated pompously at a table in a white stock and black coat, one hand clasping a volume of the " Law of Nature," the other wielding a large quill pen. He looks like a bad-tempered school-

master. His rugged features and cannon-ball head are not unsuited to
one who dreamed of playing the part of a Cromwell, but the mouth
betrays his vanity and inherent weakness.

On the 12th March, two letters addressed by Dom Pedro to his father
were read in the Cortes. One of these enclosed a petition he had
received from the local governments of San Paulo, Rio de Janeiro and
Minas, imploring him to remain in Rio de Janeiro and criticizing the
Lisbon Cortes for laying down laws for Brazil before the full comple-
ment of Brazilian deputies had reached Portugal. The debates on the
subject of this petition were so violent that no unprejudiced observer
could have failed to realize that a breach between Portugal and Brazil
was in the offing. Several of the Brazilian deputies publicly declared
their intention of no longer taking part in the proceedings.

Was there no single Portuguese capable of taking the lead at this
critical hour ? Surely it was not too late for liberal concessions to save
the situation. Palmella was in exile at Borba, the victim of petty spite.
But what of the King himself ? Dom John was at Bemposta, " very
triste and depressed," so Ward described him, and no wonder. The
debates over the Constitutional Code had made clear that the enthusiastic democrats were determined to prune the royal prerogative to the
stalk. The seventh article of the Code ordained that the Crown must be
powerless to prevent elections, or prevent the assembly of the Cortes,
or prorogue or dissolve it, or in any manner object to its decisions.
One deputy proposed that the King should be compelled to abdicate if
he undertook any of these actions, but Fernandez Tomaz argued that
such a measure was unnecessary, because " if the King should object,
they had only to ignore him, and refuse to receive him." In short, it
was evident that these foolish men would never have tolerated the
King's interference in the matter of Brazil. The only alternative course
open to him would have been to appeal to the army, to break up the
Cortes by force, and to reassume the whole responsibility of government : then to abandon the preposterous idea of dictating to Brazil
from Lisbon, and to grant the Brazilians some sensible measure of self-
government. But it is hardly necessary to point out that Dom John
was not of the stuff that dictators are made of. When the appeal to
force was made, it was not made by him. His hands had been tied by
his oath, and he made no effort to loose them. It is to be hoped that the
ritual of the royal chapel afforded him some solace in these weary days.

In May, 1822, Dom Pedro received a solemn petition from the city
corporation of Rio de Janeiro, together with deputations from all the
provinces. It appealed to him as " perpetual defender of Brazil " to
convoke a General Assembly which might proceed to deliberate on
" the just conditions in which Brazil ought to remain united to Portugal,
to discuss the constitution being settled at Lisbon, and to enter on the
legislative power *which essentially belongs to and is inseparable from the
sovereignty of Brazil.*" It was proposed that the Assembly should
assume its functions on the arrival of two-thirds of its members,
that its decisions should apply to all the provinces, and that it should
decide where the governing centre of Brazil ought to be established.

Dom Pedro acquiesced in these proposals, and on the 3rd June signed an order convoking a General Constituent and Legislative Assembly.

The news of this fresh move towards independence did not reach Lisbon until more than two months later, when it threw the politicians into a panic. In the meantime the Cortes had completed what they doubtless regarded as an immortal contribution to the glory of their country. After a labour of four hundred and sixty-eight protracted sessions they at last gave birth to the complete Constitutional Code.

The King, looking very worried and ill-tempered, went down to the Necessidades one day early in November, and swore to maintain it. A week later he sent four of his coaches to fetch a delegation of deputies, carrying a richly-bound volume containing the articles of the new constitution in full, which was solemnly presented to him. (In Portugal it is considered a matter of great importance to get a new law *on to paper*. How and in what manner the law is implemented, or whether it ever comes to be implemented at all, is another matter.) The Cortes now declared its labours at an end and " went to the country " for the election of a new parliament.

The country was still in an appalling state of disorganization. The exchequer was empty, the army and navy unpaid, the whole machine of state out of gear. In short, in spite of the Cortes having abolished certain pensions and costly institutions, including the Patriarchate and the Inquisition, it had really done nothing to remove the fundamental causes of discontent which had originally brought about the revolution calling the Cortes into existence. Indeed, they had added to them. The country now seethed with party hatred ; vested interests in church and state felt themselves menaced ; Portugal's new Free Press was disgraced by virulence and libel ; the Cortes had alienated the sympathies of the clergy, the nobles and the bulk of the armed forces.

The *exaltados*, however, were oblivious of their unpopularity. Their blind faith in the magic-working virtues of French revolutionary principles was so complete that they took it for granted that they had made the whole nation their debtors. Their complacency is well illustrated by a quaint contemporary snuff-box manufactured by some enterprising tobacconist for one of his *exaltado* clients. The lid bears an effigy of King John the Sixth, floating in a vaporous arrangement of winged figures with trumpets and cornucopiæ. And on the bottom of the box is represented the historic scene in the Cortes—the act of the *iuramento*—showing the assembly saluting the Minerva-like symbolic figure of the Portuguese Constitution. It is a ridiculous, pathetic relic of a dead ideal.

" The Constitution of 1822," wrote the Portuguese historian Rebello da Silva, whose opinions cannot be suspected of anti-liberalism, " was already a prey to political consumption when it left the hands of its authors.. . . The Crown, deprived of the right of dissolving the Chamber, or of proroguing it, or of assembling it, was silent and powerless in its presence. . . . To unjust laws the sovereign could only present a temporary opposition. Six ministers, ineligible to a seat in the house, possessed no vote in the popular senate. . . . Instead of effecting some real good for the benefit of the country, the Assembly contented itself with the proclamation of theoretical principles, and entangled itself in questions of remote and secondary interest. . . . The unnatural graft of new institutions on the decayed system of absolute government aggravated the disease. The wording of the liberal code, unsupported by regulating laws, was devoid of meaning. Men in office, having no responsibility, smiled at a document which for want of execution had become a dead letter. For the most part, those who occupied the highest positions of the magistracy and of the finance department were still the same that had contributed to the ruin of the old régime ; and the vices, the systematic and lucrative abuses of their administration, far from being restrained, had been encouraged by many who omitted no means to discredit by corruption and immorality the first steps of the liberal government. The result was that during the last months of its existence there were committed more scandals, more injustice and more illegalities than during the days of absolutism."

Dona Carlota Joaquina, as she listened to the gossip from Lisbon, saw that the hour for action was fast approaching. The Brave New World of the liberals was already tottering. A single well-directed blow would bring it crashing to the ground. But before describing the first decisive step taken by the Queen in the autumn of 1822, it will be convenient to trace the events leading up to the final loss of Brazil, for this disaster contributed to the disgrace of the liberal party and inflamed opinion in Portugal against them. In the second place, it will be necessary to say something of the international situation in Europe, where a universal struggle was going on between liberals and reactionaries, just as it was going on at Lisbon. With this wider struggle the destinies of Portugal became, to her misfortune, very closely associated. Dona Carlota Joaquina had opened a correspondence with her brother at Madrid, the reigning King of Spain, soon after her return to Portugal. She corresponded at the same time with two of her daughters who also resided at Madrid. The first of these was the Infanta Maria Francisca, who had been sent off from Rio de Janeiro in 1815 to marry Dom Carlos, Ferdinand the Seventh's brother. The second was the Infanta Maria Isobel, her eldest child, who had likewise gone over from Brazil and who became Ferdinand VII's queen. These two daughters shared all their mother's fervour for the absolutist—or, as it was known in Spain, the apostolic—cause. They seem to have been almost as subservient to her authority as Dom Miguel himself, and the importance of the influence which they in turn exerted over Spanish policy towards Portugal in the ensuing decade can hardly be overestimated. Suffice it to say for the time being that the news which Dona Carlota Joaquina received from these sources as to the general trend of events beyond the Portuguese frontiers was a decisive factor in her plan of action against the Cortes.

Chapter XV

In July, 1822, hardly a month after the convocation of the Constituent Assembly at Rio, Dom Pedro learned of further overbearing and insulting discussions that had taken place in the Lisbon Cortes on the subject of the dispatch of fresh troops across the Atlantic. He thereupon issued a proclamation justifying his decision to remain at Rio de Janeiro and declaring in the grandiloquent style that he had made his own : " Let no other cry be heard among us except *Union !* From the Amazons to the Plate let no echo ring save that of *Independence !*" On the 1st August he signed a decree which was equivalent to a declaration of war on the mother country : it denounced as enemies of Brazil whatever troops might be sent thither from Portugal without his previous consent and declared they should be resisted if need be by force of arms.

All Brazil was now in a fever. Every ship arriving from Lisbon carried reports of the Cortes' doings, and despatches from the Government, which further exasperated the feelings of Dom Pedro and the people.

In the land which he had already determined to make his own the Prince was now at the height of his popularity. It is difficult not to smile at the melodramatic attitudes he struck, but at the same time it is impossible not to admit that they were attitudes which the scene and the hour demanded. The day before he convoked the Constituent Assembly, he had been inducted into a secret society entitled " the Noble Order of the Knights of Santa Cruz," as chief of its " Apostolic Lodge." He represented in his person a tangled skein of different popular ideals—liberalism, masonic mysticism, anti-Portuguese resentment, the will for independence, and the vague but potent idea of Progress.

In August he set out on a visit to San Paulo. On the eve of his departure letters were put in his hand acquainting him with the Cortes' latest declared intention to " undertake the reconquest of Brazil." It was the one-from-last straw. His reception in San Paulo was an apotheosis. Though racked by dysentery, he was intoxicated by the cheers, the fireworks and the frenzy. A fortnight later—on the 7th September—on the road between San Paulo and Santos by the side of the Ipiranga River, he met with a courier carrying despatches from Rio de Janeiro. His attendant cavalcade halted at a short distance, while he hastily scanned their contents.

The first carried instructions from the Lisbon Cortes ; they insisted on his immediate return to Lisbon, and on the arrest and trial of his Minister José Bonifacio. The second was from José Bonifacio himself, who was already virtually the head of an independent provisional government. He informed Dom Pedro there were only two paths open to him—either to sail for Portugal and give himself up as a prisoner to the Cortes, " like Dom João," or else to proclaim the independence of Brazil and be its Emperor.

These letters were read aloud by his secretary, Father Belchior, while the Prince, still tortured by dysentery, crouched by the road-side. Then, rising in a fit of almost maniacal fury, Dom Pedro tore the despatches from his secretary's hands, flung them down, and stamped them into the ground. He turned to an aide-de-camp and cried, " Inform my guard I have decided upon the independence of Brazil."

The guards, with that genius for histrionic effect which they seem to have shared with the Parisian crowds of the French revolution— always ready, as contemporary engravings so forcibly demonstrate, to group themselves at a moment's notice into a classical chorus to acclaim a hero or deplore the death of a Patriot—his guards rode forward and with resounding cheers saluted the Emperor of Brazil.

Thus the Brazilian Empire came into being. On the 12th October Dom Pedro was officially proclaimed Emperor in Rio de Janeiro. " Citizens ! " ran the proclamation, " the God of Nature made America to be independent and free. The God of Nature retained in Brazil the Prince Regent to be he who should establish the independence of this vast continent. Why do we delay ? This is the moment. Portugal insults us. America invites us. Europe contemplates us. The Prince defends us. Citizens ! Raise the festive shout. Long live the Con-stitutional Emperor of Brazil ! "

It was an age of phrase-making. Metternich turned epigrams that electrified the chancelleries of Europe. When he declared that " Liber-alism had erased nationality from its catechism," or was heard to observe " it looks as if the dawn of a better day is about to break," his words were repeated, weighed and interpreted in every capital. Chateaubriand produced aphorisms as polished as those of the Austrian Chancellor. Even Englishmen caught the continental craze, and Can-ning proudly told the House of Commons he had " called a new world into existence to redress the balance of the old." But in an anthology of early nineteenth-century political pronouncements those of the first Emperor of Brazil would display a style all their own, in harmony with the young Empire's exuberant scenery and tropic sky.

On the 1st December, in barbaric splendour, Dom Pedro was crowned in the cathedral of Rio de Janeiro. And here for a while we may take leave of him, robed in the feather cape (made of the deep rose-red breasts of toucans) of the new American Cæsar. For this passionate, talented and still-youthful prince it was the climax of his short and strangely romantic career. The most interesting thing about him, and his chief claim to be remembered in history, is that, in his first man-hood, he had really become what he proclaimed himself to be—not a Portuguese but a Brazilian, not a European but a South American, not —as according to heredity he should have been—a representative of ancient absolutist Kings, but a product of the liberal nineteenth century. And if he was a liberal, it was because the air he breathed and had breathed since childhood was the air of the American continent. In him the Braganza and Bourbon blood had undergone a change, just as some flowers will alter almost out of recognition by transplantation to a different and richer soil. The germination and exotic flowering of his versatile powers were truly extraordinary and prodigious. Stimulated rather than enervated by a wild love-affair with the bewitching Marqueza dos Santos, he personally supervised the preparation of a Constitution for his Empire, as later on he was to prepare one for Portugal, and found time amidst affairs of state to contribute long articles to the Brazilian press, under a variety of journalistic pseudonyms, in support of his own policy and throne.

The distance between Portugal and Brazil before the age of cables and wireless is demonstrated by the fact that three weeks after the Brazilian Empire had been called into being on the banks of the Ipiranga, the Lisbon Cortes was still squabbling over what orders should be dictated to the Prince Royal. On the 20th September the deputies, after a violent session, decided that the " Vice-royalty of Dom Pedro must cease," and he " must be superseded by a Regency," and that he " must come back to Portugal." A decree annulled the convocation of the Constituent and Legislative Assembly that was already in being.

When the full news of what had happened reached the Tagus, it caused a universal despondency which the development of the international situation in Europe did nothing to dispel. Now in order to understand the causes of the prevailing tension it will be necessary to summarize the course of events in Europe during the preceding seven years.

When Napoleon was finally overthrown in 1815, the sovereigns of Europe in conclave at Vienna formed themselves under the leadership of Austria and Russia into the league which is known to history as the Holy Alliance.

Several of these sovereigns, such as the Kings of France, Spain and Naples, had been ignominiously chased from their thrones by the reverberating concussion of the French Revolution. When they returned to their respective capitals " in the baggage of the Allies " their thrones were very much less solid than they had formerly been. In the eyes of many of their subjects, indeed, there was something at once anachronistic and ridiculous about the restored kings. So it came about that though the first aim of the Holy Alliance was to provide a supreme tribunal by means of which all future disputes between nations could be settled without endangering the peace of Europe, it assumed, as time passed, the functions not so much of a tribunal between one nation and another as of a central power intent upon crushing all symptoms of revolutionary unrest wherever they might make their appearance. The reason for this was, first, that the sovereigns felt a sort of solidarity among each other, believing that a danger menacing any one of them menaced all ; secondly, the memory of how the great revolution in France had led directly to the invasion of

DONA CARLOTA JOAQUINA
from the State portrait at Queluz

neighbouring states by the French armies made any liberal revolutionary movement suspect as a possible threat to the stability of the continent.

It was agreed among the signatories that they should meet from time to time and take counsel together. They had frequent cause for anxiety. Though exhausted by war, Europe was still restless. The restoration of legitimate dynasties was accompanied by a wave of reaction which was as fierce as it was foolish, and which immediately gave a new impetus to liberal, subversive plots. Young Germany, moreover, was still effervescing with the enthusiasm of the war of liberation, and was, in fact, passing through one of her periodic and characteristic Teutonic fevers. Gymnastic establishments were being opened all over Prussia, and large numbers of earnest students clad in so-called old-German costume, eager to convince themselves or the world at large that there is such a thing as Teutonic culture, were wandering as zealous missionaries of German unity.

The Congress of Aix-la-Chapelle in 1818, at which vanquished France was readmitted into the Concert of Europe on equal terms with the other great powers, gave a new solidity to the originally rather mystic conception of the Holy Alliance. It also demonstrated Prince Metternich's rising power as the guiding spirit and master-mind of the Alliance. In the following year Metternich persuaded the confederated German princes to publish the famous Carlsbad Decrees suppressing the liberal movement throughout Germany.

England had been represented at Aix-la-Chapelle by the Duke of Wellington and Lord Castlereagh, who, backed by a Tory government at home, had participated in the labours of the Congress. But already a growing opinion in England, represented inside the cabinet by Canning, was beginning to declare itself against participation in international agreements which might hamper Britain's freedom of action. After the publication of the Carlsbad Decrees, this opinion grew very much stronger, and Castlereagh protested against the decrees as an unjustifiable interference in the internal affairs of sovereign states.

In 1820 took place the revolution in Spain. The Emperor Alexander at once suggested a joint intervention and offered, for his part, to march 15,000 Russians through the south of France to the succour of oppressed monarchy. Metternich, however, who was suspicious of Russian ambitions, managed to dissuade the Tzar from carrying out his proposal. Spain for the time being was left to fight it out, while the attention of the great powers was riveted upon a fresh revolution that had broken out in Naples. To deal with this new explosion a congress was called at Troppau, and a protocol was drawn up which was tantamount to the extension of the Carlsbad Decrees to all Europe. " States which have undergone a change of government due to revolution," so it ran, " the results of which threaten other states, *ipso facto* cease to be members of the European alliance and remain excluded from it until their situation gives guarantees for legal order and stability. . . . If, owing to such revolutions, immediate danger threatens other states, the Powers bind themselves, by peaceful means, or if need be by arms, to bring back the guilty state into the bosom of the Great Alliance." Putting this principle into practice, and disregarding Castlereagh's renewed protests, the Austrian armies marched into Italy to support the King of Naples.

Enough has been said to show how the principle of intervention had become familiar in the five years following Waterloo. We must now turn for a moment to the political situation in France.

King Louis the Eighteenth was determined "not to go on his travels again." On his return to Paris he had granted a constitution to his people and, like Dom John of Portugal, was determined to abide loyally by the Constitutional charter. But all moderate counsels were drowned by the long pent-up fury of the clerical and royalist reactionaries who were "more royalist than the King." The violence displayed by the royalists stirred up a corresponding enmity in their opponents. In short, France was rent by the fiercest political animosities. Now, when the 1820 revolution in Spain swept all before it, and Spain fell into chaos, Louis the Eighteenth recognized in the indignities being inflicted on his Bourbon cousin a menace to his own throne. But above all he saw an opportunity to distract the attention of Frenchmen from party strife at home, to restore France's prestige by a military adventure, and above all to give his own crown some of the lustre it so sadly lacked in comparison to what every Frenchman remembered of Napoleon's empire. If the Holy Alliance was not going to intervene in Spain because of Austrian fear of Russia, might not France undertake an intervention on her own ?

An outbreak of yellow fever south of the Pyrenees in August, 1821, gave the French government an excuse for posting a corps of observation on the frontier, under the pretext of establishing a sanitary cordon. In spite of the protests of the Spanish government this was gradually increased until it formed an army of 100,000 men. But it was necessary for the French government to tread warily. England was uncompromisingly hostile to the French scheme. She had not poured out her blood and treasure in ousting Napoleon from the Peninsula only to connive at its peaceful occupation by his successor. Under these conditions the French government determined, before making a move, to receive if possible the sanction of the Great Powers.

Another congress was to take place at Verona in the Autumn of 1822. The Duke of Wellington, as British plenipotentiary, was instructed by his government to object to any intervention in Spain as " objectionable in principle and utterly impracticable in execution." But the French envoy, M. de Montmorency, laid a definite proposition before the Congress ; would France, in the event of her being forced to declare war on Spain, be able to reckon on the moral and material support of the Allies ? To this question Russia, Austria and Prussia returned a favourable answer. The Duke of Wellington protested, but his protest—to use Canning's phrase—mingled with the air. He thereupon withdrew from the Congress and England severed her connection with the concert of Europe.

But France was now assured of the moral approval of the continental powers, and Louis the Eighteenth, in a speech from the throne on the 28th January, 1823, announced that 100,000 Frenchmen, under a prince of his house—the Duke of Angoulême—were about to march " invoking the God of Saint Louis, for the sake of preserving the throne of Spain to a descendant of Henry the Fourth."

Rumours of the French government's intentions filtered into Lisbon during the autumn of 1822. " The rumours of hostile measures," wrote Ward, " to be adopted by some of the allied powers assembled at Verona in order to force Spain to remodel her constitution, have produced much sensation here." There is not the smallest doubt that these reports had a decisive effect upon the mind of Dona Carlota Joaquina. If Spain was a prey to all the evils of a chaotic democracy, was not Portugal in a similar plight ? And if the " legitimate " authority of her brother was to be restored by foreign arms, had not the time come for Portugal to be forcibly purged of her liberal fever also ?

During the third week in November, the astounding news flew from mouth to mouth that *the Queen had refused to swear to the Constitution.* A pompous delegation had gone out to Queluz to receive her oath : thinking the whole thing would be a mere formality. Dona Carlota had received them standing—black, squat and rude—and had bluntly informed them of her refusal. Like those maddening people who refuse to settle an argument by a bet, saying simply they " never bet," she had told them " she would not swear ; that she had made up her mind never to swear in all her life ; which was not through haughtiness or hatred towards the Cortes but simply because she had once said so : since a person of her honour never made retractions."

According to article eleven of the Constitution, the refusal of a member of the royal family to take the oath invoked the penalty of exile. The Queen announced she was content to abide by the law, but in reality she was determined by hook or by crook to remain where she was. Her brother was as good as a prisoner of the Spanish Cortes at Cadiz, from which predicament he was about to be rescued by the Knight-errant of France. If she herself stayed where she was and the Cortes were compelled to make a state prisoner out of her, would not the Knight-errant's eyes be turned towards Portugal also ? Her two daughters at Madrid cherished a similar hope. In point of fact, the British government would never have tolerated French interference at Lisbon, and they made the fact perfectly clear at Paris, but Dona Carlota did not know as much.

The Cortes, on the other hand, was equally ignorant of what was passing between London and Paris, and though the *Perola* was lying in the Tagus ready to carry the Queen into exile, they never insisted on the law being carried out because they feared that if Dona Carlota left Portugal it would only be to plead her cause at the Tuileries, and to return with a French army at her back.

A second intimation to her to take the oath was presented to her at Queluz. On this occasion it was a written document, to which she replied in writing to the King. (It is a proof of how little assimilated to the country of her adoption she was, that she wrote in her naïf yet pungent Castilian) :

" Last night at ten o'clock I received by the hand of the Marquis of Valada the intimation to which I herewith reply as follows : (1) I have already made my solemn and formal declaration that I will not take the oath, a declaration which I now confirm ; (2) I am ready to obey the King's orders according to the law, but nevertheless I am obliged to point out that I am ill, as all know, and even more so than is believed, and that the preservation of life is a right of nature. I am sure that neither the King nor the government would wish me to die by the roadside ; it is now the depth of winter and if I undertake a journey I must succumb. Therefore, in order to show my obedience, I am ready to retire to my quinta of Ramalhâo with my two daughters (who must always be inseparable from me) until such time as I may be able to start a longer journey. It is my intention to go to Cadiz, by sea, which would be an easier journey, as soon as my strength is sufficiently recovered."

The malicious appeal to the " right of nature," in the Liberals' own abstract clap-trap phraseology, will not pass unnoticed : nor the reference to Cadiz, the goal of the Duke of Angoulême's army.

The Queen's refusal was an historic event. It was the first time that the new-fangled belief in the Constitutional creed had been openly challenged in Portugal. Among the liberal middle-classes it caused about as much sensation as if Queen Victoria in the year of the Great Exhibition had suddenly taken it into her head to denounce Free Trade. It was also the most important single action in Dona Carlota's life. Her intrigues were generally underhand ; her restless ambition found expression for the most part in a stubborn but passive hostility. On this occasion, however, she came out into the open. And as a result the strong but hitherto inarticulate sense of dissatisfaction which was felt against the Cortes crystallized round her. All eyes were turned on Queluz. From that moment she was what she had always dreamed of becoming—the acknowledged leader of a party working to obtain mastery of the state. She did not, as we shall see, choose herself to be the figurehead for her cause. She selected one more attractive to the masses in the person of Dom Miguel. But she herself was the brains behind this strange political partnership between mother and son. It was she who pulled the strings controlling the puppet prince. Her household was henceforth the acknowledged headquarters of the Reaction. Her secret agents were in contact with the troops all over the country and were active organizing everywhere, under her direction, secret societies whose aim was to counter the influence of the masons.

On the 22nd November, 1882, the new Cortes met. Its members had for the most part been elected by the grossest bribery and falsification of the voting. The majority of the chamber consisted of pushing professional men and agents of the secret societies. They were more ignorant, more demagogic and more self-seeking even than their predecessors. They resumed their interminable debates and applauded each other's long-winded oratory.

But none could devise a plan of how to deal effectively with the

Queen. Her health had been pronounced to be incapable of sustaining the fatigue of travelling by a committee of sixteen physicians carefully chosen by the Queen's party. In the end, the Cortes adopted the solution she herself had proposed, and early in December the Queen left Queluz and went into " exile " to Ramalhâo—a journey of just ten miles !

Ramalhâo was almost equally as good a headquarters for her as Queluz. Her spies from Lisbon had merely to ride for an extra hour ; her spies from the north rode for an hour less. Couriers disguised as peasants, to evade the guard set on her house by the Cortes, carried her letters to Spain, whither her thoughts persistently turned, as they had turned since childhood. The old mansion was perhaps not quite so comfortable as her palace, and was much out of repair, but there was a wonderful dining-room with its walls and ceiling frescoed with painted Brazilian foliage and birds of paradise, with cork-encrusted grottoes in the corners decorated with live ferns ; with a set of rustic chairs covered in cork-bark perfectly suitable for a court of gnomes, and with a huge centre-piece to the dining-table like a rockery, a mass of cork, ferns, and sea-shells, with water gushing out of it.

Such was the romantic council-chamber of one who was ever mindful of her rank as Empress and Queen.

Chapter XVI

Dom John spent most of his day in the royal chapel at Bemposta. " It is my considered opinion," he said wearily, " that the best thing to do is to do nothing." He had a quiet sense of humour that helped him along. When he found despatches from the Cortes on his desk, he used to say with a smile to his lords-in-waiting ; " Well, let's have a look at what they say I have done to-day." He would have made quite a good Constitutional sovereign in normal times.

His complacency irritated Dona Carlota Joaquina nowadays more than ever, for in agreeing to collaborate with the liberals he was making it difficult for her party to represent him as " a prisoner of the Cortes " like the King of Spain.

Mrs. Baillie noticed that the condition of the country was growing daily more alarming. From north to south public opinion blamed the Cortes for mishandling the Brazilian question. Everyone despised the deputies. It was obvious to any but a prejudiced person that constitutionalism was proving unworkable, while the common people felt a wave of sentimental affection for the past. A remarkable occurrence gave occasion about this time for the populace to give proof of their continued devotion to the customs and faiths of the good old days.

On the banks of a little stream in the parish of Carnaxide a few miles from Lisbon a peasant-boy was chasing a rabbit when it crept into a hole in a high bank, closely followed by his dog. The boy groped his way through the hole behind the dog, and found himself in a cave with a rocky ledge at one end, on which he beheld a tiny image of the Virgin, and the rabbit and the dog both upon their knees side by side in devout adoration beneath it.

Widely advertised by the friars, the news of this miracle threw all Portugal into an ecstasy, and an immense concourse went to pay its respects to Nossa Senhora da Barraca (Our Lady of the Cave). Every household was denuded of its servants, who hurried off to the shrine with one accord in their Sunday best. A friar was to be seen night and day at the cave's mouth, descanting on the miracles already said to have been performed there ; and in a short time the image had received numerous costly gifts, including a jewelled crown and many golden chains. An aged countess who had been bed-ridden for years caused herself to be carried to the site, and recovered the use of her limbs. The valley where the cave lay soon resembled an immense fair, with booths for the refreshment of the faithful, thirty or forty aristocratic carriages constantly parked nearby, and the hillside black with kneeling pilgrims.

Dona Carlota Joaquina observed the political significance of the occurrence. She went in state to Carnaxide, received a tremendous ovation, and made an offering of a silver lamp. But Our Lady of the Cave was not merely a barometer of public opinion ; she was a test-case. She was a litmus paper with which to distinguish sentiments throughout the country. Did you accept the whole story of the miracle? If you did, you were heart and soul of the Queen's party. If you did not, you were obviously infected by heretical liberal ideas. Immediately the country was divided into two clearly-divided camps.

Nor was this all. Our Lady of the Cave was transformed by the enthusiasm of her devotees—but especially by the fervour shown by the Queen—into a symbol of their cause. She was the banner they would follow into battle. And it was not long before Dona Carlota had succeeded in implanting in the impressionable mind of Dom Miguel a devotion to Our Lady of the Cave as frantic as her own.

The Cortes took alarm, as well it might, at the public demonstrations of loyalty to ancient traditions going on at Carnaxide. The *Astro* newspaper produced some clever modern leaders denouncing outworn superstitions, and one of the leading members of the Cortes decided to go in person to the cave and to disabuse the populace by a display of modern manners and a few pointed sneers. But he had no sooner uttered some expression of disrespect for Nossa Senhora da Barraca than a fish-wife standing by caught him a stunning blow on the ear with a heavy fish. At the orders of the government the chief of police then went to Carnaxide with an armed platoon with a view to removing the image, only to find his way barred by more than a thousand resolute country-people. Shortly afterwards, the priests announced that the miraculous Virgin was to be solemnly removed to the Lisbon Cathedral. She went by water, and was received upon the quay by a magnificent cortège of clergy, and a guard of honour.

Never has a British government read the omens of coming defeat in the adverse decision of a by-election more surely than did the nervous Lisbon deputies in the stir created by Our Lady of the Cave. Their days were in fact nearly numbered. Though in January, 1823, there were well-attended debates to discuss the French menace to Spain, Ward, who was always well informed, was writing to the Foreign Office foreseeing a counter-revolution in the north of Portugal.

It broke out in February, when the Count of Amarante, who was in command of troops stationed at Vila Real raised the shout of " Death to the Constitution ! Long live the Absolute King !" He issued a proclamation referring to " our august sovereign a captive . . . the Queen banished . . . our Holy Religion attacked . . . free-masonry rampant . . . politicians despoiling the people . . . Brazil lost . . . " Two regiments of cavalry and one of infantry joined him, and with these Amarante marched into the province of the Minho. There is little doubt that he acted in concert with advice from Ramalhão, though no letters from the Queen to him have been found. It is possible that her instructions and encouragement were conveyed by one or other of the long-haired friars that composed a kind of ecclesiastical general-staff round Amarante. But it is significant that he was supported by many men who two years earlier had been identified with the Oporto revolution. As in 1820, the true motive force behind the movement was not political principle so much as economic distress and discontent with the incompetence of the Lisbon government.

Had Amarante moved at once southwards and threatened the capital, the rotten edifice of Constitutional Government might have collapsed there and then. As it was, he hesitated and wasted time. Meanwhile a plethora of eloquent speeches in the Cortes, fiercely denouncing the enemies of Liberty aad declaring that the speakers were prepared to shed the last drop of their blood in its defence, lent a spurious air of vitality to the moribund constitutional cause. A National Guard modelled on that of the French Revolution was called into being, and the blue and white ribbons of the Constitutionalists fluttered from hundreds of hats. Many noblemen whose loyalty was suspect were hurriedly exiled to their country estates. At the same time General Luiz de Rego was ordered to march northwards to crush the revolt, and after a few confused engagements he actually succeeded in driving Amarante across the Spanish frontier.

For the time being, therefore, it appeared as if the blue-and-whites had triumphed. But the insurrection had animated the enemies of the Cortes throughout Portugal, and after long hours of communing with Our Lady of the Cave, Dona Carlota Joaquina was persuaded that the time had now come to put her long-matured schemes in motion. Her plan was this : Dom Miguel was to lead a revolutionary movement against the government ; the Constitutional System was to be declared at an end, and Portugal was to return to her ancient traditions under an Absolute King. But this was not all. The memories of Dom Pedro's successful revolution at Rio de Janeiro in 1820 were fresh in Dona Carlota's mind. Was not the immediate result of that affair that Dom John had made up his mind to bid farewell to his beloved Rio de Janeiro ? Now Dona Carlota believed that the King still hankered after that halcyon bay ; she was aware of the anxiety being caused him by the possibility of Brazil being lost to his crown. If Dom Miguel's revolution succeeded was it not possible that the King would wish to return to Rio de Janeiro, leaving the prince—her puppet—on the steps of his vacant throne ? It was with positive relish that she contemplated the imaginary picture of the old King groping from one unfeeling son to another, unwanted and ridiculous like King Lear among his daughters.

It was inevitable, however, that a woman of such passionate temper would make mistakes in her calculations. Dona Carlota made two. She forgot that in a timid man timidity often acts as its own antidote, and that if on the one hand it was perfectly true that Dom John would make almost any sacrifice in order to be able to live a quiet life, on the other hand, he still dreaded the idea of being sea-sick. Secondly, in laying her plans, Dona Carlota entirely overlooked Dom John's solid popularity with the Portuguese people. Though the Queen had lately won estimation on account of her ostentatious piety and though the King, as Ward said, had lost ground owing to his having made so many concessions to the party in power, the masses, nevertheless, liked him and detested her. But when one human being despises another, it is difficult for him to understand that the object of his contempt may enjoy the affectionate regard of the world at large. Such was the basis of the miscalculation made by Dona Carlota Joaquina.

That year, the summer came early. Already by the end of May the temperature was like a furnace. At night, the outlines of the Lisbon hills were silhouetted against fitful flashes of summer lightning. At three o'clock on the morning of the 27th, Dom Miguel left the capital secretly at the head of a troop of the 4th Cavalry, and took the road for Vila Franca, a country town which lies on the banks of the Tagus, some twenty miles from Lisbon. Four silver coins in his pocket were the only funds at the disposal of this madcap Prince for the overthrow of a government.

The commander of the Lisbon garrison was still General Sepulveda. A few days previously he had signed an order for the 23rd Infantry Regiment, which was quartered at St. George's Castle, to march at dawn of the 27th to garrison the town of Almeida, as a precaution against the Count de Amarante's forces across the frontier. The General was in a box at the Saint Carlos Opera when a message was brought him by a police agent to inform him that although it was not yet midnight the regiment was at that moment equipped and ready to move. The circumstance was suspicious. Sepulveda, therefore, sent his aide-de-camp, the young Marquis de Fronteira, to investigate. The report which the Marquis brought back to the theatre was far from reassuring, but the General took no further action. Instead, he went to bed.

The next morning he received an astonishing private letter from the commander of the regiment. It informed him that the 23rd had already marched out of Lisbon to join the Prince at Vila Franca, and added that His Royal Highness' intention was to restore the " inalienable rights of the crown." Lastly, it roundly invited Sepulveda to throw in his lot with the insurgents. The writer of the letter was a Brigadier José de Sousa, Sepulveda's closest friend. Sepulveda was aghast, but his amazement and alarm knew no bounds when the news was brought him a few moments later that his cousin, a Colonel commanding the 4th cavalry, and his own principal aide-de-camp, Colonel Gastâo, were at Dom Miguel's side. If such close associates of his had promoted the revolution, it was obvious that his own loyalty would be suspect.

Having made a tour of inspection of the Lisbon barracks and found all apparently in order, Sepulveda galloped to the Cortes, where the deputies, having heard of the Prince's movements, had declared themselves in permanent session.

Never did that august body behave with greater rashness and stupidity than on that critical day. Sepulveda was the one man who might have been able to save the situation. He had been in command of the garrison ever since the day the Cortes had been put in power. He was a capable soldier, and he enjoyed the confidence of the King. But he was no intriguer, and had omitted to flatter the vanity of certain deputies. These now made up their minds to destroy him, and easily persuaded themselves that if part of the Lisbon garrison had mutinied it was because their commander-in-chief had connived in the revolt. On entering the chamber he was met with shouts of " Traitor ! Death to Sepulveda ! " Evidently the Cortes imagined they were in sufficient security to stage yet another theatrical scene.

He with difficulty retreated out of the building. He galloped immediately to Bemposta.

The King, as was to be expected, was a bundle of nerves. He had never liked the Cortes, but he stood in far greater fear of his wife whom he shrewdly suspected of being the mainspring of the revolt. In response to the urgent advice of his entourage, however, he made some changes in his ministry. (It is not necessary to record what these changes were, for the Constitution was so unpractical a system that the King's ministers, who had no executive power, were habitually almost unknown to the public.)

Sepulveda, together with certain deputies from the Cortes, proposed to the King that he should at once promulgate a new constitution of a more monarchical type. But the King who, it will be observed, remained absolutely loyal to the oaths he had taken to the Constitution until the very last moment, refused to agree to this suggestion. He sent the Marquis of Bellas to summon Dom Miguel to return to Lisbon, an injunction which the Prince disregarded.

While these discussions were in progress at Bemposta the Cortes had called out the National Guard, and several hundreds of comical volunteers were adding to the confusion in the streets. Every quarter of an hour brought the news of some fresh defection among the nobility or the army. On horseback or muleback, with people crammed into a heterogeneous procession of vehicles or on foot, a general exodus was beginning in the direction of Vila Franca.

It would be a vain task to seek for political consistency in Dom Miguel's followers. We read how on the 29th the entire masonic lodge of the Largo do Rato followed their master the Count da Cunha on the Vila Franca road.

On the 29th, in spite of Sepulveda's misgivings, the old King insisted on taking part in the Corpus Christi procession round the Rocio Square. All passed off normally, but the shouts for the Absolute King which Dom John heard among the crowd made a deep impression on his mind. Sepulveda's embarrassments, as the day wore on, became like a nightmare. He galloped wildly about Lisbon, no sooner turning his back on the commanding officers of one barracks on his way to another than a message would overtake him saying that the barracks he had just quitted had revolted. Meanwhile, the town was full of bands of blue-and-whites shouting for his death. As he rode down the Rua d'Aurea he was assaulted by the mob, dragged from the saddle and only saved at the last moment by the intervention of some still loyal troops. That same evening, the 13th, the 16th and the 20th regiments declared for Dom Miguel, and put themselves in motion to join the Prince.

All Lisbon was in an uproar. The general anarchy was lent a final touch of horror when the convicts incarcerated in the Junqueira and Castello prisons somehow got hold of muskets and mutinied. Disaster was only averted by the presence of mind of a colonel who acted on his own initiative and succeeded in restoring order.

In a hopeless attempt to call the 16th to heel, Sepulveda sent the Marquis of Fronteira to follow them, with the result that the unfortunate aide-de-camp was promptly made prisoner and carried off to Vila Franca willy-nilly. It may be pointed out that the only three men who in spite of all remonstrances, threats and entreaties remained perfectly firm in their duty throughout the 29th were the young Fronteira, Sepulveda and the King.

The climax to three days' commotion came on the following morning. The palace of Bemposta was garrisoned by a regiment in which the Cortes placed implicit trust—the 18th Infantry. In the forenoon of the 30th, this regiment, drawn up in front of the palace, raised the now familiar shout for the " Rey Absoluto." A suggestion was then somehow made that the King should himself place himself at their head and take the Vila Franca road, which by this time must have been as crowded as the Epsom road on Derby day. The idea found general favour. It is impossible to ascertain from the records of the period who was responsible for first making this proposal, whose results were destined to be so important. It was affirmed at the time that the old Marquis de Loulé, the King's Master of the Horse, was largely instrumental in persuading him to carry it out. Certainly the whole court, intoxicated by the cheers below the palace windows, added their voices to the chorus. The Princesses clung to their father's arm, urged his faltering steps on to the balcony, and with nimble fingers removed the blue-and-white cockade from his hat. Resounding cheers greeted this gesture of recantation. Dom John was then bustled down the stairs. He was heard to mutter over and over again : " Since you all wish it, my dears, and since the nation wishes it too ; well, then, long live the Absolute King !"

So Dom John surrendered himself at last to the tide of popular feeling, and in doing so he saved his throne. Ninety per cent. of the crowd that migrated to Vila Franca were disgusted with the Constitutional System, yet they were devoted to the old King. When Dom John joined them his popularity was overwhelming. It was a masterstroke of statesmanship, though perhaps it was in reality merely a stroke of luck. Had he remained at Bemposta, and allowed the Prince to march on Lisbon, it is more than likely that Dona Carlota's dreams would have come true.

Vila Franca seethed like a bee-hive. Dom Miguel, however, had by this time, removed his headquarters to Santarem. There the Marquis of Fronteira, still under arrest, watched from the window of his cell the arrival of the Dukes of Cadaval and Lafôes, with their troops of liveried retainers glittering with badges of solid silver, like the train of some mediaeval baron; and the Marquis of Angeja followed by a regiment of rustic tenants, like a robber chief. Here, too, he witnessed the painful scene occasioned by the arrival of the unfortunate General Sepulveda, who had left Lisbon only when practically every soldier in the capital had deserted him. Dom Miguel received him with petrifying coldness. He was placed under arrest and was shamefully handled by the Prince's guards. Fronteira was himself an object of the gravest anxiety to the numerous friends and cousins he found at Santarem. They feared he might be stabbed by the villainous Manuel Vassalo or by José Verissimo, two of the Prince's bull-fighter friends who were acting as his private bodyguard.

At Santarem Dom Miguel received despatches from the King written from Vila Franca, and decided in conference with his lately appointed counsellor, General Pampluna, to obey his father's summons to join him. It is possible that Dom Miguel did not understand all the implications of the King's leaving the capital. It is arguable that he had not himself plotted to overthrow his father's throne, and was too naïf to penetrate the Queen's designs. He rode out of Santarem in good spirits, damped only by the slight repugnance he felt at having to receive the paternal embrace.

On June the 5th, the King and the Prince together re-entered Lisbon. It was a day of delirious high-spirits for everyone, except, of course, for the members of the Cortes, who, forgetting all their declarations about shedding the last drop of their blood, had now scattered and were in hiding or packing their bags. The mob broke into the deserted chamber, and vented their feelings by smashing up the furniture. Meanwhile, the royal coach, the Prince and the Infantas on horseback, a long cortège of coaches and calèches, and thousands of the populace besides the various regiments, came winding along the Vila Franca—Lisbon road by the side of the Tagus midst bouquets of rockets and a dense long trail of suffocating dust. It was christened by the people *o dia da poeira*, the Day of Dust.

It was the old King who received the loudest ovation when they came at last to Lisbon. The mob removed the horses from the shafts and dragged his carriage along. The crowd also cheered the Princesses, who rode wearing the uniforms of colonels of regiments (their skirts excepted) with superb golden epaulettes, cocked hats, and plumes of white feathers. "It is astonishing," wrote Mrs. Baillie, "how well the dress became these lovely creatures, who were perfectly wild with spirits, smiling and receiving the homage of a thousand flatterers with an air of proud delight, and nearly deafened by the noisier admiration of their humbler subjects."

Chapter XVII

It is easy enough to point out that Portugal's crying need was for a strong government under a strong ruler. There are times in the history of every nation when strong men are lacking, not necessarily because they do not exist but because circumstances prevent their coming forward, or, if they do come forward, make their task impossible. It is useless to expect even the most skilled navigator to hold a course when the ship's crew is in mutiny. And in Portugal in 1823, national discipline had broken down. Apart from this, the country needed a statesman-economist to strike at what was the root of her chronic decline—economic disorder—and in point of fact, she was to wait just over a hundred years before she found one in the person of a Coimbra professor, Dr. Salazar.

Dom John came back from Vila Franca with mixed feelings. The constitutional system that he had always found so very tiresome was no more. He had received spontaneous and touching proof of the affection in which he was held by his subjects. On the other hand, the Constitution, irksome as it had been, had at least provided a sort of bolster between himself and the malevolent Queen. Information reaching him from all sides made him perfectly aware of the part she had played in engineering the revolution. It had been as much " hers " as if she had personally led the troops on horseback to Vila Franca. He could hardly doubt that she would make a second attempt, and he felt uncomfortably vulnerable now that he was deprived of the ring of complacent busybodies that the Cortes used to nominate as his counsellors. Such was his trepidation when he thought of the future that he was sometimes tempted to regret the Constitution's downfall. He certainly entertained no thought of revenge or reprisals against the defeated liberals.

The dear old King's popularity in the nation as a whole was really as great as he deserved. Not even the ex-deputies, as they hurriedly hid their blue-and-white cockades in the lining of their hat-boxes, bore him any grudge. He had remained true to the constitution he had sworn to abide by until it had been shattered by an overwhelming demonstration of the people's will. And his good nature was so well-known that only a very few prominent politicians considered it necessary to go into exile to save their skins. Among them was José da Silva Carvalho, who had been one of the King's ministers. Dom John had grown quite attached to him, and now gave orders that his passage to England should be paid, together with a modest pension. Through the carelessness or spite of treasury officials this money was never handed over, but Silva Carvalho knew that Dom John died in the conviction that it had actually been paid. Only Borges Carneiro displayed fright, going on board a ship disguised as a servant.

There was an amusing scene at Queluz when the King assisted at Dona Carlota Joaquina's triumphant return from Ramalhâo. He rode in her carriage and with a considerable effort of self-control kissed her in front of the court. Perhaps Dom John's typically Portuguese sense of humour enabled him to play his part in this comedy with some secret amusement. Dona Carlota, for her part, found herself compelled to simper and pretend to be pleased. Had not the Constitution been overthrown ? Yet she realized, of course, that her own schemes had not succeeded. The success vouchsafed to the enterprise by Our Lady of the Cave had been only partial. Dona Carlota knew that by going to Vila Franca Dom John had saved his throne, and she believed that the man who had had a decisive influence in persuading him to act as he had done was the Marquis of Loulé.

But this was not all. When the King was at Sacavem, half-way to Vila Franca, he had issued a proclamation promising the country some sort of constitutional charter " more compatible than the 1820 constitution with the stability and peace of the state." Now no act, it might be argued, could have been more statesmanlike or more in harmony with the needs of the hour. The Portuguese were disgusted with the 1820 constitution, based on the exaggerated democratic principles of the Spanish model. But times had changed too radically to make an uncompromising return to an eighteenth-century absolutist system practicable. It would have been glaringly out of keeping with the times and would never have satisfied the majority in the long run. But the result of the Sacavem proclamation was, that though the 1820 constitution had been discarded, Absolutism—the die-hard, whole-hog absolutism of the Queen's party—could not be said to have triumphed in its place. Thus the Queen's object in the political sphere had been only half won, while in the personal sphere—in her desire to dethrone her husband—she had not succeeded at all. Lastly, Dona Carlota Joaquina had been frustrated in her burning longing to see the liberals—the hated masons—punished ; to see their blood run and the gaols crowded with the men she hated. Perhaps no woman in history was more vindictive than this Queen. And let it be borne in mind that in the matter of the Sacavem proclamation, rightly or wrongly, she again blamed the Marquis of Loulé.

The " reconciliation " at Queluz was followed by a numerously-attended hand-kissing. The sensation of the evening occurred when some beautiful young ladies dressed all in white, with breast-knots of the royal colours (red and purple, in contradistinction from the constitutional blue-and-white) presented Dom Miguel with a crown of roses. In answer the Infante pulled the plume out of his hat and, holding it under his foot, tore it hastily into small feathers which he presented to all his admirers. It became the fashion to wear bunches of red and purple ribbons with a little sprig of the princely plume inserted, and sometimes with a small cross attached in allusion to the Count of Amarante who had first raised the Absolutist cry with his sword in one hand and a crucifix in the other. These favours were everywhere apparent when the court went with all solemnity to pay its respects at the shrine of Nossa Senhora da Barraca, to whose benign influence, needless to say, the late change in government was attributed by the Queen's party. They are the earliest relics of that Miguelist cult which played so great a part in Portuguese history during the years to come, and which even today has not spent its force.

Dom Miguel had now become an acknowledged hero in the eyes of the absolutists ; he had also become a personage of European celebrity. The Emperors of Austria and Russia, and the Kings of France and Prussia, bestowed on him their most scintillating decorations. The sovereigns of the Holy Alliance congratulated themselves on the emergence of a new and effulgent champion in the cause of Legitimacy and Divine Right.

In Dom Miguel's character, however, his public triumph had so far produced no noticeable modification. The loose-boxes at Bemposta were filled with his bulls and heifers. He was to be seen leaping into the bull-ring wearing his new uniform of Commander-in-Chief of the Portuguese army, enrapturing the spectators by his dexterity with the barbs, the cloak and the sword alike, or lounging in a tavern cheek by jowl with his boon companion the Marquis of Abrantes over a bottle of rough brandy, surrounded by a bevy of bull-fighters and grooms.

It is difficult to describe Dom Miguel's entourage in English words, which give no picture of the Portuguese equivalent. They were Portuguese editions of the pugilists and mail-coachmen with whom some English Regency dandies used to surround themselves at Brighton. One was a *picador*, another was an out-rider, a third was by origin a sergeant of police. All were conspicuous for their amazing courage in the saddle, their wild and picturesque air, and their reckless devotion to the Prince.

What is the explanation of the devotion that Dom Miguel was able to inspire among his fierce associates ? He symbolized ancient traditions in Portuguese life—the sense of common fellowship between classes, which we have noticed as one of the distinguishing characteristics of the Portuguese nobleman's way of life. In defiance of nineteenth-century middle-class principles he carried on the customs which a century earlier had made the Lisbon streets at night a terror to respectable townsfolk, when young sparks of the aristocracy— the future Marquis of Pombal included—roamed sword in hand in quest of brawls, like the " Mohawks " of London. Dom Miguel's tastes were what in Portuguese would now be termed *national*; they represented a revolt against the infiltration of foreign ideas and foreign manners. Lastly, the romantic air which the Princess Lieven in later years was to find " attractive," the lower-classes in Portugal found irresistible. He shared their temperament, displayed their own virtues in his very vices, and was withal every inch a prince. The most wretched beggar meeting his smile felt its magic.

He would have been less dangerous from the political point of view had he been less hopelessly weak-willed. Though fundamentally a spoilt boy who had never even begun to acquire the rudiments of self-restraint, there was yet much solid good in him, as the evening of his life in exile in Rome and Austria was to show. But at the period under review, he was at the mercy of whatever personal influence happened to be closest to him. Palmella described him in his memoirs as " a good man when among good men, and when among the bad worse than they." Unfortunately, the predominant influence at this time was his mother, in whose hands he was as soft as wax. When the youth entered her presence and met her burning eyes fixed upon him, he felt the same awe as when in years gone by at Santa Cruz he had submitted to chastisement from her slipper. By some strange power she trajected into him her own passions and hatreds, possessing and commanding his very soul. When he was distant from her he moved like a somnambulist guided by her will, mindful only of the tie that bound them in mystic devotion to Our Lady of the Cave.

It is necessary now to remark some additions to the political chess-board which took place following the " Vila-francada." First, Sir Edward Thornton returned to the Portuguese court as British Minister. He was given a kindly welcome by Dom John, who, like all Portuguese, liked familiar faces—Sir Edward reminded him, too, of happier days in Rio de Janeiro. Secondly, Palmella was made Minister of Foreign Affairs in the King's new government. He was granted the title of Marquis (a lavish distribution of honours marked the restitution of the ancient monarchy). Thirdly, General Pampluna, whom we have seen at Dom Miguel's side at Santarem, now joined the cabinet as Minister of War with the title of Marquis of Subserra. Another new character was the newly arrived French ambassador, Hyde de Neuville.

Dona Carlota regarded Thornton as a piece on the chess board belonging to Dom John. She disliked him, as she disliked all *inglezes*, and had reason to believe the disgust was mutual. Palmella was clearly Dom John's piece also—a piece of considerable value. As for the third, Subserra, the Queen at first imagined that he was going to prove a useful recruit to her own side, which was lacking in first-rate ability. In fact, her side may be said to have consisted mainly of pawns— nameless friars, half-crazed military men such as Amarante, and the dregs of the bull-ring to act as chorus—with only one really powerful piece among them : Dom Miguel himself, powerful because of the enthusiasm he was capable of arousing. A bitter disappointment was in store for the Queen when she was made to realize that Subserra was not *her* piece after all.

Subserra was a remarkable man. He had become a soldier in early life, and in the reign of the Empress Catharine, had served in the Russian army against the Turks. At a later date, he joined Napoleon's Portuguese Legion and actually entered Portugal with Massena's invading army, acting for some time on behalf of his country's enemies as military governor of Coimbra. Then he took part in the invasion of Russia, earning Napoleon's praises as governor of Polosk. As a traitor to his country, he had been condemned to death in Lisbon, but after Waterloo he returned to Portugal and was amnestied. He accepted the post of Minister of War in the early stages of the constitutional régime, but shortly afterwards resigned, and after serving for some time as a deputy retired into private life in his comfortable house at Campolide.

Such was the adventurous previous career of this clever, much-travelled and forceful individual whom the events of May, 1823, promoted to one of the most prominent positions in the State. The part he had played in the " Vilafrancada " must be examined in order to explain the confidence which the King now placed in him and the disappointment he caused to Dona Carlota.

Enjoying a reputation as a general and known to be disgruntled with the constitutionalists, Subserra had been regarded by Dona Carlota Joaquina, when she planned the revolution, as both a necessary and a willing instrument. What better man was there, she had thought, to stand at the Prince's side and put his military experience at his disposal ? No sooner had Dom Miguel arrived at Vila Franca, therefore, than, in accordance with his mother's previous instructions, he sent a letter to Subserra urging him to join his standard. Subserra obeyed the summons, and moreover, acted with such decision that for five days he practically controlled the insurrectionary movement. But he made it perfectly clear to the Prince that although he was collaborating to overthrow the Cortes he would do nothing to defy the authority of the King, to whom he sent a letter assuring him of his loyalty. Accompanying Dom Miguel to Santarem, he advised him, as we have seen, to obey his father's summons to meet him in Vila Franca. Thus, instead of playing the Queen's game, he positively contributed to her failure. The manner in which he acted was, indeed, entirely to his credit, and considering that the new Marquis of Subserra was a man of considerable experience, it was to prove regrettable from the point of view of his own career, as well perhaps in the interests of his country, that the fact of his having fought under Napoleon against his own countrymen and against the English should have disgraced him in English eyes. The British community in Portugal were unanimous in regarding Subserra as disreputable.

In the case of the French ambassador Hyde de Neuville, again, the Queen was destined to suffer a cruel disillusion. As envoy of the King of France, her brother's rescuer, she imagined he would be her friend. As it turned out, he proved to be a piece which at her next grand attempt to seize power was to play an important part in checkmating her.

The Baron Hyde de Neuville's character and career deserve a page. He was born at Charité-sur-Loire in 1776, the grandson of an English Jacobite exile, from whom he inherited in the highest degree an all-absorbing devotion to the cause of royalty. At the age of fourteen, he went to school in Paris and there, playing truant, threw himself into every popular tumult he could find, giving proof in countless café fights of his unswerving loyalty to the tottering French throne. He later took part in a plot to rescue Queen Marie-Antoinette from the Temple. He was a marked man to successive revolutionary governments, yet his amazing good luck saved his head from the guillotine. All through the Directory, and during the first years of the Empire, he pursued his indefatigable conspiracies. In and out of prison, living under false names, assuming absurd but evidently effective disguises, he was a constant thorn in the side of the authorities. He took part in the revolt of La Vendée, escaped to England, found his way secretly back to Paris, saved himself from arrest by climbing over the roof of his house, and finally, after the Pichegrue conspiracy, baffled Napoleon's police by hiding himself in a remote country district, assuming the pseudonym of " Doctor Roland " and spending six months vaccinating his neighbours. At last, in 1805, his wife who had shared his adventures, decided to make a personal appeal to the Emperor to lift the ban under which Hyde de Neuville lay. The persevering woman travelled across Europe in the wake of Napoleon's army, came up with him at last at Schönbrunn, and as a result of her plea received the necessary passports for herself and her husband to sail to the United States.

Modern biographers have bestowed so much attention on the chief figures of the French Revolution on the side of the revolutionaries, that it is astonishing to realize that such young men as Hyde de Neuville, no less fervent than the revolutionaries, but with diametrically opposite principles, existed in the same age as Camille Desmoulins and Marat. In him the romantic enthusiasms of his epoch had become canalized in his single-minded and exalted devotion to his King. He pictured himself as a Knight of the Middle Ages, laying down his life in a hallowed cause. He treasured all his life the memory of how the Queen Marie-Antoinette had once rested her eyes on him, when he was a boy, in a public garden in Paris, and how, seeing him standing there as if transfigured by her presence, she had given him a fleeting smile.

The fall of Napoleon and the restoration of the Bourbons (a happening which filled the de Neuville's hearts with ecstatic gratitude to Providence) saw the two exiles once more in their beloved Paris. On the best of terms with everyone in the Faubourg Saint Germain, the Baron immediately entered the political arena, and was elected a member of the Chamber. From 1816 to 1822 he led two diplomatic missions as French minister to Washington.

It was during these years that he earned the suspicions of the British government, for he not only succeeded in negotiating a commercial treaty to the disadvantage of the English, but began to reveal in his conversation a deep-rooted anti-British turn of mind. He showed his colours even more plainly on his return to Paris in 1822. Brougham had remonstrated in the House of Commons against the French project to interfere in Spain. Hyde de Neuville thereupon made a sensational speech in the French Chamber, stigmatizing Brougham's speech as a calumny on the honour of France. Infected by the fever of recaptured self-confidence that was sweeping over Paris, he declared that " the arguments of the cabinet of Saint James will be as ineffectual to check the national enthusiasm within our frontiers as force of arms to check it beyond them." It is understandable therefore that his nomination as ambassador in Lisbon did not please Canning.

Considering that Hyde de Neuville was of English origin, it is curious that he should have been so typical a Frenchman. His active imagination, his dislike of English manners, his earnest preoccupation over questions of his King's, his country's and his own honour, his insistence on rules of precedence and *placement*, and his nice courtesy —all were qualities essentially Gallic. As one reads his memoirs, one comes to realize that he must have made the most typical French Ambassador that ever belonged to a *corps diplomatique*. Indeed, when all is said, it is impossible not to find both the Hyde de Neuvilles likeable—the Baroness threw herself into the diplomatic game at Lisbon with all her husband's fervour. (" She always," according to one of Thornton's despatches, " expressed a peculiar dislike to the mission of England." Both must have been maddening to meet, but there is something about the portrait we find of them in the Baron's own memoirs which is so human : they both displayed in a crisis, as will be seen in a later chapter, such real simplicity, that in the end even their conceit becomes endearing.

The Baron arrived in Lisbon in August. Canning had made a correct guess at what Hyde de Neuville's instructions consisted of. He was to point out to the Portuguese government that French intervention in Spain had also reinforced the legitimist cause in Portugal, and to persuade the King that he should henceforth look to France rather than England to consolidate his throne. He was to press the Portuguese government to abandon their neutrality in relation to the Spanish war, and to give aid to the French fleet which was blockading Cadiz. Lastly, inebriated by the rapid successes of their army, the French government had expressly instructed de Neuville to use all means at his disposal to damage, and if possible destroy, England's traditional influence in Portugal. " You know, my dear friend," Chateaubriand wrote to him, " how difficult and important your mission is. It is a question of adroitly lifting Portugal from the sphere of English influence."

Mutatis mutandis, de Neuville's instructions might have been copied out by the German Foreign Office to give to their minister in Lisbon at the time of the Spanish Civil War of 1936-1939.

Chapter XVIII

CONSTANTINOPLE in the declining years of the Eastern Empire—Peking under the Empress Dowager—had never been a more feverish hot-bed of intrigue than was Lisbon in 1823. The Queen vowed the new government a hatred even bitterer than her former hostility towards the Cortes. Discipline had broken down in the army, whose commanders had now acquired a taste for issuing proclamations and overturning governments. The troops of the Count de Amarante (now created Marquis of Chaves) marched back from Spain and entered Lisbon with their caps wreathed in laurels. They constituted henceforth a sort of Praetorian Guard that terrified the timid King. Palmella and Subserra were the only effective members of the Cabinet. Caught in a net-work of plot and counter-plot, equally detested by the extremists of both sides, their characters attacked by the slanders put in circulation from Queluz, and trusting no one, both were driven to seeking support outside the ranks of their own countrymen. Palmella turned to the British Legation, while Subserra hobnobbed with de Neuville. The proximity of the French army in Spain exacerbated the general unrest.

Thornton's chief fear was of Dona Carlota Joaquina. " There cannot be a doubt," he wrote, " that the policy of this Queen, if she can obtain the ascendancy. is to throw this country into the arms of Spain, and at any rate to carry it to all lengths in the Continental alliance. . . . The Queen, besides, is known to be of so violent and vindictive a temper, and to entertain so great a hatred towards certain classes of people, in which she is heartily joined by the Infant, that the one and the other would immediately proceed to acts of violence and even ferocity."

In some respects her position was now favourable for the further advancement of her schemes. Her tool Dom Miguel was now Commander-in-Chief. Her revenues as queen, confiscated by the Cortes when she went to Ramalhão, had now been restored to her. Living in a retired manner at Queluz, she therefore had funds at her disposal with which to reward her political supporters and bribe waverers. The friars were the most useful of her propaganda agents : " It was they," wrote Oliveira Martins, " who lived in intimate contact with the people, fraternising with them everywhere . . . inspiring them with their own gross superstitions and depravity." Nor was their action confined to the spiritual sphere merely : in the Count of Amarante's army a " Holy Platoon " had made its début on the field, consisting entirely of friars with their habits tucked up to their knees, marching with the soldiers as if on a new crusade. To these crusaders must be added the cut-throat gang composing Dom Miguel's entourage, the lineal political successors to her Corps of Cadets at Rio. Lastly, it must be noticed that conditions in the capital were fast approaching anarchy, that is to say, exactly the state of affairs in which violence can sometimes turn the scale.

In other respects, however, Dona Carlota Joaquina had lost ground. The opinion was general in Portugal, even among many of those who supported the Absolutist cause (but who found it impossible to love a Spanish Bourbon), that her policy was dictated primarily by motives of revenge. The bloodthirsty language she employed in conversation with her intimates at the time of the Vila Franca affair reinforced this impression. And it may be noticed by the way that even the most anti-liberal of the continental powers were disinclined to back the Queen because the principle of legitimate sovereignty on which their foreign policy was based was represented at Lisbon not by her but by King John. De Neuville himself, though the Queen's aims and his own were identical in so far as both wished to see Portugal adopt the policy of the Holy Alliance, consistently refused to lend himself to her plots. He rested his hopes of establishing a dominating influence over the Portuguese government on his close friendship with Subserra.

The " Vilafrancada " having, as we have seen, satisfied only a part of the Queen's ambitions, it now occurred to her that it might be possible to persuade the Powers, the people, and the King himself, that he was not fitted to rule on account of mental incapacity. Let him abdicate on his own accord in favour of Dom Miguel, who should then reign at Lisbon as Dom Pedro was reigning at Rio de Janeiro. Had not Dom John's own mother abdicated in similar circumstances owing to her insanity ? And had not she herself already on one occasion in the past dreamed of Dom John's following his mother's example ? It is a singular proof of the continuity of Dona Carlota Joaquina's schemes that the project she cherished in 1823 was basically the same as in 1805. For with Dom Miguel King, she of course imagined herself virtually holding the position of Regent.

She made her next attempt in October. A military review was to take place early in the morning of the 27th on the parade ground of Salessas, and the troops taking part included the regiments of the Marquis of Chaves. It was agreed between the Queen and certain commanders that she should herself appear " unexpectedly " on the parade ground, and that her arrival should be a signal for the troops to declare for Dom Miguel. King John was to be forcibly persuaded of his insanity.

Little contemporary evidence of this incident has survived, but it is certain that a leakage of information put the government on their guard. The parade was cancelled at the last moment, and when at eight o'clock Dona Carlota arrived at Salessas hugging some reliquaries in an open barouche she found to her dismay that the parade ground was empty save for a few patrols of city police.

She ordered her horses' heads to be turned to Queluz and drove swiftly away. That night she wrote a letter to her husband, who at the time was staying at his country-house of Salvaterra.

" My Love,

" Now I hear our enemies have spread a rumour in Lisbon affirming that this morning I tried to create a revolution in order to make myself Regent together with Miguel, and to send you into exile at Vila Vicosa. The whole thing is a monstrous libel, and I have no doubt Dr. Abrantes has a hand in it. I therefore would be grateful if you would order the Chief of Police to act with vigour. For you well know that my only desire is to live a quiet life and to see you happy."

Meanwhile the intrigues with which the capital seethed were complicated still further by the arrival of the elderly and now somewhat corpulent Marshal Beresford, come to look after his estate at Pedrouços. He caused no small annoyance to Sir Edward Thornton, who knew that he was corresponding with London on his own. Incredible as it may sound, Beresford requested Dom John to give him a place in the Portuguese cabinet. But he was not even on speaking terms with Subserra, and combined his demand with a request that the latter should be removed from the Ministry. Beresford was regarded by the King as an old friend, and it was undeniable that he had performed signal services for Portugal in the past ; but his desire to enter the government outraged national sentiment too deeply for the King to tolerate it even in his present perplexities. While Lisbon hummed with gossip about whether the Marshal would or would not succeed in his pretensions, the King fobbed him off by appointing him Chief of Staff to Dom Miguel. But the Prince did not like him.

In the autumn of 1823 Palmella asked Thornton for a promise of help from England in the event of another revolution stirred up by " malcontents." But the best that he could secure was the continued presence of the British squadron which was at that time in the Tagus. This squadron included the *Windsor Castle*.

No wonder that Palmella in after life looked back on these months as the most painful and trying of his career. He had inherited the whole aftermath of the constitutional régime's mistakes. " If only the deputies of the Cortes," he wrote in his memoirs, " at the same time as defining in polished phrases their theories of the liberty of peoples . . . had passed laws to encourage industry and develop agriculture : if they had set up a system of education which might have roused the nation from its long lethargy, perhaps the Cortes' achievements would not have proved so ephemeral."

Commerce was in fact almost at a standstill, the country was suffering from a terrible shock resulting from the loss of Brazil, and the state of the exchequer was appalling. The first political results of the overthrow of the constitution—the return of the Cardinal Patriarch and the reopening of monasteries and convents—constituted no serious contribution to economic welfare.

In accordance with the promise that King John had made on the road to Vila Franca, Palmella set to work as president of a special committee to prepare a new constitutional basis for the monarchy, and circulated a letter to the foreign missions announcing the forthcoming publication of a " Charter." Much depends on a name, and he hoped the new word would catch on. " This Charter," he wrote, " would reconcile in the highest possible degree the Rule of Law and the Happiness of Peoples on the one hand, with the dignity and solidity of the throne on the other." It was intended " prudently to avoid extremes either of absolute power or of revolutionary anarchy." The charter was to be based on the ancient laws of the Kingdom, bearing in mind the institutions of other European constitutional monarchies. It envisaged the summoning of Portugal's ancient parliament of the Three Estates.

But his intention to publish a charter excited immediate resentment among the great powers, who were not inclined, at a moment when Absolutism was being triumphantly restored in Spain, to tolerate a constitution of any kind in Portugal. In November the Spanish Ambassador, the Duke of Villa Hermosa, acquainted the King with the substance of a joint note in course of compilation by the sovereigns of Spain, Austria and Russia, declaring that they were determined to insist that Portugal should adopt no constitutional system whatever. Early in the following year the powers assembled at Paris, recalling with a shudder all that had followed the convocation of the States General at Versailles, declared their uncompromising disapprobation of the suggestion that Dom John should convoke the Three Estates.

With so much foreign pressure brought to bear at Bemposta, it is hardly surprising that Palmella should not have succeeded in his aim to provide Portugal with a new and sensible system of government. " I had no one's help," he wrote in his Recollections, " to wrestle with the King's inertia, the indifference and intrigues of my colleagues, the enmity and plots of the Queen, the more or less extreme opposition of foreign governments with the single exception of England." It is understandable that he should have looked for help in his distress to Portugal's ancient ally, though he shows in his memoirs some twinges of conscience at having appealed for the intervention of British troops, justifying his action by recalling the arrival of Dutch soldiers in England in the reign of William of Orange.

The only person who was happy in Lisbon at this time was the Baron Hyde de Neuville. He glowed at the thought that French prestige had been so brilliantly restored by the easy victories with which the French army was meeting in Spain. " Never has France," he wrote in one of his despatches, " since the misfortunes of the Revolution, held her flag so firm or so high." To begin with, his mission appeared to his imagination—which always outran his powers of observance—to be meeting with all the success his heart desired. He had arrived in Lisbon on the 10th August. Three weeks afterwards he had become entirely convinced that the customary courtesy which in reality the Portuguese extend to every foreigner, combined with the Portuguese incapacity to give anyone a straight refusal to his face, amounted to a deep desire on the part of the Portuguese government to sever there and then their ancient connections with England and to throw themselves into the arms of France. " By the 30th," he wrote in his memoirs, " I had succeeded in all my aims—even in those which my government had considered the most difficult. I had succeeded in persuading the Portuguese government not only to abandon its neutrality, but even to put ships at our disposal. . . . The new government in Portugal understood that it needed the support of that European power which by the presence of its armies was bound to exert a deciding influence in Spain." Some Portuguese men-of-war were actually sent by Subserra to join the French squadron off Cadiz, much to Canning's indignation. The fall of the city that autumn and the release of King Ferdinand brought the Spanish campaign to an end. The Baron's pride and joy knew no bounds.

As the winter passed, every packet from Rio brought news gloomier than before. In December the Marquis of Rio Maior returned with the news that the personal letter that the King had addressed to Dom Pedro had been returned unopened, because it had not been correctly addressed to " the Emperor of Brazil." At home the deterioration in public morale was growing noticeably worse. In February the swift approach of anarchy was suddenly revealed in a dramatic fashion by the occurrence of a sinister crime.

Towards the end of that month the King went back to Salvaterra, a residence customarily used by the Braganzas as a hunting box, set in pine woods to the south of the Tagus. The Queen as usual remained at Queluz, but Dom Miguel accompanied the King. The numerous gathering at Salvaterra included, therefore, not only the old King's court functionaries and nearly a hundred servants of the royal household, but also the gang of cowboys, bull-fighters and ostlers who habitually surrounded the Prince. The King's intention was to pass the whole of Carnaval in the country. Doubtless he felt relieved to be able for a few weeks to turn his back on the importunate Marshal Beresford and his ministers' worried faces. The Prince and the younger noblemen looked forward to a round of shooting, hare-hunting and cross-country riding, while some private theatricals were in production to provide a pleasant climax to the masked balls, the tomfoolery and horse-play customary in the carnival season.

Salvaterra was an even more rambling and tumble-down place than the other royal residences. A considerable part of it, including the wing connecting the King's suite of rooms with the theatre, had been severely damaged a few years earlier by fire. Some of the windows of the state apartments looked on to courtyards half choked with rubbish and fallen masonry ; certain of the rooms were connected with each other by roofless galleries and half-ruined stairs. The whole court, however, managed to find accommodation.

Among those in attendance on the King was that Marquis of Loulé whose name has already found mention in these pages. The Marquis, like Subserra, had in early life enlisted in Napoleon's Foreign Legion. He had distinguished himself on the battlefield of Wagram, had taken part in the Russian campaign and had survived the horrors of the retreat from Moscow. Though condemned to death by the Portuguese government for having served with the French, he followed the court to Rio de Janeiro in 1817. At first Dom John refused to receive him, but on Good Friday, we are told, " remembering how Christ forgave His enemies," the King sent for him, pardoned him, and restored him to his honours. The Marquis's heart was touched by the King's goodness. From that time onward he served him with devoted fidelity. We have already noted how he had earned the especial enmity of the Queen.

On the fatal night of the 28th February, 1824 (the year was a leap-year), the King retired to his apartments at Salvaterra after dinner, while numerous courtiers went into the theatre and lounged in the dimly lit, ramshackle stalls to watch their friends in a rehearsal of their play. Dom Miguel himself was taking part. There was a good deal of noise going on. While the amateur actors recited their parts on the stage, workmen were engaged giving finishing touches to a newly decorated tier of boxes. The Marquis of Loulé sat in the stalls with his cousin the Marquis of Belas, the Marquis of Tancos, Count Paraty, and many other gentlemen of the court. Scattered about the theatre were also a considerable number of Dom Miguel's bull-fighting and hunting associates—the Marquis of Abrantes, the out-rider Leonardo Joaquim Cordeiro, a soldier called Madureira Lobo, a man named Jeronimo Ferreira, who was one of the King's coachmen, and a numerous party of stable-boys and domestics. Some of them were in their shirt-sleeves, others were wearing the hooded winter cloaks of the Salvaterra country. Jeronomo Ferreira was seen wearing folded over his head a kind of Brazilian cloak such as used to be worn in San Paulo, and which was called a *poncho*. The mingling of lords and lackeys—polished old courtiers mixed up with the picturesque ruffians of Dom Miguel's train—must have presented a unique scene very typical of the Braganza's court in days gone by.

At about half-past ten one of the actors, an illegitimate son of the Marquis of Loulé, left the stage and came to speak to his father. Shortly afterwards the Marquis, who was growing bored by the rehearsal, left the theatre. He was seen mounting some steps on the left side of the auditorium, to make his way along a half-ruined, impenetrably dark corridor leading to a room called the Hall of Arches, which in turn gave access to the habitable part of the palace. This was the last time that he was seen alive. All the evidence of those present in the theatre agreed in affirming that the Marquis of Loulé retired between half-past ten and eleven o'clock.

At seven o'clock the next morning his body was discovered lying on a pile of rubbish in an inner court of the palace. Fifteen feet above him yawned a frameless window of the gutted wing—a window which stretched down to the floor of the same corridor down which the Marquis had passed on the previous night. He lay on his back with his head close to the bottom of the rubbish-heap, his head and face bathed in blood, his arms outstretched.

The rumour ran through Salvaterra that the Marquis had met with an accident, having stumbled in the corridor on his way to his rooms and fallen out of the window. But this rumour was quenched almost as soon as it began. It was only too clear that the Marquis of Loulé had been done to death in some other part of the palace and his body later placed on the spot where it had been found. Four magistrates who were instantly nominated by the King to conduct an inquiry arrived at the same irrefutable conclusion.

In the first place, it was known to have rained during the night, yet the body was dry. In the second place it was evident that the murdered man had been dealt two severe blows on the back of the head, two blows on the right temple, and others on the face. There was also discovered a mysterious wound inside his mouth. How could he have received such wounds merely by falling fifteen feet ? He was not by any means decrepit—he was fifty-three. Lastly, a footprint was found nearby—the print of a pointed town shoe—while some broken tiles suggested that some person, after arranging the corpse on the rubbish, had climbed back into the corridor through the ruined window.

The whole truth will perhaps never be known until a certain box containing Dom Miguel's intimate papers which is kept in the Castle of Siebenstein in Austria—the home of his lineal descendants—is placed at the disposal of historians. King John, who immediately after the crime was discovered hurried back to Lisbon sick with horror and never again set foot at Salvaterra—the King, as we shall see, postponed publishing the findings of the Court of Inquiry and its full records were afterwards destroyed. A résumé of the evidence taken from a hundred and thirty witnesses exists, indeed, in the national archives at Lisbon, but it is plain that much information has been suppressed.

We shall never know, until the Siebenstein papers are examined, whether when the Marquis of Loulé quitted the theatre some cloaked figure followed him with murderous footsteps or whether an assassin was lurking in the shadows to strike him as he passed. We shall not know, moreover, what is so vital a point in modern detective stories—the exact hour at which the crime was committed. According to one report current in Lisbon the Marquis had not perished on leaving the theatre, but had been summoned later that night by Dom Miguel to the Hall of Arches ; the Marquis of Abrantes under the very eyes of the Prince had pinned his throat to the wall with one hand, while another of Dom Miguel's ruffian companions had driven a skewer into the unfortunate man's mouth with such force that it pierced the brain. We may dismiss this particular story as improbable because of the mere fact that it originated among the madly hate-ridden political opponents of the Queen's and Dom Miguel's party. We may even dismiss the scarcely veiled opinion expressed by Fronteira implicating the Prince, because Fronteira also was a liberal, though of a common-sense type. But it is impossible to disregard the insistent and almost unanimous public conviction, repeated by Palmella and quoted by Hyde de Neuville in his despatches, to the effect that the Prince's entourage was responsible for the crime, acting under the orders of the Queen.

All the circumstantial evidence points to this conclusion. The Queen was in close touch with the Marquis of Abrantes, Cordeiro and José Verissimo, who often accompanied the Prince to Queluz; she bore the Marquis a grudge; she desired, moreover, to strike terror into the frightened but yet so maddeningly obstinate King. The responsibility of Dom Miguel's most intimate friends is corroborated by the reluctance shown by the King to publish the findings of the Court of Inquiry, and by the all-too-obvious distaste shown by contemporary letter-writers of fixing the blame openly. As regards the actual circumstances of the murder, it was almost certainly committed by more than one assassin; it is probable that Ferreira threw his *poncho* over the victim's head to stifle his cries, and that he was then clubbed to the ground. The body is said to have been concealed for several hours under a table in the Hall of Arches, though no bloodstains were found there.

Five months afterwards, following the second important *coup d'état* engineered by the Queen, the following individuals were officially declared responsible for the murder; the Marquis of Abrantes (who had escaped over the Spanish frontier but had been seized by peasants who, curious to relate, mistook him for a common thief, so that he was brought back to Lisbon, and imprisoned), Jeronimo Ferreira, Leonardo Cordeiro, Madureira Lobo and José Verissimo, who was the Prince's favourite attendant. The fact that this last-named had not been present at Salvaterra on the night of the 28th, but yet was convicted of participation in the murder, argues that he may have been the man who acted as the Queen's agent in conveying her·instructions to the others. All these were captured and imprisoned. A sixth member of the gang, a fellow called Cristavaô de Mascarenhas, escaped.

It may be noted that the wild Marquis of Abrantes made a last appearance on the stage of history three years later in ludicrous circumstances. One day in 1827 Palmella, who was at that time Minister in London, returned to his Legation in South Audley Street from a trip to Brighton to find that Abrantes, who had escaped from Lisbon, for some reason had called at the Legation in his absence; he had been seized on the doorstep by a dreadful paralysis which deprived him of all power of limb and speech, and had therefore been put to bed there and then by the Legation porter. So Palmella found the rascal lying speechless and gazing up at him from between a pair of his own sheets. History does not record the sequel to this curious episode.

Though it may be taken as wellnigh proven that the Marquis of Loulé was done to death by someone of Dom Miguel's intimate circle, and though the implication of the Queen seems more than probable, yet in fairness both to her and to Dom Miguel it is necessary to suggest one possible explanation of the mystery, which is as follows: At Carnaval time in Portugal in old days the coarsest and most brutal pranks were played. A box tied up elegantly in tissue paper and ribbons, but in reality full of fleas, would be brought into a party, and presented to the hostess, who would open it in the belief that it was an Easter egg. A toad would be concealed in the wine-jug and sneezing powder blown all over the table-cloth. Trouser buttons would be surreptitiously cut off, and braces severed. It was by no means an uncommon occurrence for a guest to return from a Carnaval party with a black eye or a broken limb. Is it not possible, therefore, that Dom Miguel's gang had been urged by the Queen to play some more than ordinarily odious prank on the Marquis of Loulé, with a view to paying off old scores—that he was to be trussed up all night, or frightened out of his wits somehow : that in obedience to this suggestion they set upon the Marquis in the passage, hit out wildly, and then were horrified to find they had killed him ? Such an explanation would render less surprising the fact that the Marquis of Loulé's son continued to be a close friend of Dom Miguel, and that he actually married one of the Infantas, thus becoming son-in-law to Dona Carlota.

The investigations of historians into the murder might be facilitated if it were still possible to visit the scene of the crime. But a few years afterwards a second fire ravaged Salvaterra. Then in 1858 an earthquake shattered what remained of the rambling edifice. The ruins were subsequently picked to pieces to provide road-surfaces in the vicinity. The old palace, the Hall of Arches and the theatre, the dark and perhaps haunted gallery down which the King's Master of the Horse passed on the night he met his death—all has vanished like a dream.

Chapter XIX

NERVES were on edge. The murder of the Marquis of Loulé had added an all-pervading flavour of horror to the prevailing sense of apprehension. Everyone knew that the gnome-Queen was plotting mischief. Cloaked figures were admitted at the depth of night into the corridors of Queluz, carrying messages in their shoes from secret absolutist societies. The loyalty of several regiments to the King had been undermined. Night and day the Queen instilled poison into the ear of the giddy Prince, openly designated by public rumour as the murderer of the Master of the Horse. That a plot was in existence was common knowledge, and the direction in which it was bent was shown all too plainly by the mysterious placards that made their appearance at dawn on the walls of the city: " Long live the Queen ! Let John abdicate or die !" All felt as if they were walking on the thin crust of a volcano. On the night of the 29th April, 1824, the public uneasiness reached its climax. Despatch riders were to be seen dashing about in every direction, while the heavy tread of marching troops echoed in the dark streets.

The Queen had, in fact, decided to strike again. All liberals, all moderates, all masons, were to be eliminated by her private army of desperadoes. The instrument to be used to overturn the throne was that absolutist party of which she herself was the heart and soul and of which Dom Miguel, her tool, was the theatrical nominal leader. Whether or no the murder of the Marquis of Loulé was an act of private vengeance, the Queen certainly hoped to exploit the crime politically by spreading terror in the ranks of her opponents. Now we know that the magistrates who had been charged to investigate the murder had prepared a report fixing responsibility on the Marquis of Abrantes, and though the King had for long resisted the Count de Subserra's advice that the report should be made public, the Queen heard a rumour towards the end of April that he was prepared to give way. The publication of a document which would certainly inculpate the Prince's intimate circle, if not the Prince himself, was an awkward possibility. For this reason she decided to set her conspirators in motion at once.

On the evening of the 29th Sir Edward Thornton gave a dinner and ball to celebrate King George's birthday. The diplomatic corps, most of Lisbon society, Lord Beresford and the chief members of the British community were all assembled at Sir Edward's house. " The dinner was long," wrote Madame Hyde de Neuville to a Paris friend, " and everyone was feeling worried. An error in the placing of the diplomatic guests at table had cast a certain chill. . . ." But an even greater cause of emotion than an error in *placement* was destined to be provided for her that evening. At eleven o'clock she returned to the ball-room after taking a stroll in the garden and was immediately struck—according to her own account—by the " terrified expression " of the Countess de Subserra, who had just arrived at the ball with her daughter. Drawing both the de Neuvilles into a corner, the Countess informed them that her husband had received warning that an attempt was to be made upon his life. The Count, she said, had gone as usual to Bemposta, where he was closeted with the King.

It may be imagined how the de Neuvilles thrilled to a piece of intelligence which was being imparted to them under the roof, and almost under the very nose, of their poor less well-informed British colleague. The Baron, of course, dramatized the affair in his own imagination, and decided in the emergency to behave, as he wrote in his memoirs, " in a manner becoming to an Ambassador of France." He took it for granted that not only the Count de Subserra, but also his wife and daughter, who at that moment was waltzing round the ball-room, were in instant peril of being massacred. It might be supposed that the most sensible course to adopt, if the danger were real, would have been to have requested the British Minister to offer the Countess and her daughter the hospitality of his house for the night. But such a common-sense settlement would have necessitated the Baron's suppressing both his inveterate taste for drama and his rivalry towards Sir Edward.

Let us allow the Baroness to continue the tale in her own words : " What a frightful confidence it was for us to receive, and what a situation to receive it in—a ballrooom, where we were momently interrupted by people making those aimless remarks to which it is so difficult to reply when one is absorbed by a preoccupation so dreadful as ours ! It was necessary to come to a decision quickly. Monsieur Hyde de Neuville proposed to Madame de Subserra that, when enough time should have elapsed for us to leave the ball without exposing us to comment, he should order our two carriages simultaneously : that to avoid the appearance of anything abnormal, the Countess and her daughter should enter their own carriage, and that they should then quit it at a short distance and come into our own.

" This plan was adopted, but we had to wait for the opportune moment to carry it out, and meanwhile to conceal the anxiety that gnawed us. The Countess de Subserra had one of those characters that danger elevates rather than crushes. She kept her anguish to herself and said nothing to her daughter, who was dancing, of the danger threatening her father. . . .

" After two long hours, of which we counted the very seconds, the ballroom at last cleared and we were able to make our farewells. Madame de Subserra gave instructions to her daughter in a few rapid words. Our plan was put into operation. A little way away, the two ladies left their carriage and took their places in ours. There was something lugubrious and terrifying about this change-over in the darkness (we had extinguished the lamps for safety's sake). Our gay evening dresses contrasted with the emotions we felt. No one broke the silence. A mutual pressure of our hands alone revealed all we felt.

" Our carriage started, and we ordered our coachman to go slowly, so that people might recognize and respect the liveries of the Ambassador of France. . . . Shadows glided along the walls. Out faithful manservant Bouquet was on foot, ready to rush to our assistance . . . "

Thus the Hyde de Neuvilles and their fair protégées arrived without the smallest mishap at the Subserra's house, where the Count himself arrived shortly afterwards, sound in wind and limb. Having received the warning as early as eight o'clock he had prudently left Bemposta by a circuitous route. But it is not really certain that he was in serious danger. It is hardly necessary to point out that the de Neuvilles' manœuvres at the British Minister's ball were in the true spirit of Tartarin de Tarascon. Had either the Count or the Countess de Subserra been really in imminent peril it is hardly credible that the Countess and her daughter would have put on their evening frocks and gone out to a ball.

The next morning, however, the 30th April, it was evident that things were serious. All Lisbon was in tumult. At Dom Miguel's orders troops had assembled in the Rocio Square, where from time to time he made a sensational appearance on a balcony. He had issued a proclamation (which needless to say had been concocted in the recesses of Queluz), asserting that " a subversive faction menaced the safety of his father and of the state." He was to be seen galloping like a madman from one barracks to another, surrounded by a posse of desperadoes, crying " Death to the traitors !" At his side were several of the men whose implication in the death of the Marquis of Loulé was afterwards established—José Verissimo among others. In less than two hours his minions had seized more than three hundred persons, including many of the first rank, and had conducted them under armed escort to the prisons of the Limoeira, the Castello, Saint Julian's fort and the Belem Tower. The Chief of Police and two Lords of the Bedchamber, Paraty and Vila Flor (afterwards celebrated as the Duke of Terceira), were among the prisoners. The young Marquis of Fronteira, who had obeyed orders to join his regiment on the Rocio, was ordered to surrender himself as prisoner to the Commander of the Belem Tower, and on arrival there found to his astonishment that the Count de Palmella had preceded him to prison, and was seated calmly reading the London *Times* on the terrace.

At Bemposta the King himself was a prisoner in his own palace, which was closely surrounded by troops. The wildest rumours flew from mouth to mouth. Some believed the stories spread by Dom Miguel's party, that an attempt on the King's life had been frustrated at the last moment by the Prince. Others believed that Miguel was about to depose his father and crown himself King. But the news which was more significant than any rumour was that Dona Carlota Joaquina, like one of those vultures whose shadow is seen gliding over the sand where a man lies dying, had moved into Lisbon from Queluz and was perched at the Ajuda Palace.

The sequence of events on the 30th April is best followed in the memoirs of the Baron Hyde de Neuville, who played, according both to his own account and to the accounts of everyone else, a conspicuous part in the day's adventures. Indeed, his behaviour on this occasion, together with the conduct of the whole diplomatic body accredited to the Portuguese court, constitutes what must surely be one of the most extraordinary incidents in the history of diplomacy.

" It was apparent to me," he wrote, " that my duty as ambassador was to place myself beside that throne which impious rebels were plotting to overthrow. The prestige which France at that time inspired, especially since the victory of her arms over the forces of revolution in Spain, dictated my taking steps to make the French flag respected, and to carry support to the monarch who was in such grave peril."

Having ordered his carriage to come to his door with his servants in full livery, he sent a secretary to all the chiefs of mission in Lisbon, inviting them to assemble in half an hour's time at the house of the Nuncio. A temporary interruption in his plans was created at this moment by the arrival at the French Embassy of the Countess of Palmella bringing news of her husband's arrest, and almost immediately afterwards by the arrival of the Count de Subserra, who was hiding from Miguel's men. Leaving the two of them in his wife's care—delighted that they should be under the protection of the French rather than the English flag—Hyde de Neuville set out for the Nunciature, attended by all his staff, who, as he wrote in his memoirs, were " burning to place themselves in the forefront of the field of honour."

It must be admitted that Hyde de Neuville acquitted himself with distinction on that never-to-be-forgotten day. Even though we discount the success he met with as recorded by his own romantic pen, it cannot be denied that he did in fact succeed in persuading the entire diplomatic body to follow his lead. The Nuncio, according to Hyde de Neuville, said to him, " I will follow wherever you go, Monsieur l'Ambassadeur." The Spanish ambassador and the Chargés d'Affaires of Russia and of Denmark supported him with an equal alacrity. The Baron led them into the street, where they met the arriving carriage of the old American Minister, General Dearborn. The Baron darted to his side.

" But you know, Monsieur l'Ambassadeur," drawled the American minister, " we republicans—we set little store by all your changes of governments in Europe. . . . "

" That may well be," replied the dramatic Frenchman, " but in the present crisis we have to support not merely a King, but a father."

The American Minister then fell into line. They moved off, preserving, of course, all the correct rules of diplomatic precedence. The Nuncio went first as *doyen*. Hyde de Neuville followed ; then the Spanish ambassador.

A little way along they met Sir Edward Thornton in a cabriolet, not in uniform, on his way to the rendezvous at the Nunciature. He, also, was swept into the Baron's net.

The page in Hyde de Neuville's memoirs describing this scene glows with inextinguishable pride. Was not England in the person of Sir

Edward meekly following the noble example set by France, in the person of himself ?

" I invited the English Minister," he writes, " to get into my coach. He accepted, and this unforeseen circumstance only added further weight to the moral force of the diplomatic body. For the rebels observed at once that France and England were agreed in saving the legitimate King."

So delighted did he feel that his ancient grudge against Sir Edward was quite dissipated. " I cannot," he wrote, " praise Sir Edward too highly. There was nothing of the diplomat in his first reaction. It was simply his goodness of heart that revealed itself. . . .

" We crossed the Rocio, so that the rebels might see the diplomatic body . . .

" For their leaders, our apparition was like a thunderbolt, as they watched all Europe pass through the bayonets of the rebels on their way to the royal prisoner . . . The whole of Lisbon is aware that at that very moment *several of the principal conspirators exchanged glances in silence and turned pale. . . .* "

The imposing procession, swelled *en route* by the equipages of the Austrian Minister and the Dutch Chargé d'Affaires, arrived in a body at the palace of Bemposta. Here the troop of diplomats were refused access to the courtyard by the guards, so they got out of their carriages, and began to infiltrate into the ranks in single file. The scene must have been truly risible. A soldier grabbed hold of Sir Edward Thornton's collar. Hyde de Neuville flung himself to the rescue of his colleague. He placed Sir Edward between himself and the Nuncio. Thus they arrived at the foot of the great staircase of the palace, which was crowded with soldiers.

Their difficulties were not yet over. Their further advance was imperiously barred. But now the little Baron really excelled himself. Declaring in the noble language of Racine, which none of the guards understood, that the representatives of all Europe recognized no other authority in Lisbon than that of the Sovereign to whom they were accredited, and seconding his rolling phrases with some pushing and shoving up the stairs, the Baron actually succeeded in shepherding his flock into the throne room, into the very presence of the King, whom they found prostrate with alarm. " It would be difficult to describe the deplorable condition in which we found him," wrote de Neuville. " All his faculties seemed annihilated."

Dom John, however, was not alone. The Baron Hyde de Neuville must have bit his lips with vexation to find at the King's side none other than Lord Beresford, whom he customarily distrusted almost as much as he distrusted Sir Edward. But his indignation knew no bounds when the King, having agreed, after what appears to have been a general discussion, to summon the rebel Prince to Bemposta (the Baron claims that this idea was suggested by himself) retired *with Lord Beresford* into an inner chamber. Dom John did not disappear, however, before the Baron had succeeded, according to his own account, in inflicting a snub on the English field-marshal. For Lord Beresford having himself begun to reply to a question addressed by the Baron to the King, Hyde de Neuville coldly inquired whether Lord Beresford was a Portuguese Minister of State and pointed out that the only inter- mediary between the diplomatic corps and the King was the Minister of Foreign Affairs.

A long hour later Dom Miguel cantered into the courtyard in response to his father's summons, and after being closeted for a short time with his father and Beresford, the three re-entered the throne- room. Here the King announced in an uncertain tone that the Prince had submitted himself to his authority. The Nuncio then addressed Dom Miguel, but as he spoke French with difficulty the Baron stepped forward and undertook the task. " I was," he wrote in his memoirs, " absolutely the Ambassador of the Most Christian King, and my words went straight to the heart. The Prince hung his head, the diplomats could not conceal their emotion, and my colleagues declared that I had been a worthy interpreter of their sentiments."

While this extraordinary scene was in progress, the Prince, accord- ing to Thornton, had the air of a guilty young man, " confounded at the Discovery of his Plots, and abashed at the Presence of the assembled Ministers of Europe, crowded round His Father and His Sovereign and supporting His Majesty's Cause with no other than the moral Force and Feeling derived from the eternal Principles of Justice and Truth."

The Prince having agreed to disperse the troops, release Palmella and dismiss the guards at Bemposta, knelt and kissed his father's hands and then strode with knitted brows from the room. If it is true that Beresford had advised the King during the day, it cannot be denied that it was imprudent to have left Dom Miguel still in command of the Army.

On joining his general staff on the Rocio, Dom Miguel kept the promises he had made to his father in so far as he gave instructions for the release of Palmella, and ordered the troops back to barracks. He then galloped back to Bemposta and at last dismissed the troops that had surrounded it all day. So when the Baron Hyde de Neuville and his colleagues sat down to dinner in the palace, at the King's invitation, they had some grounds for satisfaction. The Baron wished they should all take up their residence where they were until the danger of revolution was entirely removed. " Our presence in the palace," he said, " was in my opinion the most solemn protest that the diplomatic body could make before the eyes of Europe." Sir Edward, however, preferred the comfort of his own roof, so the party broke up. Needless to say, the Baron rushed back to Bemposta early next morning.

Hyde de Neuville's misgivings were only too well justified by events. For the space of no less than eight days Dom Miguel and his ruffians continued their reign of terror. Forty mule carriages, heavily escorted by armed guards, conducted a batch of prisoners from the Belem Tower on a wearisome three days' trek to the fortress of Peniche. On the way, the long cavalcade was joined by similar convoys from other prisons. And anyone who visited the gaols of Portugal before the late reforms will realize in what frightful conditions these unfortunate prisoners found themselves. The fact that they were the victims of vengeance on the part of the Queen's party and were not suffering on account of any political misdemeanour is proved by the fact that three of their number, Santa Marthe, Taipa and Portella, had been until a few months earlier among the recognized leaders of the absolutists. All these prisoners, including many courtiers and their ladies, were treated with callous cruelty by their guards. They were all in fear of their lives. Dom Miguel actually ordered the execution of the Peniche prisoners, who were only saved by the events of the 8th May. We must hasten to add, however, that the terror of these nine days, though imposed in Dom Miguel's name, was largely the work of his entourage. Nor must we overlook the fact that the primary responsibility for the revolt belonged to the Queen. She sat at Ajuda, exulting over the messages that informed her of the development of events, and chuckling over the news of every fresh arrest. The Prince was constantly to be seen galloping backwards and forwards at break-neck speed, receiving her instructions.

The Count de Subserra was smuggled on board the English frigate *Lively* by Hyde de Neuville and Thornton working hand-in-glove. Dom Miguel, learning of the Count's escape, dashed on his fastest horse to Saint Julian's fort along the coast and fired sixteen shots from a cannon at another English ship, a packet crossing the bar, under the impression that the Count was on it. He missed, however.

On the 5th the terror was at its height. Respectable citizens of every class were being arrested right and left. On this day the diplomatic body assembled at the French Embassy and decided unanimously, Thornton concurring, that the King should be urged to go on board the British man-of-war the *Windsor Castle*. Hyde de Neuville, who was incessantly bustling in and out of Bemposta, went off to convey this advice to Dom John. (It is astonishing to observe that part of the diplomatic corps may be said to have assumed at this juncture the functions of the Portuguese cabinet. But by this time the Count de Palmella was himself on board the *Windsor Castle*, while Subserra was cruising about the Tagus in the *Lively*.) The Russian and Danish Chargés d'Affaires had followed the example set by the Portuguese ministers, and had gone on board a Danish frigate.

The measure proposed to the King by the diplomats was contrary to the advice of Lord Beresford, who was the only counsellor still permanently at the King's side. Dom John, however, found the proposal to his taste.

The Baroness Hyde de Neuville spent a considerable part of this day on the roof of the French Embassy, her eye glued to a telescope commanding the river, sending excited messages to her husband below to say she could see Palmella reading his newspaper on the deck of the *Windsor Castle*, or had descried Subserra blowing his nose on the *Lively*. It was a painful thought for the French Ambassador that the King should have no other alternative but to seek refuge on a British ship. De Neuville had sent a courier post haste to Cadiz to summon the French man-of-war, the *Santi Petri*, but as the hours and days passed the

Baroness's telescope espied no French sail at the river mouth. So he generously suppressed his disappointment.

" Every day that passed," he wrote, " the King's situation grew more precarious. In spite of the bitter regret I felt at the lack of a ship flying the French flag, I urged the King to go on board, adding that his safety was the first consideration occupying my thoughts and that, as Ambassador of France, I would not hesitate to follow him on to an English ship. In such grave circumstances all rivalry between nations ought to disappear."

King John, with no more will-power than a jelly, took three long days to make up his mind to disregard Lord Beresford and to follow his own inclinations. On the 9th he slipped out of Bemposta with the two princesses who lived with him, drove to Belem in a closed cab, got on to a barge, and was wafted over the river. A short time afterwards the Portuguese royal standard was seen to break from the mast of the *Windsor Castle*. At this signal the Hyde de Neuvilles and the Spanish ambassador rose hastily from their luncheon-tables, hurried to the quay, and tumbled into a dinghy.

The scene on board the *Windsor Castle* now resembled the last act of a well-constructed comedy in which the various actors, after inconceivable adventures and vicissitudes, find themselves all happily reunited. Palmella, Subserra, Beresford, the diplomatic body all complete, the two Infantas, their ladies-in-waiting and such loyal courtiers as were not in prison, crowded round the exhausted monarch on the deck. The King immediately signed two orders, the first commanding the release of the prisoners at Peniche and the second removing Dom Miguel from the command of the army. A despatch was then sent to the Prince ordering him to come on board the *Windsor Castle*.

According to the Marquis of Fronteira, Dom Miguel, who was not very clever at reading and writing, understood the gist of the King's order without realizing the severity of tone in which it was couched. At any rate, he now took a step which destroyed, completely and instantaneously, the whole absolutist plot, all the hopes of his party, and the ambitions of the Queen. He went on board. Possibly the excitement of the past week had overstrained his nerves and he was too tired to think of the consequences of his action. When he arrived on deck he flung himself on his knees in front of his father and exclaimed, hysterically, " Oh, father ! If I had been at the ends of the earth, I would have come to you !" The King and the Princesses retired into the royal cabin without replying, and the Prince then burst into tears. An hour later he was admitted to his father's presence, and threw himself on the King's mercy.

" This artful and ferocious young man," as Sir Edward Thornton described him, was now put under arrest, and it was promptly decided that he should be sent to travel abroad. Confined in the stern of the *Windsor Castle*, he behaved in a manner almost demented, hailing the boats in the river, asking them to cry " Viva " and " Hurrah " to him, and flinging papers and furniture out of the port-holes. When, on the evening of the 12th, he was transferred to the Portuguese frigate

Perla, in which it had been decided he was to make the voyage to Brest, the ship was watched all night by English boats in case an attempt should be made by his supporters to kidnap him. The *Perla* sailed at three o'clock the next day but one, accompanied by the *Lively* and the French corvette *Le Tibre.*

On the 13th May, the King's birthday, hundreds of people came on board to kiss hands. The numbers were swelled by all the prisoners who had come streaming back from Peniche. And thus Dom John welcomed them, in Palmerston's picturesque phrase, " with our hardy sailors as his pages-in-waiting and our menacing guns as his guard of honour." It is to be supposed that Captain Dashwood was forced to exercise some self-restraint at the spectacle of his ship transformed into the picturesque but rather eccentric court of San Christoval or Bemposta. To mark his gratitude the King bestowed the title of Count of Cacilias on Thornton, and that of Count of Bemposta on Hyde de Neuville. He returned to Bemposta on the 14th, midst much popular enthusiasm.

The little Baron glowed with satisfaction over the conspicuous part he had played throughout the crisis. The King received him in audience on the 15th. " I have had," wrote Hyde de Neuville to his government—and his pen must have trembled with emotion as he wrote—" a long conference at Bemposta. I am embarrassed to repeat the words the King used to me. ' Write to your Sovereign,' he said, ' that here, in this palace, his Ambassador saved me. I will never forget it '."

On the 16th arrived the so eagerly awaited *Santi Petri.* It was, alas ! several days too late, but better late than never. " The King," wrote Hyde de Neuville, " wished to pay a visit to our ship, to show that it was only the absence of the French fleet which caused him to ask of the English flag that protection which he would have preferred to receive from the English and French nations together."

And so the Hyde de Neuvilles gave a wonderful party on board the *Santi Petri,* and French national vanity was assuaged. " You would have imagined," wrote the delighted Baroness, " that a magician's wand had transformed the imposing *Santi Petri,* which only four days earlier was still bristling with cannon, into the palace of a fairy-tale. Imagine two thousand lanterns . . . and a huge ballroom all hung with white, with the Portuguese arms in the centre and garlands of fleur-de-lis, and laurels and roses all round. . . . Imagine two hundred ladies in their loveliest gala frocks, and the gentlemen all in uniform or court dress."

Each lady as she arrived up the gangway was presented with a bouquet by a gallant French officer. There was a throne set for the King, and opposite was hung a portrait of Louis the Eighteenth, surrounded by flowers and garlands " all arranged with taste." When the Baroness recalled that portrait, she all but fainted from the overpowering effect of the recollection. " But do not let your eyes," she wrote, " be monopolised by the ballroom ! Look beyond the mainmast where is revealed Gérard's beautiful picture ! On either side are cradles of laurels and roses perfectly lit up by coloured lamps, and beyond is a galaxy of lights and the words Long live John the Sixth !"

The King arrived at seven o'clock, accompanied by the Infantas. Hyde de Neuville opened the ball with the Duchess of Lafôes. At midnight there was supper, and the King's health was drunk by all present. Captain Dashwood had kindly promised to provide a salute at this moment, but owing to the unfortunate explosion of a rocket a few minutes earlier, the *Windsor Castle's* gunners, believing that the rocket was a signal, fired their pieces unexpectedly. The roar of cannon so startled the Princess Isabella-Maria that she was miraculously cured of a pain in the shoulder that had hitherto obliged her to carry one arm in a sling. She was now able to dispense with it, and the supper for six hundred guests continued merrily till dawn.

Meanwhile four hundred sailors of the French ship, who had been put on shore to make room for the party, sat down to supper in the illuminated gardens of the French Embassy, and the echoes of their revels floated over the water to the ears of the glittering company on the ship.

Chapter XX

THE " Abrilada," as the April revolution was nicknamed, was a victory for the King's government and a resounding defeat for Dona Carlota Joaquina.

For nine intoxicating days, but for no more, she had tasted the sweets of power. The prisoners arrested by Dom Miguel's gang had been seized at her orders : she had come from Queluz with all her lists of enemies already made out, counting upon success as certain, bringing her shabby regalia with her in a trunk, merely awaiting the summons to join her son on some appropriate balcony, to put her emblems of sovereignty on.

Her calculations had been based once again upon her recollection of Dom Pedro's revolution at Rio de Janeiro. She had been convinced that the good-natured timid King who hated disturbances, would be frightened into abdicating. She had misjudged the loyalty of the capital, had misjudged the paradoxical strength inherent in the King's weakness and, lastly, she had not foreseen the intervention of the diplomatic body.

She now drove back in her coach to Queluz filled with indescribable rage. Her recorded comment is : " If when that old fool went on board the English ship Miguel had come to me instead of obeying his father all would have been well : the Lisbon streets would have run with blood !" The words have the true Spanish ring, reminding one of the popular assertion that Dona Carlota had imbibed mancillares wine with her nurse's milk.

She now found herself in isolation. Many of the frenzied friars and agents that formed the inner ring of her party were arrested or had gone into hiding. Instead of Queluz being a hive of activity as it had been all through April, its approaches were now deserted. To the ruin of her hopes must be added the personal sorrow of Dom Miguel's exile. She had not even been given the opportunity to bid him farewell. Only a last message from her had somehow been conveyed to him in his cabin-cell, together with a tiny image of Our Lady of the Cave. The clatter of his horse's hooves as he dashed into the courtyard, the ring of his spurred footsteps as he strode down the corridors to her boudoir, no longer broke the silence of Queluz. And all at Lisbon who hated her were smiling over her defeat.

For several months, her spirit was wellnigh broken. She did not rally even when she learned of the dissensions that were splitting the camps of her enemies, and heard the news of the discomfiture of first Thornton, then de Neuville, then Subserra.

A bitter quarrel broke out between Beresford and Thornton over the parts which they had respectively played during the late crisis.

Beresford went off to England in a temper, affirming that in spite of the happy turn which events had in fact taken, it had been absolute madness to put the King on board the *Windsor Castle*. What would have happened, he asked, if instead of obeying his father Dom Miguel had gone to the Ajuda and brought back the Queen as Regent? Contrary to Beresford's view and in self-defence, Thornton affirmed that the army would never have supported the Queen and the Prince. He not only defended his own conduct, but criticized Lord Beresford's. He argued that Beresford had given wrong advice to the King at Bemposta on the 30th April, that he ought not to have allowed Dom Miguel to continue in command of the troops, and that the Royal Proclamation which had been issued that evening, drawn up by Beresford, had caused harm. For, wishing to spare Dom Miguel's feelings, it had more or less accepted the truth of his tale about a masonic plot, and had thus given Miguel an excuse to make his wholesale arrests.

It may befall the most circumspect of diplomats that after he has successfully avoided, during a long career, falling into any of the pitfalls that beset his footsteps, at the very end of his career luck deserts him. He takes on his own initiative some decision which he subsequently finds to his horror is contrary to the views of his government. Such was the fate of poor Sir Edward Thornton. Fortune had seemed indulgent to him. He enjoyed, in a peculiar degree, the confidence and even the affection of the King of Portugal. But his peace of mind had no sooner been shattered by Lord Beresford's strictures than he received a despatch from Canning reprimanding him for having encouraged Palmella to sue for the intervention of British troops, and for having sent to the Foreign Office a " reasoned opinion in favour " of the suggestion. It was, said Canning, a plot hatched by Subserra and de Neuville, who guessed that the House of Commons would never sanction the necessary expense, and who intended, when England's refusal was made public, to acclaim it as an excuse to summon French troops in their place.

There is a saying that misfortunes never come singly. Thornton's run of ill-luck was only beginning. The great problem facing the Portuguese government when the April crisis had passed was what to do with the termagant Queen. Palmella called de Neuville, the Spanish Ambassador, and Thornton to a conference to discuss the matter. He laid before them conclusive evidence proving that Dona Carlota had been directly responsible for the movement of the 30th April. It was agreed at the conference that the Queen should be invited to reside abroad.

When Canning learned that the British Minister in Lisbon had been sitting round a conference table with the representatives of France and Spain, to whose schemes for meddling in the internal affairs of other nations Canning's own views were diametrically opposed, he penned him a despatch which must have made Thornton turn pale. " The actual intervention of the diplomatic corps on the 30th April," Canning wrote, " was quite right, as that concerned the personal safety of the King and might be regarded as clearly exceptional. But a standing council of Foreign ministers, convened for no special purpose growing out of previous obligations of Treaty . . for the guidance, in its internal details, of the conduct of the Government to which they are severally accredited, is a thing unknown to the Law of Nations. . ."

Thornton admitted his fault. " I suffered myself," he wrote in reply, " to be diverted from a salutary line of conduct. You cannot think me on these occasions more wrong than I own that I feel myself." But his apologies did not appease his chief. In August he was recalled. " He has been cowed and cajoled," Canning exclaimed, " till he forgot he was Minister of England."

Thus Thornton made his ignominious exit from public life. His enemy Beresford continued to flourish, and five years afterwards the old busybody was astonishing Lady Holland by driving down to visit the young Queen Maria da Gloria at Laleham dressed in full Portuguese Field-Marshal's uniform, kissing her hand on bended knee, and making " a complete offer of duty and obedience to her commands."

Old King John was much distressed at the news that he was to be deprived of Thornton's advice. Palmella's unfortunate conferences had not even succeeded in getting the problem of the Queen settled, for Dona Carlota simply refused to budge. She declared that nothing but force would carry her out of Queluz. She declined to receive the Spanish ambassador, or to reply to his letter enclosing one from her brother the King of Spain, offering her a residence across the frontier. When the Archbishop of Evora and the Cardinal Patriarch went to Queluz with a letter from King John inviting her to leave Portugal, she demanded a public trial and protested she was guiltless of any crime. She fell back on her old excuse that she was too ill to make a journey, which at this time may have been the truth.

Nevertheless, her refusal to visit her beloved Spain is not easy to explain. Was she really feeling ill and old, or did she feel intuitively that her day would come again, that Dom John could not live much longer, and that she must at all costs keep the nest warm for her darling son ? Or did she know that her brother, though he wrote to her (at Dom John's request) to invite her to Madrid, did not really want the presence of an elder sister who might cause the question of the Salic law to be revived and thus encourage the formation of a party of opposition ?

Certainly, there were two circumstances that helped her to make up her mind to stay where she was. In the first place, her reputation as a menace to the state and the fear she inspired in Dom John's mind constituted the major political problem of the Portuguese government during the eighteen remaining months of the reign. This fact was sufficient to flatter her and to keep the embers of her vitality aglow. Secondly, she had abundant occasion during these months to observe that Portugal was still a prey to internal political feuds at the same time as becoming to an ever-increasing extent the battleground of contending foreign influences. This contributed to the slow revival of hope in the Queen's breast, for factions and feuds were the troubled waters in which she fished.

In the summer of 1826, French influence was in the ascendant. Subserra was altogether a more forceful personality than Palmella, while de Neuville had let it be known that during the April crisis he had summoned to Lisbon the French garrison of Badajoz. The summons had not been answered, but he claimed credit for having made it. The continental powers meanwhile were bringing all available pressure to bear upon Dom John to persuade him to relinquish his already-published intention to call together the Three Estates. (Several allied conferences were held in Paris during the course of 1824 to remonstrate against the proposal, while a sort of permanent committee of ambassadors at Lisbon worked for the same end.)

Canning's position was clear. It had, indeed, never been otherwise, from the day he became British Foreign Secretary. Inspired by his own intense belief in the virtues of vigorous independent nationalities, and supported by public opinion at home, he was determined that England should under no circumstances be a party to the plots of the greater continental powers to browbeat small nations. He had, as we have seen, severed England's connection with the Holy Alliance at the Congress of Verona, and when the French had persisted in their plans to occupy Spain, he had warned them flatly that England would not only contemplate recognizing the independence of Spain's revolted colonies if the French occupation were prolonged, but also that she would be prepared to go to war if French troops violated the territorial integrity of Portugal. The French for their part, had respected Canning's warning, and Villèle had told the Duke of Angoulême " not to get mixed up in Portuguese affairs for, if so, England would intervene."

Canning was perfectly firm in holding to the line he had laid down, being determined to intervene in Portugal only in the event of her being definitely threatened in a military sense. Thus his policy was throughout in entire accordance with the terms of the treaties existing between Portugal and Great Britain. When the time came—as we shall see it did come—for him to send military assistance, it was in circumstances in which the Anglo-Portuguese Alliance was plainly affected, and in which he could count upon British public opinion being behind him. But in 1824, Palmella's call for help was not against any existing external threat ; it was for support against internal intrigue—the eternal conspiracies of the Queen's party. The authority of the government was to such an extent enfeebled that King John saw no guarantee of stability except the presence of English red-coats. But the only concession that Canning would make was to keep the British squadron at Lisbon, to augment the strength of the marines to 750, and to instruct them to occupy the Tagus forts in case of emergency.

Sir Edward Thornton said farewell to Lisbon in August, and the Baron Hyde de Neuville did not long survive him. Canning dished him by complaining to Polignac in Paris on the grounds of his having appealed in April to the French at Badajoz. As de Neuville had acted in this matter without authority, and as moreover he had fallen out with Villèle for having in a rash moment expressed his approval of Dom John's proposal to summon the Three Estates, he was removed a few months later.

The Queen had the curiosity to send for him one day before he left Portugal, and he was received in audience. She caused him no little amusement by telling him that he was a fine enough fellow, but that his friends at Lisbon were a pack of rascals. When he retreated to the door after the interview was over, and then turned round rather quickly to make a final obeisance, he was startled to see the Queen standing immobile on the daïs *putting her tongue out at him.*

Once back in Paris, de Neuville threw himself with his habitual gusto into Parisian politics. He continued to be a picturesque and still meddlesome public figure until the fall of Charles the Tenth, when he retired to his estate at Lestang. There he finished his days in an atmosphere of great sanctity, surrounded by mementos of an already vanished age, white banners growing slowly threadbare, and other dusty relics of the last Kings of France. His chief delight— perhaps memories of Lisbon haunted him too—was to take part in religious processions in his village. The awestruck peasants of Lestang would watch this illustrious, forgotten old man, wearing on his breast a faded Grand Cordon of the Legion of Honour and holding with trembling fingers a cord of the canopy shading the holy image.

Sir Edward Thornton was succeeded as British minister in Lisbon, in September, 1824, by Sir William a'Court, a diplomat who at Naples, in 1820, and at Madrid, in 1823, had shown great firmness amid almost unprecedented difficulties. Lady Holland described him in a letter to her son, whom she hoped to see appointed to Sir William's staff, as " just what you wish as a school to learn your business. He is by far the first man in his line." His capacities for diplomacy were certainly to be put to the test in his new post also. Palmella was thoroughly disgruntled at Canning's refusal to send troops. " If England," he told Sir William at their first interview, " persists in saying she can assist us only in a case not likely to occur, and deserts us in a danger that is imminent (*i.e.*, yet another revolution engineered by the Queen), can it be a matter of astonishment to her that her counsels should not have that weight which they would otherwise have commanded ?" The old King was disgruntled likewise. It is a chilly welcome for any ambassador on arriving at a new post to be informed by the Minister of Foreign Affairs that the departure of his predecessor at the Embassy is deeply regretted. This is what Palmella told Sir William in so many words. " His Majesty," he said, " cannot but feel that he had lost a person sincerely devoted and attached to him, in losing Sir Edward."

Sir William's first interview with Dom John was hardly more agreeable. " Oh, yes," the old King burst out, " I have done everything for the English. I left my country for the English, and went to the Brazils. Lord Strangford danced for joy upon the quarter-deck when I crossed the bar."

Dom John had returned to his old lair at Mafra. As old age crept over him the salient traits in his character became accentuated. As far as his consort was concerned, his fear now amounted to a persecution-complex. She had poisoned his manhood, and now was the dread of his declining years. He had learned by long experience how to hedge himself round with trusty old favourites, who served not only to act as buffers between him and Queluz, but who also each contributed to create a small world, where he could still move among them as King. But even when buried in the priest-hive of Mafra, concealed in a smoke-screen of incense, he never felt secure.

He confided his incessant gnawing nervousness to Sir William a'Court. " If the Queen were once convinced," he told him, " that you English would not oppose her, should she declare herself in favour of a constitution, she would change her colours immediately, and come at the head of a constitutional mob to dethrone me." Sir William, while firmly discouraging the King's hopes, which he still cherished, of seeing some English regiments in the capital, assured him that he could count upon the British squadron in all circumstances. He pointed out that there was a useful force of marines to hand. " Excellent men !" replied the old King between grunts, " but too few, Sir, too few !"

Canning's principle of not interfering abroad " except in exceptional cases when duty was clear " was proof against the Portuguese Government's vexation. Nevertheless, though undoubtedly sound in the long run, Palmella was right in saying that this policy involved, at times, a diminution in British influence. " The events that are now passing in the world," a'Court wrote in September, " and the principles now struggling for pre-eminence, have thrown something of contradiction into our relations with this country, which renders the part we play less obvious to common apprehension, and more obnoxious to suspicion, than the general protecting influence we formerly exercised. . . . It is not the country that is in danger now, but the Government." So for the time being Portugal continued a prey to sharp diplomatic pressure from the continental powers, and while the English press called for the summoning of the Three Estates according to the King's promise the whole of continental Europe urged its abandonment.

The economic situation was still parlous. The proportion of expenditure to revenue was as 27 to 15 in peace-time. The army and navy absorbed two millions of cruzados, which was the entire revenue, yet Portugal had little to show for it except 1,200 soldiers and a navy consisting of one ship of the line, three frigates, and some smaller vessels. The expenses of the court, and the maintenance of the nobility and the judicature, were heavy charges only to be met by extraordinary means. " Every establishment," wrote Sir William, " is continued upon the same scale as when Portugal possessed an active trade with India and the exclusive commerce of Brazil. The same crowds of useless employees encumber the public offices, the same state offices are kept up, and the crown lands, under the title of commanderies, etc., still continue to be re-granted, as fast as they fall in, in order to enable a host of new-made nobles to support titles which ought never to have been bestowed."

The master of the government, such as it was, was still the Marquis of Subserra, whose gifts for political wire-pulling were just those that keep unscrupulous, clever politicians prosperous in degraded times. He was the recognized leader of the French party, and had become as cordially detested by the British Foreign Office as by the English community in Portugal. It is not surprising, therefore, that a'Court should have received instructions to press for his removal. But Subserra well knew the weak side of every man's character, including the King's, and he had succeeded in convincing Dom John that he— Subserra—was his only solid guarantee of protection against the Queen.

" But if I lose Mr. de Subserra," moaned Dom John to Sir William, " who is to defend me against my wife and son ? They want to shut me up as mad. They say that I must be mad, because my mother was mad. Will you engage to defend me against them, if I get rid of Mr. de Subserra ?" He asked for a written promise, a *petit certificat*, to this effect, and on the 17th December, Sir William, who had evidently come to the conclusion that the Queen was not in a position to stage another revolution at present, wrote out a *petit certificat* which he took to Mafra. Thereupon the King promised to dismiss Subserra within a month.

He kept his word. On the 21st January, 1825, a decree was published nominating this troublesome man as Ambassador to Madrid. His removal from the government represented a purge of the entire anti-British clique both in the government offices and in the palace, where all the key-men including the Court Chamberlain, had been in the pay of Subserra's chief of police. To give an impression of fairness, the pro-British Palmella was relieved at the same time of his office of Minister of Foreign Affairs, and went back to London as Portuguese minister to resume his distinguished place in the salon of the Princess de Lieven.

Thus the Marquis of Subserra passed from the political stage in Portugal, but his exit was by no means a quiet one. Before leaving for Madrid, he put in circulation a number of virulent anti-British pamphlets, one of which accused Marshal Beresford of the murder of the Marquis of Loulé. And he had no sooner arrived in the Spanish capital than he became the centre of a resounding scandal. Not that this extraordinary, this tragic and yet at the same time comic affair, was any fault of his own. It happened that he had ordered the liveries for his new embassy (and even, it is said, his own uniform) from a Lisbon tailor who, being niggardly-minded, had saved a cruzado or two by using up some old buttons. They were not plain buttons. They were liberal buttons. That is to say, they displayed in minute letters the dynamic words " Long Live the Constitution." So when the new Portuguese ambassador appeared at the arch-Legitimist Court of King Ferdinand of Spain, and some hawk-eyed Spaniard perceived the preposterous, the outrageous buttons, there resulted an explosion of indignation that reverberated through every chancellery in Europe. To find any modern parallel to the flagrant impropriety of Subserra's blunder one would have to imagine an ambassador arriving in Madrid in 1940 with a hammer and sickle as the mascot of his motor-car. It was in vain for Subserra to protest the purity of his monarchical principles and to denounce the wickedness of his tailor. He was cold-shouldered, and publicly insulted. Finally he threw in his hand in despair and returned without leave and on the pretence of illness to Lisbon. Thus ended his public career.

Chapter XXI

THE Queen received orders from Bemposta that she was not to appear in public. Queluz was now her prison. Government spies took lodgings in the village nearby and watched her. Their suspicions were much excited by the weekly visit of the Infanta Ana's piano-teacher who, as they reported to the chief of police at Lisbon, " seemed to have plenty of money always in his pocket." A policeman disguised as a market gardener was instructed to make friends with the head gardener of the palace " on the excuse of buying shrubs." He honestly reported that the place was almost as lifeless as a desert.

It veritably appeared as if the Queen was no longer dangerous, and as if her decrepitude was not feigned. Her condition at this time is well illustrated by the following story : Two young cavalry cadets who were out on a stroll somehow managed to gain access to the gardens. Having explored the orange groves, they at last penetrated on to a terrace below the palace. Suddenly a French window opened close beside them, and they were startled to see an old hag limp into the sunlight. Her appearance was so dishevelled and grotesque that one of the cadets made a joke, and asked the old woman whether Queluz did not provide anything more succulent in the way of female charm than herself. He was surprised to be met with a glance of haughty authority, but he continued to tease. At that instant there emerged on to the terrace four ladies-in-waiting who knelt before the old woman and inquired whether Her Majesty would deign to dine. A moment later she had disappeared from view.

Horrified by their mistake, the two youths took to their heels, vaulted over the balustrade of the terrace without looking where they were going, and both sprained their ankles at the bottom of a ten-foot drop. They were rescued by some servants, and put into a room of the palace, where a doctor attended them. At the end of a few days, when they were well again they were summoned to the Queen's presence and found her seated magnificently on a throne, dripping with jewels. She reprimanded them in a caustic, affable manner and dismissed them.

The daily reports prepared by the Chief of Police provide an interesting sidelight on the condition of the country beyond the walls of Queluz. His main duty consisted of keeping watch on the state of opinion among the clergy, and on the morale of the barracks ; it was the former who caused him the most anxiety. The conflict between liberal ideas and the inherited superstitions of two centuries still fed the fever which for so long had been wasting Portugal's strength. News reached Lisbon from time to time of inflammatory sermons preached by half-demented friars in the provinces, exciting the population against the freemasons and free-thinkers. " The blood of the

151

Portuguese must be set flowing as the blood of the Jews once flowed!" had screamed the ex-Franciscan, Joâo Mariano, on the eve of the "Abrilada." Then, with his voice sinking to a lugubrious, thrilling whisper: "Expiation is necessary! I, myself, feel transported! I, myself, desire to see my hands smeared with blood!" The prevailing tension which existed in spite of the country's outward calm is demonstrated by the fantastic rumours that the Chief of Police chronicled from day to day. The two chief manufacturies of these rumours, or *boatos*, always so typical a feature of life in Portugal where every coffee-sipper has the imagination of an Arabian story-teller, are noted as being the promenades on Black Horse Square and the Cais de Sodré. There was a rumour that the King had been initiated as a freemason on board the *Windsor Castle*; that the colony of Goa had declared for Dom Pedro; that the King of France was stricken with St. Vitus' dance; that the royal cabin on board the *Dom Joâo VI* had been lined with crimson velvet in preparation for King John's departure. But the most persistent rumour of all was that Dom Miguel (who by this time was in Vienna) was really in Spain at the head of an army about to invade Portugal.

Meanwhile Portugal, metaphorically speaking, was on the operating table, suffering a far from painless dismemberment in the final, publicly acknowledged loss of Brazil. The separation of the two countries had, of course, been virtually complete ever since Dom Pedro's proclamation of the Brazilian Empire in 1823. But the fact was too painful a one for the Portuguese to accept without the most desperate efforts to restore the old connection at least in name. At least in name! The Portuguese mind has a perpetual tendency to shrink from unpalatable realities, and even when the substance of some long-prized privilege has faded for ever, to cling tenaciously to the shadow. Dom John was typical of his countrymen in this respect. He clung obstinately, almost desperately, to the illusion of undiminished sovereignty.

Dom Pedro's reign had opened in an ominous atmosphere of precariousness and strife. His first task as emperor was to suppress incipient insurrections in various provinces. That he achieved his object in a comparatively short space of time, was due to his good fortune in obtaining the services of an English sailor whose name at this time enjoyed a great and awful reputation.

Lord Cochrane had lately played a glorious part in the liberation of Chile. Being now free to undertake new adventures, he accepted Dom Pedro's invitation to assume command of the Brazilian navy. He issued a farewell manifesto to the people of Chile, most typical of his romantic personality and of the exalted spirit of freedom of his age. "The sacred cause of your independence," ran the manifesto, "called me to Chile four years ago. I have assisted you in establishing it. I have seen it obtained. You have now only to preserve it. I absent myself from you for a time ... Chileans! You know that independence is gained at the point of the bayonet. Know then that Liberty is preserved by good faith and the laws of honour, and that

DOM MIGUEL

from a portrait painted during his exile at Vienna, now at Queluz

those who break them are your only enemies, among whom will never be found—Cochrane."

The darkened footlights and the roll of drums which accompany the entrance of the bad fairy at a pantomime could not create a more effective thrill among the audience than did Cochrane when he sprang on to the quay at Rio de Janeiro. He wasted no time in putting again to sea, and at once blockaded Bahia, which had defied the new imperial authority under the leadership of General Luiz Madeira. When Madeira realized that resistance was hopeless, and attempted on the 2nd July, 1823, to cut his way out of the harbour by night, together with the Portuguese troops who had been defending the town, Cochrane attacked, captured eleven transports, and scattered the remainder of the fleet. Rebellious Pernambuco surrendered a few months later and lastly Maranham. Such was the immortal Cochrane's effective contribution to Brazilian history.

Dom Pedro's second great task was to establish political as well as territorial unity in his empire. He had inaugurated the National Assembly on the 3rd May, and had been acclaimed as Constitutional Emperor. But this assembly had no sooner begun its labours than the deputies revealed a spirit hardly less exasperating than that of the Cortes at Lisbon. Their debates were particularly unruly when they discussed their favourite question as to whether the Emperor should or should not be allowed the power of veto.

The democratic party, which held a third of the seats in the assembly, dragged out the discussion of every article and detail of the constitution, while the press, in full enjoyment of its democratic liberty, disseminated an atmosphere of bitter contention. The worst offender was the violent radical Barrata, whose paper was called " The Sentinel of Liberty." It is permissible to suppose that Barrata was not quite sane. He looked like a gorilla, and his career had been punctuated by all kinds of violence. In his youth he had been condemned to death for exciting a revolt among the slaves at Bahia. Later on he had been one of the Brazilian representatives to the Lisbon Cortes, where he had on one occasion publicly assaulted an elderly colleague at the entrance of the parliament, hurling the unfortunate old gentleman down a flight of fifty steps. But the Emperor himself, though engrossed by his passion for the Marqueza dos Santos, and shaken by recurring attacks of epilepsy, as a bright day in the tropics may be broken by seismic disturbances, showed a clear comprehension of the aim he wished to achieve. He was determined to compel Portugal to acquiesce in the recognition of his independent sovereignty, even if the price to be paid was war against his own father and against the mother country of whose throne he was himself the heir apparent. He proved himself a ruthless fighter. He began by confiscating all Portuguese property in Brazil, and by authorizing his ships to seize Portuguese vessels on the high seas.

He soon gave further proof of his metal in his dealings with the Assembly. Throughout the summer of 1823 he made every effort to conciliate the deputies though, as a result of their behaviour, the condition of the country was going from bad to worse. But in the following month he realized that the existing state of affairs could not be permitted to continue. There was resentment in the army at the language being used by both the assembly and the press. So Dom Pedro signed a decree declaring the assembly at an end and placing himself in supreme command of the armed forces. Then, acclaimed with enthusiasm by the mob, he personally led the troops through the city. The chamber was summarily surrounded and the deputies were dispersed. Seven were imprisoned. Barrata was arrested at Pernambuco and brought to Rio to captivity in Fort Villegaignon. A new and, as it proved, more workable constitution was promulgated shortly afterwards.

When the Marquis of Rio Maior returned to Lisbon empty-handed from his conciliatory mission at the end of 1823, the Portuguese government decided to invite the mediation of Great Britain. And so it came about that Canning exercised a decisive influence, not indeed in the creation of Brazilian independence—that, as we have seen, was already a *fait accompli*—but in discovering a formula that Portugal might accept in order at long last to acknowledge reality. Canning acted like a competent midwife, whose first duty is to clear busybodies from the scene of operations. His task was facilitated because the Holy Alliance, in this question of Brazil, did not present a united front. Their overriding aim being to settle all matters in conformity with the interests of legitimate monarchy, their counsels were divided by the fact that Brazil's revolt against Portugal was not simply the revolt of a democracy against a monarchy. An hereditary Prince had revolted against his father, and was himself now wearing a crown and carrying a sceptre. So, though France and Russia urged for the parental authority to be restored, and to be restored if need be by force of arms, Metternich took a different line. He looked upon the foundation of a new hereditary monarchy in Brazil as a potential balance to democratic tendencies in the American continent, and he therefore allowed Canning a free hand.

Negotiations opened in London in July, 1824. They were preceded by some preliminary skirmishes in which Canning flatly refused to countenance the interference of the Allied Powers—" who have not," he wrote to a'Court, " a transmarine Colony belonging to them, nor a single sail on the ocean which washes South America, nor a bale of goods in the ports either of Portugal or Brazil," but who nevertheless " discuss very much at their ease, the relation of a mother country to its Colonies, and recommend perpetual war between them, by which both may be destroyed : rather than any influence dangerous to legitimacy may be drawn from a compromise by which both may be saved." He consented, however, to the participation of Austria in the London conferences.

After four months of sterile discussion Canning's patience grew threadbare, and it is probable that he welcomed the opportunity that presented itself in November to suspend the conference altogether. He learned that the Portuguese government had been guilty of what he termed "astonishing duplicity." They had sent round a circular inviting the mediation of other powers (France, Russia and Prussia), thus implying that Austria and England had failed.

In December, Canning decided to undertake direct negotiations. "Tell me," he wrote privately to the Portuguese representative at the London discussions, " if you believe any government here could throw away the trade with Brazil in order to avoid the simple admission that *what is, is, viz.*, that Brazil is separated from Portugal. . . . The King of Portugal has it yet in his hands to decide whether Brazil shall be independent by his act, or in spite of him."

On the 16th March Sir Charles Stuart set out on his memorable mission, first to Lisbon and then to Rio de Janeiro. He persuaded King John to accept a draft agreement, and having been nominated his plenipotentiary, sailed for Brazil in June. He obtained his treaty on the 29th August, 1825.

By Article 1, His Most Faithful Majesty recognized Brazil " as an Empire independent and separate from Portugal and the Algarve : and . . . Dom Pedro as Emperor, ceding and transferring, of his own free will, the sovereignty of the said Empire to his said Son and to His legitimate successors : His Most Faithful Majesty only taking and reserving the same title for his own person." By Article II, Dom Pedro agreed to permit his father to assume the imperial title for his life-time. Article III prohibited Pedro from accepting the proposals of any Portuguese colonies to unite themselves with the Empire of Brazil. Article IV agreed that there should be oblivion of past differences, and an alliance and perfect friendship between Brazil and Portugal for the future. The remaining articles stipulated for the mutual restoration of sequestered property and the payment of certain indemnities to Portugal.

This treaty was ratified at once by Dom Pedro and sent off to Portugal on a British ship. It reached Lisbon on the 9th November. On the 20th ratifications were exchanged and the separation and independence of Brazil were complete.

It was the last great event of Dom John the Sixth's troubled reign, and for the King himself it was perhaps the most bitter. Though he was not an old man—he was fifty-nine—he had long been in failing health. The loss of Brazil proved a mortal blow. On the 4th March, 1826, he went by carriage to the royal pavilion at Belem to watch the procession of the sacrament that was to issue from the church of the Ajuda. He supped while waiting for the procession to pass. On his return to Bemposta he was attacked by convulsions and fainted. Six days later he was dead.

The Queen never came to his bedside to say farewell to him. She was too ill, she said, to be able to cover the few miles from Queluz. Yet, when Sir William a'Court was received in audience by the invalid two months later, she talked for two hours, standing straight as a poker throughout the interview, and showing no signs of fatigue. "The conversation," wrote Sir William, " was an unconnected series of the most improbable stories, picked up from all sorts of persons, from which she drew inferences the most extraordinary, and, as it appeared to me, the most unjustifiable." She informed him that the King had been poisoned by a dose of *agua tofana*, and that she was convinced she was about to be poisoned also (no doubt by the masons). "They have declared," she said, "that the country will never be quiet, *till I have had my dose.*"

The Queen was not alone in whispering darkly of poisons. The Portuguese, as we have already had occasion to observe, show extraordinary talent for the invention and dissemination of tales. While the Queen's party accused the Secret Societies, the liberals swore that the King had been done to death by the agents of the implacable Queen. He was said to have imbibed a certain bowl of broth, to have instantly exclaimed, "This broth has killed me !" and to have collapsed. Investigations had disclosed, it was said, that the servant carrying the broth to the King had met the Court physician, Dr. Aguiar, in an ante-room. "Here is the King's tonic," the doctor had whispered, emptying a small bottle of liquid into the soup. A drop had been spilled on the napkin, immediately eating a hole into the cloth. At this the servant had paled, and had reported the incident to the head cook, by name Caetano ; and that same night Caetano and the lackey had both been found strangled in their rooms. In pointing out that this fantastic story had no more solid basis than the gossip of the cafés, it may be added that the drop burning a hole in the napkin is one of those touches which sometimes raise Portuguese rumours to the level of artistic creations.

The only poison which the poor King had tasted was the venom which had embittered his life. Slowly but surely his vitality had been sapped by the Queen's hatred, to which must be added not only the ceaseless political anxiety which had dogged his footsteps with increasing persistency ever since the day he had set sail with a heavy heart from the halcyon shores of Rio de Janeiro, but the grief caused to this tender-hearted man by the conduct of his sons.

It has been said of him that he would have made a good constitutional King in normal times. He well represented those traditional characteristics of the Portuguese monarchy which his countrymen had learned to look for in the Braganzas. He was accessible to the humblest of his subjects. He was a fervent son of the Church, a patron of music. Lastly, it is always pleasant to find in the pages of history a monarch who, like Edward the Third of England, or the Tudors, has embodied the essential qualities, even the faults as well as the virtues, of his people. King John the Sixth was a typical Portuguese. He was charitable, intensely loyal to his friends, loyal to his country's allies, sentimental, easy-going, much attached to familiar faces and familiar scenes. The affection and respect he enjoyed among his people were proved on numerous occasions. The defects of his character were mostly the excess of his good qualities. A less kindly man might have freed himself of his difficulties by a divorce, or by severity might have established discipline among his sons. A more energetic statesman might have forcibly stemmed the rise of liberal enthusiasm. But let it be remembered how many sovereigns of the liberal epoch allowed themselves to become identified with reaction, and by meddling with the tiller lived to see their ship capsize.

Dom John appears to have floated somewhat helplessly down the rapids, but he retained his throne to the end. It remained a symbol of national unity, so that until his death, Portugal was spared the horrors of civil war. It may be said with conviction, that the disasters and disgrace into which his country was plunged so shortly afterwards, were in no way due to him. The spirit of fanaticism was awake, and had to burn itself out.

Chapter XXII

PRINCE METTERNICH'S comment on King John the Sixth's death was : "He would have been doing me a signal service in abstaining from dying." It did not call for the talents of a Metternich to foresee storms ahead. Not merely the whole of Portugal but the whole of Europe was apprehensive of the future.

A few days before his death, the King had signed a decree appointing his daughter the Infanta Isabel Maria regent until such time as the wishes of the "legitimate heir" should be made known. This was one of the two Princesses who had always lived at their father's side. Dona Carlota Joaquina was given no place on the Council of Regency.

The "legitimate heir" was, of course, Dom Pedro. He had been recognized as such by a royal decree of the 13th May of the previous year. But Dom Pedro was Emperor of Brazil, and it was equally unthinkable that Portugal should become a Brazilian dependency as that Brazil should revert to being a Portuguese colony. Who, therefore, was to reign at Lisbon ? It seemed logical that Dom Pedro would give the Portuguese crown to Dom Miguel. Tradition and popular sentiment (as a'Court was the first to recognize) alike demanded that a King should be found somehow.

Two aspects of the succession problem must be briefly mentioned. In the first place, Dom Miguel's name was unfortunately associated with his mother's party, an association which the ill-judged enthusiasm of her supporters contributed to rendering indissoluble. In the second place, there were many who affirmed that the decree of the 13th May had no validity, for if Dom Pedro had made himself a Brazilian, they argued that he had *ipso facto* made himself a foreigner and had, therefore, according to the ancient laws of Portugal, deprived himself of all rights to the Portuguese throne and of all right to dispose of it. Thus from the very beginning the legal aspect of the problem was hopelessly confused. Party prejudices and hatreds usurped the place of law.

Since the fatal afternoon when Dom Miguel had gone on board the *Windsor Castle*, he had been living in exile. First, he had gone to Paris, where he had made his bow to Louis the Eighteenth at the Tuileries, but where the effect of his romantic good-looks had been somewhat offset by his rustic manners. The story that he relieved the tedium of his idle hours by vivisecting cats may be dismissed as an invention of Lisbon liberals, but the Marquis of Fronteira was an eye-witness of the fantastic scene at the Hotel Meurice when one day the Prince took it into his head to shoot with his pistol at a flock of Sussex sheep penned in the courtyard, to the despair of his chamberlain, the Count of Rio Maior, and the frightful alarm of the hotel servants. From

Paris he had proceeded by easy stages to Vienna, where he was now residing, living in as good order as the strait-waistcoat of Austrian etiquette could keep him, spied upon by the Portuguese Minister, and carefully watched by Metternich, who saw in Vienna's illustrious visitor a potential hostage, a priceless pawn on the European chess-board.

From the beginning Europe took sides. The government in Spain plumped at once for Dom Miguel. Russia and France leant to the same side. But Metternich, always prepared to uphold the principle of strict legitimacy, sent round a circular recognizing the rights of Dom Pedro. which was grudgingly approved by the other powers with the single exception of Spain.

Metternich persuaded Dom Miguel to sign a letter addressed to his sister the Regent, expressing approbation of the Regency " until the intentions of the legitimate heir and successor, who is our much-loved brother and Lord the Emperor of Brazil, should be made known." The letter asked his sister to declare publicly his disapproval of " pernicious designs " taking his name in vain. Dom Miguel also signed a letter to his brother acknowledging him as legitimate sovereign. He *signed* these documents, but it may with certainty be inferred that he neither composed nor wrote them. It is probable that he scarcely took the necessary pains to understand them, though their significance was doubtless explained to him in some interval between a shooting picnic and a supper party with the *corps-de-ballet* of the Imperial Opera. However, so far so good. According to the views of both Austria and England, the pawn had made the right opening.

What was to be the move to be made by Dom Pedro ? For six weeks the fate of Portugal lay in the hollow of his hand. It is not easy to follow the workings of his mind, nor to calculate how far he was influenced by the necessity of satisfying public opinion in Brazil. Certainly he was preposterously conceited, and fancied himself in the rôle of a benefactor of mankind. Suffice it to say that at the end of April his decision became known in Rio and was dispersed to the world at large. To the bewilderment of Austria, to the rage of Spain, and to the astonishment of the civilized globe the youthful Emperor announced his intention of bestowing upon Portugal the blessings of a liberal constitution. It was not to be any exaggeratedly democratic system on the Cadiz model, but was to imitate the British variety. Portugal was to be equipped with a House of Commons with a wigged Speaker complete, and a House of Peers in robes. In the tropic climate of Brazil the Constitution was designed, was drafted and was printed with the rapidity of growth of a mustard-tree. By a decree dated the 26th April, Dom Pedro then confirmed the Regency of the Infanta Isabel Maria until such time as his wonderful Charter should be formally promulgated and a new Regency chosen according to the Charter's stipulations. On the 29th, the Charter was signed by Dom Pedro as King of Portugal and the Algarve.

Then three days later Dom Pedro issued a *Carta Regia* abdicating the Portuguese throne in favour of his infant daughter, Dona Maria da Gloria. *But by yet another decree this abdication was made conditional, first, on the betrothal of his daughter to Dom Miguel ; secondly, on the acceptance of the new constitution by the Portuguese.*

The proposed marriage between the tender Dona Maria da Gloria and her lusty uncle, shocking as it may sound to modern ears, had a parallel in the marriage of Queen Maria the First, and from the political point of view approached the " sound domestic arrangement " being urged by the British government. But Dom Pedro's abdication presented one grave disadvantage in addition to the inconvenience of its being a conditional abdication merely. Dona Maria da Gloria was a child of seven. It would be necessary for a regency to continue to govern Portugal until her majority. There was thus no prospect of the country acquiring a strong and stable government for a number of years.

Sir Charles Stuart left Rio de Janeiro in the frigate *Diamond* with the famous Charter in his pocket. It was an unpolitic thing to do, for it looked as if England sponsored the Constitution, contrary to her principle of non-interference in the political concerns of other countries. Canning realized the danger at once. He sent a circular note to all foreign governments explaining that England had not sponsored Stuart's action, and he ordered Sir Charles, on his arrival in Lisbon, to come home at once to avoid further complications. Sir Charles also carried to Lisbon a decree issued by Dom Pedro ordering general elections for the new Lower Chamber and another naming a chamber of peers. The news of his imminent arrival preceded the *Diamond* on a faster ship by seven days. The liberals went wild with delight and made a demonstration at the San Carlos theatre. a'Court wrote to Canning : " All parties and all passions are roused."

The publication of the Charter had other important results besides the inspiration of a plethora of liberal sonnets in a pseudo-classic style full of references to Cato and Brutus ; it instantly galvanized Dona Carlota Joaquina's party into a fresh burst of life. The vested interests represented by pensions and monopolies, no less than the priests and the monks, felt themselves directly threatened by certain of the Charter's stipulations. Lastly, it evoked the open hostility of the Catholic-absolutist court at Madrid. The Regency, therefore, immediately found itself faced by enemies both within and beyond the Portuguese frontiers.

Though Beresford once said that the daughters of King John the Sixth all had fits but that none hád any political opinions, the Regent Isabel Maria was good-looking and reasonably level-headed. Unfortunately her standard of education was little superior to that of her brothers and sisters. On one occasion she informed her Minister of Foreign Affairs, the Count of Lavradio, that she intended to persuade one of his colleagues to resign by arranging for him to receive an anonymous letter ; tactics to which, she said, she knew the minister in question was peculiarly susceptible. She soon began to cause her advisers acute anxiety by her habit of lending an ear to dubious dependants of her private household. At the present critical juncture, moreover, she was suddenly deprived of the use of her limbs for twenty-four hours, and as a result, left Lisbon with a small suite of back-biting toadies to take medicinal baths at Caldas da Rainha, leaving the capital in the throes of a political crisis behind her.

Before describing the subsequent events of the Regency, which must be grasped in order to understand how it came about that Dona Carlota Joaquina was enabled to re-enter the political stage in triumph, it will be necessary to give some description of an individual who played a prominent part in them, namely, General Saldanha.

João Carlos de Saldanha was the son of the Count of Rio Maior, the eighth of twenty-two children, and a grandson on his mother's side of the Marquis of Pombal. At an early age he became one of Beresford's most brilliant officers in the Anglo-Portuguese army of the Peninsular War. A keen soldier, and as brave as a lion, he was just the type of Portuguese who caused the Duke of Wellington to refer to the Portuguese troops as " the most solid foundation of the hopes we have of freeing the Peninsula."

In 1815 Saldanha accompanied the troops that had been summoned to Brazil to take part in the campaign of Montevideo. It was an extraordinary kind of warfare. The troops of the rebel Artegas were composed chiefly of well-disciplined Indians who carried no less than six weapons : the carbine, the pistol, the sword, the knife, the lasso and the *bolla*. At full gallop they could throw a noose round a flying enemy and unhorse him. They used the *bolla*, an iron ball at the end of a long cord, for the same purpose with equal dexterity. If, at full tilt, their horses fell, they themselves invariably alighted on their feet like demons, instantly ready to fight on.

In battle with this ruthless and cunning foe, Saldanha distinguished himself by a hundred acts of personal valour. His name became a legend to his men. When Montevideo was captured by the Portuguese and the province annexed to Brazil he was appointed Captain-General of Rio Grande.

Saldanha was a child-like character with what nowadays would be called a single-track mind. His loyalties were few, simple and absolutely firm. He therefore found no difficulty in coming to a decision (not always the right one) in any emergency. In the first place, he felt himself to be a Portuguese, and when the severance between Portugal and Brazil took place he stoutly refused to consider himself a Brazilian. On the day that Dom Pedro was crowned, Saldanha appeared at the opera at Rio de Janeiro in the box of his relative, the Countess da Ponte, ostentatiously dressed in mourning. The Minister of Marine said to him : " The Emperor wonders why you are in mourning." " Can I be otherwise," replied Saldanha, " on the day that the dissolution of the Monarchy is effected?" Two days later, he sailed for home and landed in Lisbon in January, 1823, with £6 in his pocket. Bronzed by the sun of the pampas, and of brave bearing, he created a favourable impression on the Lisbon populace.

The Cortes, like most assemblies composed almost exclusively of " intellectuals," regarded with acute suspicion the presence in their midst of an individual of Saldanha's physical magnetism. He was ordered to return quickly to Brazil " to take supreme command of all the forces at Bahia." He refused the appointment, and was promptly imprisoned in the castle of Saint George. From this predicament he was ultimately rescued by the *Vilafrancada*. He escaped from his cell, galloped to Vila Franca, and was at once given command of the 2nd Division of the army. The next landmark in his career was his appointment as Military Governor of Oporto, which took place shortly after the old King's death.

Saldanha was a moderate liberal, like Palmella. He believed that Dom Pedro's constitution suited Portugal, and that, therefore, the sooner the country adopted it the better. Unfortunately, though he had all the qualities of an ideal scout-master, the great energy which he had inherited from his maternal grandfather was mixed with a strong dose of Pombal's overbearing temper. He was one of those who think men can be made to agree by having their heads knocked together. He thought that the ills from which Portugal was suffering could be cured simply by exercising the discipline of a sergeant-major. He was not, in fact, a very clever man, and though he was entirely opposed to the excessive democratic ideas of the first constitutional experiment, there is little doubt that at various stages in his career he became the unconscious dupe of the masons. Secret societies had been " abolished " by decree after the *Vilafrancada*, but in reality they were more active than ever. Saldanha detested them (his liberal English biographer writes roundly : " Freemasonry became, in Portugal, a secret society devoted to the worst purposes "), but by the discreet supply of false information, masons who, unknown to him, might exist inside his very staff were sometimes able to use Saldanha as a cat's-paw. They used him as a gang might use a bull, to drive him into a china shop to avenge themselves on the proprietors.

As Military Governor of Oporto, Saldanha won the devoted affection not only of the troops under his command, but also of the middle classes—who here, as in Lisbon, were mostly liberal-minded—and, above all, he earned the love of the populace. This popularity was due mostly to his knack of imposing the rough-and-ready justice of an Englishman in small matters, combined with his stern refusal to take a bribe or to fill his pockets at the expense of other people. Indeed, he earned for himself throughout the whole of the north of Portugal, a reputation for probity which never faded during his long life and which stood him in good stead in the years to come.

Sir Charles Stuart and the Charter arrived on the 7th July. For three dangerous weeks the Regency hesitated to carry out that public act of acceptance which was the first of the two necessary steps if Dom Pedro's abdication was to become a reality. The only positive measure towards putting the Charter into effect was taken by some naïf noblemen who with the greatest pride hurried, as newly created peers, to order their pale-blue uniforms with buttons stamped with the words " Peer of the Realm." Meanwhile, plots to acclaim Dom Miguel Absolute King there and then were being hotly fomented by the

Spanish ambassador. The priests were conducting their usual potent propaganda. Worst of all, the loyalty of whole regiments stationed in the central and southern provinces—who as usual had not been paid for months—was being rapidly undermined.

To all these malcontents, Queluz had again become a centre of resistance. Dona Carlota Joaquina was not only in constant touch with certain military commanders, but was in contact with the Spanish government through the Spanish Princesses who were her daughters. Together the Queen, the Spanish ministers, the Infantas at Madrid and the rebellious Portuguese generals plotted night and day.

There was not a moment to be lost. Saldanha had made up his mind on the 9th. "The one who has been acknowledged the legitimate sovereign," he wrote to a'Court, "has given us a Constitution. Our ally Great Britain approves it (else Sir Charles Stuart would not be its bearer). The Brazils will maintain it, and therefore I am determined, if the intrigues of Spain and Russia prevail, to put myself at the head of the troops in all the northern provinces, of whose obedience I am sure, and act according to the orders of my King."

He wrote a letter to the Regent to inform her that if the oaths to the Charter were not taken by the end of July, he would publicly take them himself and make all the northern provinces follow his example. At the same time he addressed the Minister of War, threatening to march on Lisbon.

This bombshell woke the Regency from their stupor. Oblivious to the fact that it was a bad precedent to give way to the threat of military force, the Regent replied by choosing the 31st July for the oath-taking of all state functionaries and officers of the armed forces throughout the country. When the day arrived the ceremony was performed with due solemnity, and there was a Te Deum in the churches. The liberals celebrated the occasion at Lisbon and Oporto in high glee. Illuminated arches, obelisks and temples decorated the main streets, and on her way to the cathedral the Regent stopped her carriage in the Rua Augusta to receive a delegation of thirteen school girls dressed in blue and white, who presented her with twenty-five white pigeons tied up with blue ribands.

This act of submission to Dom Pedro's wishes calls for two comments. In the first place, it must be pointed out that the multiplication of solemn oaths is never a desirable thing if circumstances offer no guarantee that the oaths will or can be respected. The multiplication of pacts and treaties between nations during the years immediately preceding the Second Great War did much to rob them of their value. The Portuguese had already once sworn to maintain the constitution of 1820. It had proved a failure and had been smashed with general consent. The swearing of oaths and their subsequent revocation looked like becoming a habit. In the second place, the act was too late to prevent a rebellion in favour of Absolutism which had broken out in Traz-os-Montes on the 26th July. It spread to the Alemtejo on the 1st August. Two regiments of infantry and one of cavalry, besides many officers and men of other brigades, joined the revolt. On the 3rd, the artillery mutinied at Elvas.

A rapid reshuffle was made in the Ministry of the Regency, and Saldanha became Minister of War. He came to Lisbon by ship and was acclaimed by swarming crowds excited to the highest degree by the news coming in from the provinces. Dom Miguel had been proclaimed Absolute King at Vila Maior. The governor of Almeida had deserted into Spain with 250 soldiers of the 11th infantry.

Saldanha took instant steps to deal with the situation. With a stroke of the pen, he ordered the rebel regiments to be disbanded and struck off the list of the army. A wave of arrests among officers and priests followed. The new minister was certainly reminding Portugal of his grandfather.

a'Court wrote to the Foreign Office : " Saldanha is indefatigable in his inquiries into the characters and conduct of all those in command. His appointment has had the best effect." And in this opinion, it may be added, General Saldanha himself would have very heartily concurred. For he was not lacking in self-confidence. In the lengthy report which he presented to the Regent he blithely announced that his " measures of severity and well-merited punishment had paralized the revolt of whole regiments." The truth was, however, that the revolt had merely been scotched and not killed. While the whole country seethed with seditious pamphlets and proclamations attributed to Dom Miguel, the temporarily discomforted rebels merely passed over the frontier into Spain. Here they received a cordial welcome from the Spanish authorities who, on instructions from Madrid, fed and clothed the footsore rabble and waited for a propitious moment to push them back again. Meanwhile Saldanha's disciplinary measures were resulting in what remained of the army becoming infected with a sort of pernicious anæmia. He was like a man who goes on cutting out the rotten parts of a melon until there is hardly any melon left. An English resident summed up the situation in a phrase. " The state," he said, " was full of ulcers, and Saldanha was a heavy-handed physician." Perhaps the most drastic of his acts was his dissolution of the entire Royal Police Cavalry. As the maintenance of order in the capital was the charge of this body of police, it may be presumed that Saldanha became particularly popular among the pickpockets.

All through the summer the country was kept on tenterhooks by rumours of plots and counter-plots. In August the Count of Lavradio appealed to England to send a military force to Portugal as the only means of steadying the situation. The Regent also agreed to a message being conveyed to Lord Beresford inviting him to return to Lisbon to assume command of the Portuguese army. Wholesale desertions over the Spanish frontier continued.

In October there were fresh disturbances in the south. Saldanha, always in his element in a crisis, received a great ovation in Black Horse Square when he left Lisbon with 4,000 troops to dominate the revolt. He succeeded in a few weeks. Most of the rebels, however, made their escape into Badajoz, while Saldanha's customary severity damaged the Regent's popularity. It is difficult to say whether it was fortunate or unfortunate that at this moment he should have been taken seriously ill following a dinner in the palace of the Bishop of Beja. (Perhaps the dinner had followed Portuguese ecclesiastical tradition, opening with a succession of seven different soups, and closing its thirty courses with an infinite variety of egg-sweets.) As a result the Regency was deprived of his services for six months, but at the same time they were freed from the embarrassment that his ardour sometimes caused them.

The month closed under happier auspices than it had opened. The new Cortes assembled on the 30th October to listen to an inaugural address from the Regent in person. The House of Peers consisted, besides the Duke of Cadaval, of 24 marquesses, 41 counts, 3 viscounts, 4 archbishops and 11 bishops. The Lower House contained 111 deputies. By a lucky chance the news reached the Regent on that very morning that Dom Miguel had " sworn to " the Charter in Vienna. " Huzza ! " wrote Canning to Palmella. " Twenty-four hours later, and who can declare the consequences that might have resulted from the belief in which the members of the Chambers were, that Dom Miguel was hostile to the Constitution ? " The Infanta Isabel Maria was able to insert the great news into her speech. She added the information that measures were in train for procuring Papal dispensation for Dom Miguel's betrothal to Dona Maria da Gloria.

" This day," wrote the Count of Lavradio, in his memoirs, " gave me hopes that I might live to see my country happy. Everything seemed to be combining towards the union of parties. The elegance and dignity shewn by the Regent, the dignified demeanour of the deputies . . . all seemed to promise the revival of better days. . . ."

Alas ! the optimists were ignorant of how deeply the spirit of fanaticism and party passion had bitten into the character of the Portuguese people, and were feeding on an already half-derelict nation. They overlooked the malign influences holding sway at Madrid, and the inveterate grudges nursed by the Queen at Queluz.

Chapter XXIII

THE affairs of Portugal at this period were the subject of voluminous correspondence between the Great Powers. In March, 1826, both England and Austria agreed that it would be inexpedient for Dom Miguel to return to Lisbon until his situation had been clarified. The Austrian Chargé d'Affaires at Lisbon received instructions to follow a'Court in supporting the existing regency for the time being. Both powers agreed, also, in believing that the end to be achieved was an association between Dom Miguel and Dona Maria da Gloria on the throne. But the infant Princess would not come of age until her fourteenth birthday, which would fall in 1833. Dom Miguel would come of age at twenty-five, namely in 1827. The most immediate problem, therefore, was not who should eventually occupy the throne, but how Portugal could best be governed in the meantime. In this question, Canning and Metternich were again in agreement in believing that the reins of government in Portugal needed a man's hand. " From the beginning of the Regency of Dona Isabel Maria," wrote Lavradio in after years, " the British Government showed a great tendency to support the claims of Dom Miguel to the Regency as soon as he should be twenty-five."

The difficulties and the differences arose as a result of Dom Pedro's action in giving Portugal a constitution. " The abdication of Dom Pedro in favour of his daughter," wrote Canning, " and her betrothal to Dom Miguel, was in accordance with the advice of England, France and Austria . . . but the Constitutional Charter was really unforeseen by all the governments of Europe, including Great Britain." Dom Pedro's action not only offended Spain, but also alarmed Austria in the highest degree. The existence of a constitutional government in Portugal was regarded by Metternich as a menace to the stability of the whole continent. He was particularly annoyed because this was the second time that Dom Pedro, a legitimate sovereign, had betrayed the old school tie. Dom Pedro, and not the people, had made the Brazilian revolution of 1822. And now it was Dom Pedro who with his own hand had drafted and signed a Charter. Such behaviour was to be expected from liberal apothecaries in Naples or masonic journalists in Munich, but not from a crowned head. In spite of his loathing of Dom Pedro's constitution, however, which he described as a mere " system of anarchy," Metternich remained loyal to his own principle of the sanctity of legitimacy. He recognized Dom Pedro as heir to the Portuguese crown ; he recognized Dom Pedro's abdication in favour of his daughter, who therefore would become, in course of time, the undoubted Queen of Portugal. In re-reading the diplomatic despatches of the period, one is struck more by the general conformity of views between England and Austria than by their occasional diversity.

The British government was in no sense positively in favour of the Constitution. It was unfortunate that an Englishman had carried it to Lisbon " Mr. Canning," wrote Martineau, " protested against the doctrine that Constitutional rights are conferred by the royal pleasure . . . the English nation could not be expected to subscribe to this principle, nor could any British statesman uphold or defend it. . . . It is indeed a principle which strikes at the roots of the British Constitution." But Canning had long since taken his stand against the principle of interference in the internal politics of other countries. He would not brook any revival of the principle of intervention as practised by the Holy Alliance. Moreover, he made it quite clear that if foreign intervention was ever proved to be necessary in Portugal, that intervention must be British intervention. Nor would it be exerted on ideological principles, but only if Portugal's territorial sovereignty were threatened. As far as the Charter was concerned, the English point of view was that it was no good crying over spilt milk. On the face of it, it looked a fairly sensible document. It might have been a great deal worse, and it deserved a trial. As regards the problem of the Regency, Canning considered that on the whole the safest policy would be to keep Miguel away from Lisbon until his twenty-fifth birthday and then to allow him to return with the least possible fuss.

But meanwhile, Portugal was directly threatened by Spain. With Spanish contempt for compromise, the government at Madrid swore undying enmity against Dom Pedro's Constitution. They were equally hostile to the Regency, to Dom Pedro, and to Dona Maria da Gloria. They declared for Dom Miguel alone : for Dom Miguel *rei livre e absoluto*. It was his misfortune that this intransigent attitude adopted by the Spaniards should have increased the tendency already noticeable inside Portugal for the Prince to be regarded not as the leader of a nation, but as the chief of a party.

Canning had been delighted by the news that Dom Miguel had " sworn " to the Constitution, because it appeared to him that in doing so the Prince had broken down the dangerous identification between himself and the Absolutist Cause. And English public opinion agreed with Canning, since for an Englishman an oath is an oath. Unfortunately the continental mind is less straightforward. If Metternich approved of Dom Miguel's swearing to the Charter it was rather on the principle that Paris was worth a mass, while the absolutists as a body were encouraged in declining to take his oath very seriously by the fact that Dom Pedro himself, though theoretically a constitutional monarch, actually chose and dismissed his ministers according to his pleasure and ruled in a more or less despotic fashion.

There was another and even more serious reason why the oath was worthless as a guarantee that the Charter would be given a fair trial when the time came for Dom Miguel to return to Lisbon. The state of affairs inside Portugal was such as to render any commonsense solution impossible. It was in a continuous paroxysm. Though

Canning knew Lisbon personally—he had begun his career as minister there—he did not realize to what extent the country had deteriorated both economically and morally since his day. He did not accurately gauge the degree of fanaticism that existed among absolutists and liberals alike. Saldanha was perfectly clear-sighted in this matter. " Even if the Infante Dom Miguel," he wrote to Dom Pedro, "were to arrive here with the firm resolution to support the institutions which Your Majesty in your wisdom granted us, still their existence would be but of a few days' duration." " The anarchy of the nation," wrote Oliveira Lima, " was crystallized in the anarchy of political parties. . . . The confusion existing in the Portuguese Government, the confusion of thought in European politics, a Regent who was hysterical—all combined to make of the Portuguese problem an imbroglio so great that the force which in the end predominated was the only decided, affirmative one, that is to say, the Catholic exaltation of the population."

The prestige of Dona Isabel Maria's regency, and of the Charter which the Regency had dutifully adopted, was meanwhile being seriously weakened by the Portuguese politicians' complete lack of experience in governing according to constitutional principles. The various secretaries of state spent half their time in intestine squabbles. They showed not the smallest appreciation of the necessity of maintaining loyal co-operation among each other.

Palmella in London had adopted the English standpoint. He wanted to see the Charter given a trial undisturbed by foreign intrigues. And he encouraged a bevy of liberal newspapermen to give the Constitution their support in the British press. But what these well-meaning journalists had never learnt, and what Palmella apparently had forgotten, was just this fact that there existed in Portugal no inherited traditional code of public conduct such as existed in England and such as alone can make a democratic system of government workable. In October, 1826, one half of the Portuguese cabinet held a secret meeting unknown to the other half, and excluding the Minister of Foreign Affairs, to discuss fantastic plans for ham-stringing the Spanish by exciting a liberal revolution at Madrid. In November of the same year, when Portugal had been invaded by large forces of rebels and Spanish, the Minister of Justice announced in the Chamber of Deputies that he had decided to adopt the drastic measure of suspending individual liberties as established by the Charter. His colleagues in the government had heard nothing of his intention until the moment he rose to speak. The spirit in which the cabinet must have met to discuss business is well illustrated by the following amiable descriptions which the Count de Lavradio gave of his colleagues (writing not in the heat of the moment, but with what one must suppose to have been the calm detachment of later years, for these notes are to be found in his memoirs) :—

" Pedro de Mello Breyner, Minister of Justice. . . . I never ceased to wonder at the lack of dignity and the puerilities of this conceited man. . . ."

"Moura Cabral, Secretary of State. . . . Devoid of talent, of education, and of dignity, losing his temper at every small vexation, his character and abilities corresponded to his degraded appearance, and well merited the nickname that a man of great experience gave him—Old Dirt."

" Antonio Manuel de Noronha, Minister of Marine . . . one of the most idiotic, the most ignorant and grossest creatures I have ever known. . . . It was an affliction to have to conduct business with such a Donkey."

Sir William a'Court's task of attempting to keep this team in hand must have been a hard one. He drove in his carriage all day from one minister's house to another, smoothing down their ruffled feathers and threatening to have the English squadron removed from the Tagus for good and all if they did not mend their ways.

The invasion that took place in November was a deliberately planned operation. In spite of their promises to disarm the Portuguese deserters, the Spanish government had been breaking their word flagrantly for the past four months. General Maggessi, in agreement with Dona Carlota Joaquina and with her daughters at Madrid, marched into the Alemtejo with a regiment of cavalry and one of infantry, at the same time as the irrepressible old Marquis of Chaves with two foot regiments and a large force of Spanish guerillas invaded Traz-os-Montes. Their aim was the overthrow of the Regency and the destruction of the Charter, to be followed by the dispatch of a summons to Dom Miguel to return as Absolute King. It was a new application of the old principles of the Holy Alliance, applied by a single power, and an open defiance of Great Britain. Inside Portugal the Spaniards counted upon the collaboration of half the nobles, all the clergy, half the Portuguese army and the official functionaries—the *men in place*, as a'Court called them—who saw in the revival of an absolute monarchy the best hope of their keeping their places and receiving their salaries. And let it be remembered that in Portugal, as in Spain, the *men in place* compose a compact political force.

First and foremost (in the minds of the invaders) it was a Holy War. The legitimate rights of Dom Miguel were proclaimed in manifestos in which there predominated a note of mystical hallucination. The Marquis of Chaves was himself the prototype of the Queen's devotees. His uniform was hung with reliquaries and crucifixes. He moved surrounded by his " Holy Platoon." When provisions failed, he horsewhipped his victuallers ; and he liked to explode rockets at full gallop down the main streets of sleepy provincial towns. He was accompanied in the field by the Marchioness, in facial type a caricature of Dona Carlota Joaquina herself. She wore a cartridge-belt slung across her shoulder, and a huge hat encrusted with small tarnished silver images of Saints tied on to her head with a scarlet bandana. She was in personal command of a cut-throat company of volunteers which she had herself recruited. The news of the long-expected invasion reached Lisbon on the 27th November, whereupon the Regency immediately lost their heads. Lavradio had time to send off yet another urgent appeal for assistance to London but was so violently attacked in the Chamber on the 4th December (possibly the scene was staged by Miguelist sympathizers with the deliberate aim of causing confusion) that he resigned in a huff. It took a'Court the inside of a week to calm him down and persuade him to withdraw his resignation.

Everything depended on such army units as remained loyal. But who was to command them ? Saldanha was still on his sick-bed. Valença, acting Minister of War, was a feeble person whose only recorded utterance in the emergency was that " there was nothing to be done except to go fall down a well." Beresford was now at hand, in his quinta at Dafundo, but he had already snubbed Lavradio and was hobnobbing with Miguelists. He seems to have lost his grip of Portuguese politics altogether, and his appointment as Commander-in-Chief was never confirmed by the Regent. Luckily there did exist one good soldier in Portugal—the Count of Vila Flor, a liberal of good family who had been one of Dom Miguel's prisoners on the day of the " Abrilada." In later years he was to win a fame equal to Saldanha's as general to Dom Pedro, and was to earn the title of Duke of Terçeira.

Vila Flor put himself at the head of the loyal troops in the Alemtejo and gave Maggessi a sound beating at Arronches. Then he turned northwards, where Chaves had seized Viseu. It was a bitterly cold winter. Both armies lived on the country like brigands, stealing a goat here and a pig there. At Guarda, Vila Flor's troops broke up all the doors in the town for firewood. The convents offered shelter to first one army and then another, the constitutionalists eating up what egg-sweets the absolutists had left behind. The Marquis of Fronteira, who was Vila Flor's aide-de-camp, has described the anti-quated manners and customs which he met with in the remote country districts. At one house he found the squire and his family dressed in the fashions of the Napoleonic wars, grouped waiting to receive Vila Flor like a party of ghosts.

Slowly the Constitutionalists gained the upper hand. Chaves gave away his position at Montgualde by indulging in an orgy of rockets and was so nearly surprised that in his flight he left behind a mass of documents compromising to the hilt the Spanish government, the two Portuguese Infantas at Madrid, and the Queen. Then he was soundly beaten at Coruche de Beira. By this time Maggessi had re-entered Portugal in the north (the Miguelists kept up their Tom Tiddlers Ground tactics for months), but his effort petered out and he rejoined Chaves on the other side of the Spanish frontier. Vila Flor was the victor.

But in the meantime, the British government had decided to respond to the Regency's appeal for help. That appeal had been handed to Canning by Palmella on the 3rd December. On the twelfth, the King's message to Parliament announced that His Majesty had received " an earnest application from the Princess Regent of Portugal, claiming, in virtue of the ancient obligations of alliance and amity between

His Majesty and the Crown of Portugal, His Majesty's aid against an hostile aggression from Spain." It went on to refer to the great exertions which the British government had made at Madrid to persuade the Spanish government to desist from mischief-making. It stated that notwithstanding the assurances given by the Spanish, hostile inroads into Portuguese territory had been concerted in Spain, and executed under the eyes of the Spanish authorities by Portuguese regiments which the Spanish government had repeatedly and solemnly engaged to disarm and disperse.

At the close of the King's message, Canning rose in his place and delivered a speech of surpassing brilliance. He said : "Among the alliances by which, at different periods of our history, this country has been connected with the other nations of Europe, none is so ancient in origin, and so precise in obligation—none has continued so long and been observed so faithfully—of none is the memory so intimately interwoven with the most brilliant records of our triumphs, as that by which Great Britain is connected with Portugal. It dates back to distant centuries ; it has survived an endless variety of fortunes. . . . This alliance has never been seriously interrupted, but it has been renewed by repeated sanctions. It has been maintained under difficulties by which the fidelity of other alliances was shaken, and has been vindicated in fields of blood and of glory."

After reviewing the various treaties binding the two countries, and taking pains to argue that the measure being presented for the approbation of the House was " for the defence of Portugal, and not a vote for war against Spain," Canning defined the policy of the British government towards Portuguese politics. He said : " I have already stated, and now repeat, that it has never been the wish or the pretension of the British government to interfere in the internal concerns of the Portuguese nation. Questions of that kind the Portuguese must settle among themselves. . . . I am neither the champion nor the critic of the Portuguese Constitution. But it is admitted on all hands to have proceeded from a legitimate source—a consideration which has mainly reconciled continental Europe to its establishment ; and to us, as Englishmen, it is recommended by the ready acceptance which it has met from all orders of the Portuguese people. To that Constitution, therefore, . . . it is impossible that Englishmen should not wish well. But it would not be for us to force that Constitution on the people of Portugal, if they were unwilling to receive it. . . . It is no business of ours to fight its battles. We go to Portugal in the discharge of a sacred obligation, contracted under ancient and modern treaties. When there, nothing will be done to enforce the establishment of a constitution—but we must take care that nothing shall be done by others to prevent it from being fairly carried into effect. Internally, let the Portuguese settle their own affairs ; but with respect to external force, while Great Britain has an arm to raise, it must be raised against any power that should attempt forcibly to control the choice and fetter the independence of Portugal."

He pointed out that England's position must be one of neutrality

" not only between contending nations but between conflicting principles," and he ended : " Let us fly to the aid of Portugal, by whom-
soever attacked : because it is our duty to do so : and let us cease our
interference where that duty ends. We go to Portugal not to rule, not
to dictate, not to prescribe constitutions—but to defend and preserve
the independence of an ally. We go to plant the standard of England
on the well-known heights of Lisbon. Where that standard is planted,
foreign domination shall not come."

The Princess Lieven listened to this famous speech locked in a small
cubby-hole in the gallery of the House of Commons called the venti-
lator. Overcome by his chief's eloquence, Canning's secretary forgot
to release her in time for her dinner engagement and she hurried away
tearfully exclaiming " My husband will beat me."   No one realized
better than she that the speech marked the end of an epoch—the final
defeat of the principles of the Holy Alliance and the emergence of
England as the recognized champion of the liberty of peoples.

The speech was a masterpiece of lucidity, but it contained one
misstatement ; Canning was hardly justified in referring to the
" ready acceptance " which the constitution had met from " all orders
of the Portuguese people." In the second place, it must be noted that
however scrupulously the British government maintained neutrality
" between conflicting principles " it was in fact, impossible for the
Portuguese to resist interpreting the arrival of British troops as an
act of intervention on the side of the constitutionalists. When Sir
William Clinton and his force of 5,000 men landed a fortnight later on
the Lisbon quays the smiles of welcome were all on liberal faces.
Whereas the Queen's party, and above all, Dona Carlota Joaquina,
herself, were almost speechless with indignation. Her presence having
been requested for the transaction of some business at the Ajuda,
the Queen refused to set foot there, because, she declared, the spectacle
of British men-of-war in the Tagus, clearly visible from the palace
windows, was a sight she could not stomach. She who had always
detested Englishmen individually now expanded her hatred to envelop
the entire heretic British nation.

Chapter XXIV

THE year 1827 was one of small events inside Portugal. Military operations came to a successful end in March when the rebels who had made yet another incursion into the north were forced to surrender. The pestilential Marquis of Chaves and his comrade-at-arms, Maggessi, again skipped over the frontier, but the Spanish government this time consented to expel them and they took refuge at Bayonne. At Lisbon, the presence of English red-coats imposed a fictitious atmosphere of calm. Hatred and anxiety seethed beneath the surface.

The fate of Portugal continued to be moulded at Vienna, London and Rio de Janeiro. On the 26th October, Dom Miguel would attain his twenty-fifth birthday, and early in that year, 1827, Prince Metternich took a fateful decision. He decided to come forward and support the Prince's claims to the Regency when that day should arrive. So an envoy from Dom Pedro having arrived in Vienna, in March, inviting Dom Miguel to go to Rio de Janeiro, Metternich sent an emissary of his own across the Atlantic to persuade Dom Pedro to approve the idea of his brother going straight to Lisbon, there to remain as Regent until Dona Maria da Gloria should be old enough to join him as his wife and Queen. Metternich also addressed a circular note to the European powers, arguing that Dom Miguel's rights to the Regency were incontestable, and informing them that the Austrian court had tendered advice to Dom Miguel not to comply with his brother's summons to go to Rio until an answer had been received to the Austrian envoy Neumann's mission. The Austrian chancellor furthermore intimated to the powers that Dom Miguel would no longer be regarded as a welcome guest at the Austrian court after his twenty-fifth birthday, and would therefore be urged to take up his residence "in Spain or elsewhere." The implied menace to the tranquillity of the Peninsula was obvious.

The British government were willing to fall in with Metternich's suggestion. That Dom Miguel, now he was about to come of age, should be allowed to assume the Regency seemed to be common-sense. He was clearly indicated by the clause in the Charter which laid down that the Regency should be held by " the person nearest to the throne." Moreover, Dom Miguel had appeared of late to be acting in a proper and correct manner. He had sworn to observe the Charter ; he had obediently become betrothed to his niece. No one, again, disputed the fact that the majority of the Portuguese, whether for the Charter or against it, were agreed in longing for Dom Miguel's return. The Regency of Dona Isabel Maria had proved itself deplorably weak ; a man's rule might succeed. Lastly, the British government were quite as suspicious of Dom Pedro as they were of Dom Miguel. His abdication had not yet been declared absolute, in spite of the fact that the necessary conditions had been fulfilled. The British government suspected with good reason that Dom Pedro was bent upon post-poning the final act of severance between his two crowns as long as possible. (He actually wrote to the Regent Isabel Maria in the spring of 1827 declaring his intention not to make his abdication effective until his daughter should come of age in six years' time.) The British government also agreed with Metternich over the undesirability of Dom Miguel's going to Brazil. If he obeyed his brother's summons and went to Rio, might not Dom Pedro arrange matters so that he stayed there indefinitely? Dom Miguel's presence in Brazil would certainly represent a trump card in the hand that Dom Pedro was not playing too scrupulously.

The news that Dom Miguel had been restrained from accepting his brother's invitation produced a wave of nervousness in Portugal, where the absolutists were filled with hope and the liberals correspondingly depressed. Saldanha, who had now recovered from his illness and had returned to the War Ministry, decided that yet another purge was necessary in the army. He also insisted on the dismissal of the Intendent of Police. The Regent, however, refused on this occasion to be browbeaten. Saldanha resigned, and as a consequence the Lisbon mob rioted for three days. It was a sinister symptom of the condition that Portugal had fallen into. Shortly after these events Saldanha went into a self-imposed exile in London.

In July, Dom Pedro changed his mind. Yielding to the advice of the European powers, he published a decree nominating his brother Lieutenant-General of Portugal, and granting him " all the powers that are mine as King of Portugal and the Algarve as specified in the Constitutional Charter that he may govern in conformity with the said Charter." It will be observed that this decree implied that the Regency of Dom Miguel was to be a Regency on account of the absence of Dom Pedro, not a Regency on account of the minority of Dona Maria da Gloria, and that Dom Pedro reserved for himself in entirety his rights as heir of Dom John the Sixth. There is little doubt that Dom Pedro already foresaw the possibility of a revolution in Brazil depriving him of his Brazilian diadem and that he did not like the prospect of one day finding himself without any throne at all.

At the same time as publishing this decree, Dom Pedro addressed the King of England and the Emperor of Austria, asking them to adopt a benevolent attitude towards the arrangement he had made. To the former he wrote : " I ask Your Majesty to give assistance, not only that this Regency may be installed without delay, but also that the Constitutional Charter, granted by me and acknowledged by the nation, may be the fundamental law of Portugal." While one imperial envoy carried the first letter to London, another carried the second to Vienna, where he was furthermore instructed to make it plain to Dom Miguel that the Emperor of Brazil would revoke the delegated powers and reassume his royal authority the day the Prince should lend an ear to any suggestions made by factions inside Portugal so far as to violate the Emperor's rights, those of his daughter, or the laws of the Charter.

The news of Dom Miguel's appointment was received with relief by the British and Austrian governments, who both hoped that the wearisome problem of the Portuguese Regency had at last found a solution. Diplomats hurried to Vienna, to make the last necessary arrangements preliminary to the Prince's departure. They may be compared to scene-shifters putting up as solidly as possible the *décor* for the great scene of Dom Miguel's return. It is essential to understand what exactly their labours consisted of.

All reports emanating from Lisbon foretold that Dom Miguel's appearance in Lisbon would cause an explosion of popular feeling. The governments of England and Austria were, therefore, determined to make Dom Miguel's legal position as clear as pen and ink, contracts, oaths and protocols could make it. Villa Secca, Portuguese minister at Vienna, the British minister Wellesley, Villa Real, who had come specially from the Portuguese Legation in London, Lebzeltern, Neumann and Bombelles (the three last acting on behalf of Austria) gathered round the conference table. To use another metaphor, these distinguished persons may be compared to a firm of family lawyers bent upon tying up as securely as possible a great fortune about to be inherited by some rather erratic and wild young man.

To begin with, Dom Miguel showed signs of sulking. He bit his lip and his brow darkened when he was informed that it would be utterly impossible for him to return to Portugal *via* Madrid, and that he must go *via* Paris and London. He was prejudiced against both these capitals, because he still bore a grudge against all Frenchmen and all Englishmen on account of Hyde de Neuville and Sir Edward Thornton. But a last Viennese love-affair monopolized his thoughts, and he could not be bothered to argue the point. He gave Villa Secca and Villa Real *pleins pouvoirs* to act on his behalf.

The conference decided all matters to their satisfaction. Three protocols were signed on the 19th, the 20th and the 23rd of October, regulating the whole manner of Dom Miguel's return to Portugal and of his future conduct there. The most important part of these protocols were the copies of letters which Dom Miguel, who was now entirely conciliatory, addressed to his brother Dom Pedro, to the King of England, and to the Regent Dona Isabel Maria. All three spoke specifically of his intention to rule in his brother's name *according to the Charter*. The words used in the promise addressed to Dom Pedro were : " . . . according to the Constitutional Charter which Your Majesty granted the Portuguese nation. All my efforts will be bent to-wards maintaining the institutions by which Portugal is governed and towards contributing, as much as is in my power, to maintaining public tranquillity in that country, and to preventing its being troubled by factions which will never have my support whatever their origin." Nothing could have been expressed more clearly. The delegates to the conference congratulated each other on the apparently complete success of their labours.

Dom Miguel left Vienna on the 6th December, reached Paris on the

19th, and London on the 30th, where he received a friendly welcome from the public. In political circles his reputation was improving. Had he not shown himself to be a most reasonable young man ? Even Metternich had written of him, " he firmly intends to support the Charter." The " Abrilada " was an incident of the past, and was regarded, if it were ever remembered, as a passing folly of youth. After all, some of the most respectable English statesmen had once led rebellions at Eton, and had broken the windows of Christ Church. Palmella shared the general optimism. " My prayers," he had written to Villa Secca in September, " were never more sincere and ardent than those I now make that the memory of this Regency may be considered in future times as one of the most glorious epochs of Portuguese history." The fashionable world endorsed the good opinion of the public and the politicians. Society was particularly impressed when the Prince went down to stay at Windsor, went out with the stag-hounds in a pink coat, and " rode over the fences," as Greville said, " like anybody else." King George the Fourth had himself fitted out with an extra dozen pairs of doe-skin breeches for the occasion.

To those who had opportunity of watching Dom Miguel closely, however, there were signs—somewhat ominous signs—that the hand-some Prince had more than one side to his character, and that his graceful manners might possibly be nothing more than a veneer. The fact did not escape the penetrating eye of the Princess Lieven. " Dom Miguel," she wrote to Lord Grey, " has a sweet smile, but at times has fits of passionate gesticulation amounting almost to fury in their intensity. The moments of passion, however, only occur at long intervals. The first impression he makes is much in his favour."

She was not long enough in his presence to note that these sudden moods of petulance, when his black eyes flashed and his whole expression was distorted, were caused by his catching sight of a face, or hearing a name mentioned, which recalled certain memories of the past. If someone spoke to him of Vila Flor, or of some other liberal who refused to pay court to his mother, and whom consequently she hated, the transformation would take place in an instant. It was, in short, evident that Dom Miguel still nourished many old feuds.

Palmella deliberately closed his eyes. He excused the insolent hostility which the Prince showed when he gave audience to Saldanha, reminding himself that Saldanha had offended the Regent Isabel Maria so that he deserved no better reception. But it might have been supposed that Palmella would have been caused some uneasiness by an incident that took place at Strathfieldsaye. Palmella had accompanied the Prince to stay in a house-party with the Duke of Wellington, and one night in the library after dinner the conversation took a serious turn. Palmella and the Duke (he was then Prime Minister) discussed the form of oath which Miguel should take in the Cortes on his return to Lisbon ; would it be more correct to swear fidelity to Dom Pedro, or to Dona Maria da Gloria ? Dom Miguel paid not the smallest attention to this conversation, though the common courtesy of a guest should have prompted him to listen to what the Duke was saying. He sat on a sofa nearby, flirting with the Countess Esterhazy. At last the Duke, who was nettled, said to Palmella, " This will never do. He must settle the terms of the oath, and *if he is so careless in an affair of such moment, he will never do his duty.*" To which Palmella, whose confidence was still unshaken, replied, " *Oh, leave him to us. We will manage him.*"

The fact of the matter was that Dom Miguel resented the incessant meddling in Portuguese affairs being carried on by foreign powers. His national pride was wounded by this tutelage, and in feeling as he did he represented—consciously or unconsciously—the sentiments of the large majority of his own countrymen. His failure to pay attention to what the Duke was saying may, therefore, have been intentional ; in which case the sentiments which inspired it were from one point of view understandable, though the act was not diplomatically expedient, or even well-mannered.

But whatever the actual motives behind his conduct on this occasion, it was certainly national pride that caused him to decline to be transported to Lisbon in a British man-of-war, though one was offered to him. He insisted upon going on a Portuguese ship. After being delayed at Plymouth for several days by contrary winds he set sail on the 9th February on the frigate *Perola*. Before describing the fateful events that followed his return home it will be convenient to sum up exactly what his legal position was, as settled by the various protocols to which he had given his assent before leaving Vienna.

His office was clearly defined. He was to govern as Lieutenant-General in the name of the rightful sovereign of Portugal, Dom Pedro. In the expected event of Dom Pedro issuing in the near future the decree making his abdication absolute, then Dom Miguel was to govern in the name of the Queen Dona Maria da Gloria until she should come of age, when she should ascend the Portuguese throne in her own right, Dom Miguel then becoming her consort. Such was the interpretation of his office which he himself had agreed to, which the Powers had approved, and which they had bound themselves to respect.

But distinct from the question of the succession was the question of the Charter. Dom Pedro, the legitimate sovereign, had insisted upon Dom Miguel's promising to govern as Lieutenant-General in conformity with the Charter. Whether this condition was pleasing to Austria or to the other Powers is not important. The fact remains that the Powers had accepted it as a condition of Dom Miguel's Regency ; Dom Miguel had repeatedly given his word to respect this condition, and therefore it was unthinkable that Dom Miguel, whatever his personal views might be (in point of fact they were, of course, known to lean to absolutism), should ever dare with his own hand to destroy the Constitution he had sworn to uphold. But there was another possibility which was foreseen. It was obvious that public opinion in Portugal was turning against the Charter. It was possible that Dom Miguel would in time find himself unable to govern as Lieutenant-General under the existing constitutional system. He, himself, could not legally destroy the Constitution, but the Constitution might conceivably be destroyed by the will of the Portuguese nation. In such circumstances, Dom Miguel would in no sense lose the sympathy of the European Powers if he continued to govern in the name of Dom Pedro under a different system.

The views of the British government are illustrated in a despatch which the new Foreign Secretary, Lord Dudley, addressed to a'Court in August. He wrote : " If the Constitution ' *crumbles to pieces* ' it will be because its destruction is due to its own intrinsic debility . . . the reason must be that the will of the nation does not favour the régime. We can guarantee constitutional Portugal against an invasion by apostolic Spain ; we can *recommend* to Dom Miguel as Regent a strict adherence to the free institutions of his country as essential to his own honour, as the best means of maintaining public peace, and of preserving the ancient alliance which has always been a political principle of the House of Braganza. If all fails, we for our part will have done all that good faith and policy require, and the failure can only be attributed to causes over which we can exercise no legitimate control."

Liberal historians have been tempted to blame England for having " deserted " the cause of the Constitution in 1828. They seek significance in the fact that Canning had died in the previous August and that in January a new Tory Ministry had come into office. But had Canning been alive, there is no reason to suppose that his policy would have been different to that of his successors. No Englishman could support a Constitution which was demonstrated to be hateful to the majority of the nation where it had been planted. In the second place, there is no doubt that after two years of ceaseless correspondence and negotiations over the affairs of Portugal the British government were growing somewhat weary of the whole question. Dom Miguel, therefore, carried to Lisbon the best wishes of everyone. Let him make the best job of the Regency that he could. Everything depended upon his own abilities. If he were wise, steady and conciliatory, he might hope to weather the storm. But if he were ignorant and revengeful—above all, if he were careless and weak—he would be like a leaf flung hither and thither by the winds.

Chapter XXV

DONA CARLOTA JOAQUINA had dragged out the past two years at Queluz in futile exasperation. She was still in contact with Madrid, in contact with Chaves and Maggessi; still indomitably cheering the absolutist party by her example. Moreover, she was rich : and in a country on the verge of bankruptcy money was power. But the presence of Clinton's troops had frustrated her latest hopes. It looked at times as if her dreams would never be realized : as if the day would never dawn when she might have a firing-squad at her disposal and the blasphemous free-thinkers at her mercy. She was growing old now. The thought haunted her sometimes that she might never see Miguel again. In her rage and helplessness she turned to Our Lady of the Cave. To *her* miraculous intervention she had always ascribed the success of the revolution at Vila Franca. But why had not the sacred image realized that that success had only been partial ? And why had she refused her blessing on the attempt of April ? The Queen sank on her knees before the shrine. She moaned a prayer. The devout dog and the holy rabbit were portrayed to the life in the sacred niche, they too kneeling in ecstasy before our Lady of the Cave suspended in baroque clouds of golden wire.

The news from Rio de Janeiro of Dom Miguel's nomination as Lieutenant of Portugal was Our Lady's answer to the Queen's prayers. It roused the Queen like a trumpet call, transforming in a moment the weary monotony of Queluz into a whirl of movement. She summoned her numerous attendants about her. On her breast she pinned a miniature of her beloved son. " Behold ! Your King ! " she whispered like a priest at the confessional to each in turn, as kneeling and with tears streaming down their faces they bent their lips to the likeness. At her side a wild-eyed friar, her confessor Macedo, held a crucifix aloft. The thrilling news flew from mouth to mouth, spreading far and wide the demoniacal hysteria of the palace. The imagination must conjure up the frenzy of dancing dervishes to picture Portugal at this time. The forces of superstition, bent like a bow to breaking point by twenty years of liberal pressure but still drawing their sap from the hearts of the people, were to spring back now with irresistible recoil. The fluid of modern ideas injected little by little into the body of the state was to produce a last violent paroxysm. Dark, grotesque instincts rose now to the surface among a people maddened by misery. Could it be that age-old messianic tendencies of the Portuguese lost in the mists of antiquity but nourished for centuries by the cult of Dom Sebastian—the mythical saviour who was to return across the seas in the hour of need—now caused the people to hail Dom Miguel as a supernatural apparition ? He was the Messiah, the " Prince-Saint," the " Angel-Child " !

Pins, brooches, and boxes were everywhere on sale depicting the Infant already crowned, with sceptre in hand. In the grotto at Carnaxide a gaudy votive picture made its appearance representing Dom Miguel decorated with all the insignia of royalty, with the Archangel Michael directing his footsteps towards the royal palace of the Ajuda, where the old Queen was seated upon a daïs surrounded by devout soldiery, all kneeling.

The police no longer even attempted to maintain order. Excited by stories of tumultuous scenes taking place at Queluz, the Lisbon populace poured through the streets cheering for the " Holy Religion Unique and True," and beating up the blue-and-whites. A liberal was termed a Hottentot, a cannibal, a fiend, a minion of the anti-Christ.

A conjunction of circumstances favoured the Queen in addition to the anarchical delirium of the mob. In January the Bank of Portugal suspended payment, and the economic situation of the country turned a degree worse, if worse were possible. Then there was the wave of popular feeling sharply hostile to incessant foreign interference in Portuguese affairs, a sentiment which, as we have already noticed, Dom Miguel shared. It was felt to be a disgrace that Portugal's concerns should be wrangled over by foreign statesmen and should be a subject of debate for every foreign newspaper. Indignation was swollen by a fresh movement of antagonism against Brazil. The liberals proclaimed their strict loyalty to Dom Pedro, but the masses were angry that a Brazilian should lay down the law for the Portuguese. Above all there was a general conviciton that what Portugal needed was a sovereign of flesh and blood, " not a roll of parchment."

Apart from the personal popularity of Dom Miguel in distinction to Dom Pedro, there were substantial sections of the nation who disliked and feared the Charter. The priests recognized in it the 1820 Constitution under a new disguise, and remembered how one of the principal aims of the first Cortes had been the expropriation of ecclesiastical property and the revocation of the Church's senorial rights. The country magistrates and the local military governors were no less hostile in the fear that the Charter would sooner or later put an end to a system under which they had for years waxed fat on the receipt of bribes. And it will be recalled what a'Court said about the " *men in place.*"

If the reactionary party thus drew its strength from several sources ; the liberals were correspondingly weak. Distrust had been caused between the upper and lower chambers of the new Cortes by the divergence of their views on issues of property and taxation. The liberal politicians had been discredited by their own abuse of each other, by their recriminations and their maliciously false statements. The government was in fact a chaos of intrigue, while British policy, which was attempting to hold an even keel and was neither in favour of revolution nor reaction, was simply one more element of confusion.

While Dom Miguel lingered in London, Dona Carlota Joaquina set herself feverishly to work with her confessor. There were lists of friends and enemies to be corrected and completed. The names of all army officers had to be tabulated according to their past records. Miguel must, of course, clap all Saldanha's nominees into prison, though a prison seemed too good a place for them; the ideal thing would be a Saint Bartholomew's Day—that was the goal to aim at. And, of course, she herself must be on the scene of action. In January, the Queen took up her residence in the Ajuda. Her plans were laid, her projects concrete. They included not merely placing the crown on Miguel's head, not merely a sanguinary vengeance—the sweeter for having been so long postponed—on her enemies, but the setting of England, Brazil and all Europe at defiance.

What a magnificent, delicious panorama! Nor was she contemplating any longer a remote dream. The execution of her plan was more than possible; it was going to be easy; the sequence of events was almost inevitable. Not an insult that she had ever suffered—and she remembered them all—but would now be revenged. Lord Strangford was still alive, and Sir Edward Thornton. They would read of her triumph. Palmella would find himself a penniless exile. Of all the men she had longed to crush beneath her heel, only Dom John was beyond her reach in his grave.

A single doubt yet worried her. Was Miguel still the obedient darling son whom the detestable English had seized on the *Windsor Castle*? Was he still *hers*, heart and soul? Had the letters which she had sent him to Vienna ever reached his hands? " If you are coming back," she had written to him," disposed to govern according to that vile Charter, you might as well bury a knife at once in your mother's heart."

With feminine intuition she realized that the first hour after the Prince set foot in Lisbon would be critical for herself and the Absolutist Cause. Either he would succumb instantly (she knew his passionate temperament) to the effect of old memories and familiar scenes, or else the influences that had surrounded him at Vienna and London would survive and might never be eradicated. So the Queen took with her to the Ajuda her whole Queluz establishment, including the old woman who had been Dom Miguel's nurse, and a bevy of ageing servants who had hugged and spoiled him from his earliest infancy. She also arranged for the *Perola* when it sailed to England to carry on board one of Dom Miguel's boyhood friends, Raposo, a wild youth, who had been at his side during the Abrilada. It was an adroit move. Engrossed in recalling old days and old faces, the Prince, when the *Perola* left Plymouth on its homeward voyage, found little time to be affable to his fellow-passenger, Sir Frederick Lamb, the new British Minister who was to replace a'Court. But probably he was not encouraged to be civil by knowing that Sir Frederick carried a cheque for £50,000 in his pocket, the fourth part of the Rothschild loan that had been raised in London to give the new Regency a good start. Lamb had been instructed to withhold the money in the event of the Prince not behaving himself. Considering the vein of romantic chivalry in Dom Miguel's character, this whole proceeding was tactless on the part of a country whom her enemies are ever eager to denounce as a nation of shopkeepers. Nor was Lamb a happy choice as an envoy whose first preoccupation should have been to win the Prince's confidence and friendship. He was a sour-faced misanthrope who was once described by Alvanley as " hating half mankind, and wishing the other half dead." A culprit was reprieved. Alvanley said in a whisper, " How shall we break it to Frederick ?"

On the 19th February, a violent storm burst over the Portuguese coast, giving rise to much anxiety as to the safety of the Prince, who was known to be at sea. But our Lady of the Cave, who had already granted the Angel Prince her benign protection on the day he break-fasted in the Thames tunnel (there was a dreadful *contretemps* : everybody was nearly drowned), continued to protect him across the Bay of Biscay. The storm blew itself out and the memorable 22nd was a cloudless day. The fact is not unimportant, for Portuguese sunshine is a powerful alchemy. Standing on the deck of the *Perola* as she crossed the Tagus bar, recognizing first one and then another landmark of the Cintra hills and the river-mouth—Saint Julian's Fort, the Tower of Belem, the irridescent silhouette of St. George's Castle in the distance—as he saw the splendid panorama stretched beneath the glittering Portuguese sky, that alchemy was at work in Dom Miguel's veins. The tedius etiquette of Vienna ; the absurdly solemn diplomats wrangling over the choice of a phrase and the placing of a comma ; the fogs of London and Palmella's last grave words on the quay at Plymouth—all suddenly became unreal. Time was telescoped, so that it seemed to him as if his two years' exile had been simply a dream, and as if he had now woken from it on the very morning after the " Abril-ada." The tumult and the clatter of his horse's hooves rang again in his ears.

The representatives of the government and the municipality were awaiting him at Black Horse Square, turning worried glances towards the bar and rehearsing their carefully-prepared speeches. At two o'clock the thundering salutes from the various shipping, answered by the castle cannon, proclaimed the Infanta's arrival. But the *Perola* had not dropped anchor in front of Black Horse Square. The ominous intelligence flew from mouth to mouth that it had been stopped in front of Belem by a boat containing a messenger from the Queen. The government officials soon learned that their addresses of welcome were to be of no use to them that day. Dom Miguel had leaped into the boat. He had been rowed to the Belem quay, where an enormous and picturesque multitude had met him with shouts of " Long live the Absolute King ! Death to the Constitution !" Disentangling himself with difficulty from the embrace of friars and fish-wives, he had gained a waiting carriage. Amidst a volcano of rockets and a forest of lifted crucifixes he had driven to his mother's side.

She was gibbering in her palace, waiting for him. From a window she had seen the *Perola* cross the bar. Probably she had even been able to watch her messenger stopping the ship in the river and with a sudden sense of triumph had seen that her summons to her son had been obeyed. So the first victory was hers ! Now she hears shouts beneath the palace walls. The great moment in her life has come—the moment for which she has awaited, not for two, but for thirty years. She is to be a Queen at last ! She hears her son's quick footstep. The next instant he is on his knees before her, covering her hand with kisses. A single piercing glance and she knows that all is well. She stands as if transfigured in her exaltation. Yet he has caught that first swift look of inquiry in her blazing eyes. He takes from his bosom the image of Our Lady of the Cave. " Behold this relic ! " he murmurs " It is your parting gift ! Mother, you see before you the same child you lost ! "

From that moment the royal attendants knew what Lisbon and the whole country was to know in a few days' time : that Dom Miguel's political tendencies were unaltered, his mother's influence over him unimpaired, and the fate of the Charter sealed. His aged nurse and other retainers now pressed forward to play all unconsciously the part that the cunning Queen had assigned to them. They knelt before him, sobbed and acclaimed him King. The lackeys on the stairs, the ostlers in the stables, a score of bull-fighters who had been loitering there since dawn to welcome their hero home, cheered themselves hoarse. They had brought a bull into the court-yard. They were frying sardines on the grand staircase. They were throwing squibs out of the windows. Nor must it be imagined that their joy was in the slightest degree affected. The good old days had returned, and Dom Miguel's capacity for inspiring personal devotion was his outstanding gift.

For Dona Carlota Joaquina, who had largely stage-managed it, his reception was a triumph. All night long the echoing cheers for the *rei absoluto* were mingled with hoarse shouts for the Empress Queen. As an apotheosis it hardly needed the crowning news that the same night was carried post-haste from St. Ubes, of a miracle—a radiant vision that had appeared in the evening sky. A friar looking towards the sunset over the bay had noticed, resting on rose-tinted clouds, two angels robed in blinding white, raising aloft an imperial crown entwined with a scroll whereon were inscribed the words : " Long live Miguel the First, Anointed King !"

Chapter XXVI

The following day, Dom Miguel drove to a Te Deum at the cathedral and was again greeted on all sides by "vivas" for the Absolute King. The Constitutional party were much dispirited. The Prince's intention to take the oath in the Cortes, however, was made known the same evening and somewhat revived their hopes. After all, his own views had not yet found expression in any public statement and it was not positively established that they were really identical with those held so notoriously by his mother and the Ajuda camarilla.

The truth was that his political views were nebulous. He was vaguely aware that he had undertaken to swear to the Constitution all over again on his arrival in Lisbon, and though already under his mother's spell it seemed impossible for him to evade his obligations at this moment. The stage had been too carefully set in advance. The whole political question was in fact inexpressibly boring. What he would have liked would have been to spend the day in the bull-ring with Raposo. As it was, he took the worst course possible. He decided to do what was expected of him and so gain time, but his sense of honour was wounded by what he knew was a mean expedient and he was not a good enough actor to carry the scene off. The ceremony was thus foredoomed to failure, even whithout the Queen's firm intention to turn it into a fiasco.

Lord Porchester, afterwards the third Earl of Carnarvon, was on a visit to Lisbon at this time and was present at the oath-taking in the great saloon of the Ajuda on the 26th February. The peers (all dressed "like Roman senators") sat on the right hand of the throne, with the peeresses in a tribune above and the deputies opposite to them. The Regent Isabel Maria, who was formally to hand over her powers to her brother, entered with Dom Miguel at one o'clock and seated herself on the throne. Then, noticing that Miguel was standing beside her, she touched his arm and insisted on his sharing her seat while she read her speech. The spectacle of brother and sister squeezed into a single chair was comic.

As she began to read she was frequently interrupted by shouts from Dom Miguel's bull-fighting friends in the court below, placed there— it is hardly necessary to add—by Dona Carlota. Her voice was at one time so completely lost in the clamour that she was obliged to pause, while Dom Miguel's eyes flashed with a fury so volcanic that more than one deputy shifted uncomfortably on his bench. Having concluded her speech, the Infanta retired gracefully from the daïs. The written oath of adherence to the Charter was then presented to Dom Miguel, who, in Carnarvon's words, "regarded it with apparent confusion and seemed unable or unwilling to read it." At the same time the young Duke of Cadaval drew near with a missal, but his wide spreading toga so effectively concealed the Prince that it was impossible either to see him kiss the sacred book or hear him pronounce the solemn words. "I was not far from the royal party," wrote Carnarvon, "but cannot give any decided opinion upon that much debated point, whether Dom Miguel really went through or evaded the prescribed forms. Many of his adherents declared then, and still assert, that he neither repeated the words nor kissed the book ; and the Infant himself is said to have assured his favourite nurse on the same day that in subverting the Charter he should incur no moral guilt as he had not bound himself by any oath to maintain it."

The opinion of the British public on Dom Miguel's conduct on this occasion was voiced in the House of Commons by Sir James Mackintosh. He said : " There was such a mixture of cowardice and superstition in this dastardly and unprincipled attempt to escape the responsibilities of wilful perjury, that it is impossible not to feel indignant at this effort to evade the sanctity of an oath ; more especially where a member of a family illustrious in history condescends to an unprincipled meanness, which on some occasions is practised by the very lowest orders at the Old Bailey, with a view to deceive mankind and cheat as it were the Searcher of Hearts."

It was expected by all present that Dom Miguel would address the Chambers on the subject of future policy. But immediately the sorry scene which we have described was over, he strode angrily from the room. "During the whole proceeding," said Carnarvon, "his countenance was overcast, and he had the constrained manner of a most unwilling actor in an embarrassing part. I read the approaching fate of the Constitution in his sullen expression, in the imperfect manner in which the oath was administered, and in the strange and general appearance of hurry and concealment."

That night was announced the formation of a new cabinet which was of a markedly Absolutist complexion. The precincts of the Ajuda palace were invaded by bands of the Queen's ruffians, shouting for the Absolute King, and openly encouraged by persons that appeared at the windows waving white handkerchiefs and joining in the " vivas." Dom Miguel, himself, was invisible. He seems to have accepted his mother's assertions that his life was in imminent danger from assassination. He ate no food that had not been cooked by his old nurse. It is also permissible to suppose that he was suffering from some twinges of conscience.

The 1st of March was marked by serious disorders, for which Dona Carlota Joaquina was again wholly responsible. On that evening, Dom Miguel was to give audience to a grey-headed delegation from the Academy of Sciences. Their astonishment was extreme when they found the corridors at the Ajuda and the flight of steps leading to the throne room completely filled by the dregs of the populace. The Cardinal Patriarch was compelled by threats of physical violence to make the sign of the cross, to call down heavenly blessings on the excited people and to join in the cry of " Down with the Charter !"

General Cunha, the Military Governor of Lisbon, was severely wounded in the street outside when his carriage was literally broken to pieces under him by the mob. The hub-bub was such that the address which the Secretary of the Academy was reading was inaudible, while the troops drawn up in the main courtyard, indignant at the insults being heaped on their officers (Saldanha's men), added to the general chaos by playing Dom Pedro's hymn, the anthem of the Constitution, as loudly as possible all through the night.

Already numerous officers of moderate opinions had been dismissed from the army and their places filled from the Queen's and Friar Macedo's lists of friends. Vila Flor, whom Dom Miguel had inherited as Minister of War from his sister's Regency, was forced to hand in his resignation. All the military governors of the provinces were then removed. The Queen was following her prearranged plans with a recklessness that frightened even her own supporters. " We have done in a week," exclaimed the new War Minister, " what could not have been effected with safety in a year." He knew that the rank and file of the regular troops were hostile. They struck up the Constitutional anthem on every possible occasion, until forbidden to play it. " As a dismasted ship is driven upon the breakers by an uncontrollable tempest," wrote Carnarvon, " so the Government, deprived of its better judgment, was compelled to adopt . . . perilous expedients by the secret but powerful influence of a fanatical priest and the frantic energy of the Queen mother." The behaviour of the Prince himself was as reckless and as odious as theirs. When Villa Real, who had assisted in the drafting of the protocols at Vienna, stooped to kiss his hand, Dom Miguel slapped his face. " Instant death," wrote the Princess de Lieven, " whatever might have been the consequences to himself, should have been the return for such an outrage."

Panic spread. It was evident that even moderate liberals, men who had been perfectly prepared to welcome Dom Miguel, were to be persecuted on account of past opinions even though some of them had already relinquished them. Henceforth none felt safe. Hundreds of respectable families began to pack their trunks.

The climax came on the 12th. The troops remained under arms all that night. The belief was prevalent that the leading Constitutionalists were about to be arrested. They no longer ventured to remain in their houses, but concealed themselves during the day in various parts of the city and, when night fell, escaped to vessels lying in the Tagus. The Count and Countess de Vila Flor and the Marquis of Fronteira were received on the *Spartiate* by the Admiral, Lord Amelius Beauclerk, who gave orders that his ships should be extended in a line up the river so as to make them more easily accessible to the fugitives. Soon every ship was crowded. The emigration continued throughout the 13th and the 14th. It was on the latter day that a decree was published dissolving the Cortes.

The preliminary stage of Dona Carlota's programme was accomplished. Dom Pedro's constitutional edifice was now virtually demolished. It only remained for the English army to leave Portugal for the forces of vengeance to be let loose, and for Dom Miguel finally to usurp the throne. During the ensuing days, pamphlets that might have been penned by lunatics made their appearance, denouncing the English as heretics and promising that the lately-defeated absolutist troops not yet returned from Spain would come back to cut off the Englishmen's ears. An arch-absolutist of the Queen's gang, a ruffian so horribly bloodthirsty that he was said to have " hairs on his heart," was appointed chief of police ; and the taverns and cafés that took their orders from the Queen's agents received instructions to arrange an " acclamation."

The Queen counted upon the benevolence or at least the indifference of the European powers. Spain was behind her. In France, a reactionary government was presiding over the last years of the Restoration. Austria and Prussia would not interfere in what was regarded as a British sphere of influence, and the Duke of Wellington's government was not inspired by any pro-liberal fervour. Nevertheless, when accounts of what was going on in Lisbon reached the European capitals they caused amazement. It is only doing justice to Metternich to say that his indignation at Dom Miguel's conduct was untempered by any satisfaction he might have been tempted to feel at the destruction of Portugal's liberal régime. His reactions, in fact, were those of a gentleman. In his view, Dom Pedro was the legitimate sovereign. This legitimate sovereign had abdicated in favour of his daughter (who was also, by the way, the Emperor of Austria's grandchild). Dona Maria da Gloria was, therefore, the rightful Queen of Portugal, and Dom Miguel merely her Viceroy. He penned a stern despatch to Bombelles, his minister at Lisbon, asserting that Dom Miguel's conduct left no doubt in his mind that " this young Prince, who held in his hands the means of establishing the Portuguese monarchy on solid and durable foundations, and who, moreover, had the certainty of being supported in this noble enterprise by all the great powers of Europe " was going to become " the artisan of his own ruin." He instructed Bombelles to keep in the closest possible touch with Lamb and, if circumstances should result in Lamb's being recalled to London, to go with him, there to await instructions.

Dom Miguel was too ignorant and the Queen too transported to realize the gravity of deliberately squandering his international reputation. Every act of both proclaimed their insane determination to ignore all foreign opinion whatsoever.

The ensuing sequence of events may be briefly tabulated. If we except the beatings and assaults going on in the Lisbon cafés, the first blood to be spilt was not spilt by the Queen's men, but by some hot-headed students of Coimbra who waylaid a university delegation on its way to Lisbon to compliment the Prince. Three of the dons were forced at the pistol point to leave their carriages and enter an adjoining field, where their brains were blown out by their pupils.

On the 1st April, Clinton's troops were ordered to return to England and quitted without regret scenes of which they had been unwilling and helpless spectators. Their departure, needless to say, had not the smallest connection with Dona Carlota's spiteful and puerile pamphlets : Portugal was no longer threatened by Spain, so that the *raison d'être* of the English army's presence had ceased to exist. But its departure was hailed as yet another triumph for the Queen. She now hurried forward with her preparations not only to wreak vengeance on all remaining liberals who had not succeeded in escaping from the country but also on foreign residents without distinction of nationality. At her instigation opinion became inflamed to such an extent that Carnarvon was compelled to disguise his identity ar St. Ubes, and was later thrown into prison at Evora. At both these towns he found the people rioting in favour of the " *Rey absoluto,*" smashing up the property of the constitutionalists—the " blasphemers," the " masons," the " infidels "—and all night long sending off rockets. If a rocket failed to explode it was declared to be a " liberal " and stamped into the earth by the infuriated rioters.

The Lisbon press participated in the frenzy of enthusiasm sweeping the country. The *Last Trump* published an article defending the " legitimate rights " of Dom Miguel. The pulpits—the great organ of propaganda in the provinces—reiterated to the people the argument that the Charter was the origin of all their misery. By the middle of April there was only one section of the community that was neither crushed nor won over to the Queen's side—that portion of the army which had defeated Chaves and Maggessi under the command of Vila Flor. These regiments were proud of their victories, and were still loyal to the exiled Saldanha's memory.

The 25th of April was the Queen's birthday. The Ajuda camarilla decided that this was the ideal date for the " Acclamation." Though the Lisbon garrison declined to take part, a very numerous mob mustered in Black Horse Square. The President of the Municipality was fetched from his house and made to appear at a window, where some aldermen unfurled the royal standard and " acclaimed " Dom Miguel King. Meanwhile copies of a petition printed in the President's name were carried from door to door. In twenty-four hours of indescribable popular excitement hundreds of thousands of signatures were collected, from rich and poor, old and young, and the signed petitions hurried in sheaves to the town hall. What more touching birthday present indeed for Dona Carlota Joaquina ?

On the 3rd May the peers of the realm (the very nobles who had been nominated by Dom Pedro) met in the palace of the Duke of Lafões and invited Dom Miguel to convoke the ancient Three Estates with a view to deciding the question of the legitimate succession to the throne. This petition was graciously acceded to the same day.

The Three Estates met at the Ajuda in June. Dom Miguel presided. The Bishop of Vizeu proposed in his presence that he should assume the crown, and in a speech in support of this motion it was declared that " the hand of the Almighty led Your Majesty from the banks of the Danube to the shores of the Tagus to save his people, who sighed for their liberator as the people of Israel once sighed in captivity at Babylon." •

When the speech was concluded " His Majesty," according to the *Gazette*, " descended from the throne, and, preceded by the court musicians playing their instruments, returned to his apartments, where a hand-kissing ensued."

At the end of the month Dom Miguel officially assumed the title of King. On the 11th July took place the festivities that customarily marked a Portuguese coronation.

The Queen mother was triumphant, and felt her power. What did it matter if the entire diplomatic body with the exception of the Nuncio, the Spanish ambassador, and the American minister, had been ordered to ask for their passports by their shocked and outraged governments ? It was good riddance to bad rubbish. What did it matter if three thousand liberals were in exile ? Portugal was well rid of them. She had heard that some regiments in the north were in revolt. They would be exterminated by the archangel Michael's sword. To punish these infidels and to wipe out the last traces of the anti-Christ would be a fit task for the Messiah-King.

Chapter XXVII

On the 18th May, 1828, the 6th Regiment of Infantry stationed at Oporto declared for " Dom Pedro the Fourth, Queen Maria the Second and the Charter." The troops seized the city, drove out the battalions that resisted them, and on the 22nd formed a provisional Junta. The garrisons at Aveiro, Almeida and Coimbra joined the movement, while a troop of gowned undergraduates, spouting self-composed odes in honour of Virtue and Liberty, marched with the Coimbra soldiers to Oporto. Before a week was out twenty regiments in all were involved, amounting to half the Portuguese army.

There was despondency at the Ajuda, where several of the court talked wildly of flying to Spain. But the Queen did not flinch. She gave her orders. In the course of a few hours hundreds of fresh suspects were rounded up by the police and incarcerated in the Tagus forts. The squadron sailed to blockade Oporto, while the regiments loyal to Dom Miguel marched northwards under the command of General Povoas.

" Cut off heads for me !" Dona Carlota croaked to him when he took leave of her, " Cut off heads ! Why, the French revolution cut off forty thousand and there are as many Frenchmen as ever !" The Miguelists scored the first success in a skirmish near Condeixa, and slowly chivied the Constitutionalists northwards. The weakness of the liberals consisted first in the fact that they had proclaimed for a Trinity that was nebulous ; Dom Pedro and the infant Queen Maria were in far-off Brazil, the Charter was a mere rallying cry. Secondly, the members of the Oporto Junta were no better than inept doddards, none of whom possessed any personal prestige. When some real leaders did arrive—from London—it was too late.

In London the news of Dom Miguel's headlong career had already caused the Portuguese funds to fall ten points. It looked as though the whole Brazilian-Portuguese problem, which statesmen had imagined to have been satisfactorily settled, was about to be reopened, for if Dom Miguel broke his word and abolished the Charter, Dom Pedro would certainly refuse to make his abdication absolute. Lord Dudley wrote to Palmella on the 22nd April to say that " the events which have signalized the regency of His Highness have produced a feeling of disquietude in the mind of His Britannic Majesty and have frustrated his hopes and expectations."

Palmella's position was most painful. He had " backed " Dom Miguel, and he had been left completely in the lurch. He had refused to listen to Saldanha's warnings about Dom Miguel's character, and now Saldanha was proved to have been in the right from the beginning. There was no love lost between these two. Their temperaments were too dissimilar. Palmella was a cosmopolitan, tailored in Savile Row; Saldanha was a sort of Buffalo Bill. But now they both found themselves in the same boat, and allies by the force of circumstance. On the 23rd May Palmella made known to Lord Dudley that he could no longer deceive himself as to the events passing in Portugal and that he must resign his diplomatic functions.

Saldanha was meanwhile nursing a madcap plan to rush to Italy, charter a frigate at Genoa, and to land at some place on the Portuguese coast, there to unfurl the flag of Queen Maria da Gloria. He had received assurances of financial assistance from two envoys of Dom Pedro who were then in London, the Marquis of Rezende and the Viscount of Itabayana. They promised to put at his disposal certain moneys that were owed to Portugal by Brazil under the 1825 Treaty, but which in the present circumstances they, of course, had no intention of handing over to Dom Miguel.

The news of the rising at Oporto and the formation of a Junta caused him to change his plans. It was decided to charter a ship at Plymouth, called the *Belfast*, and to sail at once to the Douro. Together with Vila Flor and some other of the liberal exiles already arrived in London, Saldanha persuaded Palmella to accompany them.

Poor Palmella! In his heart of hearts he detested the whole enterprise. What was he, whose " intelligence and conversation were all velvet," as the Princess Lieven described them—what was he to do on a rolling and (as it turned out) leaking ship ? But it was necessary to show his colours without hesitation. So he laid in a store of his favourite cigars, and an extra supply of his indispensable eau-de-Cologne, and after arranging for the *Belfast* to be provided with a respectable cook, went down to Plymouth.

Their journey was horribly uncomfortable, but their arrival was even worse. In comparison to Bond Street the Matosinhos beach where they landed might have been the shore of a cannibal island. If the Princess de Lieven could have seen their luggage, including the precious cigars, being loaded on to an ox-cart! And when the expedition—Palmella, Saldanha, Vila Flor, and half a dozen liberal fidalgos besides—made their entrance into Oporto, which they found *en fête* to welcome them, it was palpable to everyone that the liberal cause was in desperate plight. Povoas was already half-way on the road to Oporto from Coimbra.

The next five days were disgraced by pusillanimity, cowardice and muddle. Palmella was elected President of the Junta, but had already come to the conclusion that all was lost. Saldanha received command of the army, dashed southwards to review the disposition of his forces, dashed back again to declare he was prepared to stand and fight, discovered that the Junta had dissolved itself and that his party had all scrambled back on to the *Belfast*, rushed on board, succumbed to the fatigue of five days and nights spent consecutively in the saddle, and fell into a sleep like death. When he opened his eyes he found that the *Belfast* had dropped down the river and was already at sea on the way back to England.

The return journey was a nightmare. The crew were all drunk on port-wine. The ship sprang a leak, and had to put in to Corunna for several days. The dejected members of the expedition hardly spoke to each other : their glances were loaded with mutual recriminations. Palmella smoked his last remaining cigars in gloomy silence and cursed himself for ever having left South Audley Street. Yet their lot was better than that of the unfortunate Constitutionalist army they had abandoned. Refusing to surrender, drifting northwards foot-sore and almost without provisions, 5,000 men under the leadership of the intrepid Sá de Bandeira struggled towards the Gallician frontier. Many Oporto citizens, in fear of the approaching Miguelist forces, swelled the forlorn crowd on the road. Carrying sheaves of corn to sleep on, fired upon by Miguelist guerillas at the crossroads, sometimes forced to fire upon companies of their own men who in mad despair turned and tried to bar their way, the same soldiers that once covered themselves in glory at Bussaco and Talavera—Wellington's " fighting cocks "—had been reduced now by the vice and misery of their governments to a mob of beggars, homeless, half-starved, and lost. It is one of the saddest pages in Portuguese history.

The cause of the infant Dona Maria da Gloria was indeed at a low ebb. Her father had sent her off by ship from Rio de Janeiro that summer in charge of the Count of Barbacena. They had arrived in Gibraltar on the 2nd September to learn for the first time of Dom Miguel's usurpation. Barbacena decided that the best thing to do would be to take the Princess to England, and they arrived there on the 24th at the same time as the first batch of wretched refugees from the Constitutionalist army and the remains of the ill-fated Junta who had managed to secure a ship at Corunna.

Who would have laid a bet that the little Dona Maria would ever reign at Lisbon unless she followed what the Wellington government thought was the only possible course and married her uncle " without the Charter "? Portugal appeared to be firmly in Dom Miguel's grip. Dom Pedro was absorbed in the ever-thickening problems of his Brazilian Empire. The Princess's only acknowledged supporters at present were several hundreds of political exiles in London, totally destitute, who used to sit down twenty and thirty strong at Palmella's table every day for dinner—the only square meal they ever got. Besides these there were soon three thousand hungry and almost naked Portuguese soldiery that Sá de Bandeira had succeeded after titanic exertions in sending out of Spain—where the Spanish government refused them a refuge—and that were confined in a dreadful concentration camp at Plymouth. Their plight was appalling. They received no money except a pittance that Palmella sent down to them from his rapidly evaporating Brazilian funds—his own property in Portugal had been sequestrated. " Poor Palmella," the Princess de Lieven was writing soon afterwards to Lord Grey, " finds himself in a deplorable condition . . . if he remains here he will be sent to the King's Bench within the week."

The exiles' only consolation was that Dona Maria was recognized as

Queen of Portugal by the British government, received a royal salute on her arrival at Falmouth, and was invited to a children's party in honour of Princess Victoria. (" Our little princess," wrote Greville, " is a short, vulgar-looking child, and not near so good-looking as the Portuguese.") She also scored a personal success with old King George the Fourth. Unable to express adequately her thanks for his good wishes, the little girl put up her arms and kissed him, which " completely captivated him."

As for the British public, it shared the view of the Princess de Lieven that " it is all a piece of confusion such as never was before." If Dona Maria was Queen, what was the position of Dom Pedro, whose abdication had never actually been confirmed ? And what was Dom Miguel doing at Lisbon ? The British public regarded him as typical of the rather picturesque but at the same time utterly undesirable person that foreign countries are apt to produce owing to their unfortunate lack of free institutions and the Public Schools system. Landor with his somewhat heavy humour wrote an Imaginary Conversation between the Prince and his mother, whom he imagined discussing the cooking that the Prince had been made to sample on his late visit to England :

" *Miguel :* I once was served with what I flattered myself were snails, but I found they were only oysters. Another time, when I fancied I had a fine cuttle-fish before me, they put me off with a sole.

" *Mother :* Heretics ! Heretics ! Poor blind creatures ! Little better than Moors, Jews and Freemasons !

" *Miguel :* I have tasted in England eight or nine different soups : and vainly have I sounded the most promising of them for a single morsel of fat bacon or fresh pork.

" *Mother :* Strange uncivilized people !" Etc., etc.

In the House of Commons the Whigs seized on Dom Miguel as a useful stick with which to beat the Government, whom they charged with having lent him support.* Thus Mackintosh argued that the Tories were responsible for the " disgraced and degraded condition of England's ancient ally . . . whom they had now abandoned to the yoke of a usurper—a man who laboured under the imputations of private crimes—imputations uncontradicted and unrefuted, which rather reminded us of Commodus and Caracalla than of the tame and commonplace character of modern vice." Palmerston, winding up for the opposition, informed the House that " the civilized world rings

---

* The whole debate on British Foreign Policy during which these speeches were made (June 1st, 1829) deserves the attention of the student of Anglo-Portuguese relations in no less a degree than Canning's speech, referred to in a preceding chapter, on December 12th, 1827. The numerous references they contain to England's policy of non-intervention in the private concerns of other countries—" That principle is sound," said Palmerston. " It ought to be sacred "—provide quotations most apposite to modern times. On the subject of the Anglo-Portuguese Alliance Peel's language was hardly inferior to Canning's. " The Portuguese," he said, " are well entitled to the name of ancient Allies ; the inhabitants of the respective countries have united their arms in many fields, and almost always in fields of victory."

with execrations upon Miguel . . . this destroyer of constitutional freedom, this breaker of solemn oaths, this faithless usurper, this enslaver of his country, this trampler upon public law, this violator of private rights, this attempter of the life of helpless and defenceless woman . . ." (a reference to a report that Dom Miguel had attempted to do away with his sister the late Regent).

But on the banks of the Tagus the Queen's triumphant party were deaf to ridicule and abuse alike. For three halcyon months Dom Miguel reigned over a people as unconscious of realities as if wrapped in a mesmeric trance. It was the swan-song of the Portuguese eighteenth century ; a last desperate attempt to wipe out all that had occurred in the past quarter of a century and to return to the golden age of the Solomon King. The sacred images emerged in procession from the Lisbon churches and with ancient pomp wound their way through the prostrate throng. Bull-fights by day, fireworks and brawls by night, revived the traditional care-free life of happier days, while the poorer classes swarmed to share the open hospitality of the great houses, or clustered in contented indigence to receive their plate of soup at the convent gates. It was an almost flawless illusion, during those few swiftly passing weeks, of the return of an era when the Portuguese people were mendicants living on the kindly abundant charity of Church and Throne, while those ancient august institutions were themselves dependants of Brazil. But it was a theatrical performance without a booking-office. The Brazilian mines no longer existed to pay for the scenery and the costumes. The state was bankrupt at last. When Sir Frederick Lamb had been instructed to come home, he had carried with him the Rothschild loan for which the British Government were guarantors. So, in Lady Holland's words, we " saved our pence."

Heedless of the reverberating collapse which sooner or later was inevitable, Dom Miguel played the leading part before the footlights with unsurpassable charm. He was to be seen careering through the streets on horseback, radiant with happiness, his whip stuck into his saddle as in the past, while every face on the pavements seemed to reflect his youth and joy. The beggars crawled to him on their knees, and he emptied his purse among them. The women lifted up their eyes to heaven to invoke divine blessing on so sweet a King. Children in arms were held aloft to catch a glimpse of him. When he appeared at the Opera, all eyes were turned from the stage and riveted on his box. Popular songs, psalms, odes, hymns and *fados* celebrated his fame in archaic phraseology, crammed with fantastic biblical and classical allusions, acclaiming him " King by Law Divine, Liberating Hero to Europe Entire." Every public appearance was a triumph. One day, passing in his carriage through a small village on the road to Queluz, he suddenly found himself surrounded by a mob and his horses at a standstill. It was a spontaneous demonstration of love. No one had organized it. It was something springing from the very soil, like the magnolias at Queluz. The crowd removed the horses from the shafts and pulled their beloved *rei absoluto* several miles along the road, cheering like mad all the way.

Meanwhile his government was scarcely worthy of the name. Apart from the readmittance of the Jesuits into Portugal, the principal achievement of his reign was the institution of a new order of Knighthood, the Order of San Miguel-da-Ala. Dom Miguel became the Order's Grand Master; its aims were defined as the defence of the Holy Catholic Religion, the restoration of the legitimacy of the Portuguese Throne, and the suppression of masonry: its symbol was the five wounds of Christ.

The weird, sparkling dream of Dom Miguel's reign was disturbed on the 9th November, 1828, by a shock of a most dramatic and terrible nature. On that day the insouciant Prince, accompanied by two of his sisters, was driving a pair of piebald mules at reckless speed on the road between Queluz and Caxias. The off-wheel hit a rock lying in a rut; the carriage capsized. The Infantas were thrown clear, and escaped with a severe bruising. But Dom Miguel became caught in the reins of the panic-stricken mules. The wheels of the swaying carriage passed over his body, breaking his thigh. He was picked up, like Hippolitus, covered in dust and blood. Mangled and bleeding he was carried to his mother's apartments at Queluz. His life hung by a thread.

A thrill of horror shot like an electric current through Portugal. At first glance it seems strange that so deep, so lugubrious an impression should have been caused by an accident which any Sandhurst cadet might meet with on a motor-bicycle or out hunting. But it must be borne in mind that the idolatry—there is no other word for it—with which Dom Miguel was regarded by the people was based upon a fanatic mysticism. He was to them the Angel-Prince, the Messiah, chosen by Divine Will and moving among them under the benign protection of the Saints. How could the Divinity and His Archangels permit this thing? In vain the less bigoted among the priests, fearful of the effects of the accident upon the public imagination, argued that his narrow escape from death was a proof of yet another miraculous intervention on the part of Our Lady of the Cave. Her shrine was hung with votive offerings and crowded to suffocation with the mourning people, but the disaster disseminated disillusion far and wide. " Society," wrote Oliveira Lima, " fell suddenly sick with the King."

Here again we can discern the nefarious influence of Dona Carlota Joaquina. The wave of barbaric cruelty that now swept Portugal, based like most cruelty on sheer fear, was bound to produce disgust. It was not Portuguese in character but entirely Spanish, utterly at variance with Portuguese traditions. It resulted not only in associating Dom Miguel's name with a Reign of Terror that antagonized civilized Europe, but destroyed one of the chief reasons of his popularity in his own country—the belief that his reign was in all things typically Portuguese. It is only fair to add that the Prince was not wholly responsible for what happened. The persecution was inspired and directed by the Queen's party.

The piebald mules were slaughtered to assuage the fury of the people. But this stupid sacrifice was not enough. The nickname " piebald " was attached to everyone in the slightest degree suspected of liberal sympathies, and every " piebald " was hunted from house to house by a pack of half-demented apostolics. Mystic frenzy demands a symbol of darkness as well as a symbol of light. The same devil that had inhabited the mules must be exorcized from every corner and cranny. " In the name of the Lord ;" shrieked the Benedictine monk Joâo Boaventura in the royal chapel where the crippled Prince lay stretched in the royal tribune, " in the name of the Lord here present amongst us in the Holy Sacrament, I implore Your Majesty to stamp out these liberal vermin. Your Majesty is aware that there are three ways of finishing them off ; let them perish on the scaffold, or let them die of hunger in the gaols, or let them be given poison to eat—POISON, O LORD !"

The Prince was soon convalescent. Three weeks after his accident he held a hand-kissing in his private apartments. But the evil forces that his mishap had let loose could not be stemmed by his recovery. The Absolutist party were driven rabid by the very hopelessness of the task they had set themselves ; by the obvious impossibility, which they yet refused to acknowledge, of sealing up Portugal hermetically against modern ideas. The fearful and rapidly-spreading misery, increased by the issue of a worthless currency, turned the spirit of opposition and criticism into a hydra-headed dragon which it was beyond human power to destroy.

In June the nine Coimbra students who had murdered their dons were publicly put to death on the Cais de Sodré. In March of the following year were executed five soldiers convicted of plotting against the state. They included a youth of nineteen. The ghastly ritual of the Inquisition was revived to intensify the horror of the proceedings, while the windows overlooking the square provided front-stalls for Dona Carlota Joaquina's ladies, dressed up to the nines in the Miguelist purple and scarlet, gorging egg-sweets and peering through opera-glasses at the gruesome operations below, the hanging, the mutilation and the quartering of still-quivering flesh. In May ten wretches implicated in the 1828 rising were executed in almost similar circumstances at Oporto—" a bold and deliberate defiance," Mackintosh called it, " of civilized Europe and of Christendom."

But the total number of executions that took place during Dom Miguel's reign did not number more than 115. More intolerable than the shadow of the scaffold was the incessant and universal insecurity, the secret betrayals, the incessant anonymous denunciations paying off private grudges, the menace which hung over every citizen of finding himself dragged at night from his bed by the police and thrown into the Limoeira gaol. More than fifteen thousand souls are said to have languished in the state prisons. Nearly two thousand were deported to Africa. The *Courier* calculated (in 1831) that thirteen thousand besides had chosen voluntary exile.

The crumbling and vermin-infested walls of the Limoeira served as a sort of clearing house for the unfortunate prisoners. Here they were flung promiscuously among thieves and lepers, compelled by their venal gaolers to purchase at exorbitant sums every small alleviations to their sufferings. But the prison most closely associated with the

Miguelist terror was Saint Julian's Fort at Carcavelos, the place where half a century before an English visitor had once caught sight of the Jesuits imprisoned by Pombal gazing wistfully through their bars in the mildewing robes of their Order. Here, in surroundings which would have defied the pencil of Hogarth or Cruikshank to portray, a brutal gaoler, the infamous Telles Jordâo, rattled his rosary and his relics in one hand as he brandished his heavy whip in the other. The wretched " piebalds," fainting from lack of food and reduced to the condition of animals, were forced under the lash to lift their voices in plain-song. A cretin named Barata-Feio, ex-chorister of the Patriarchate, who had purchased immunity from punishment for various crimes by offering his services as a prison-spy, and a horrible fourteen-year-old youth known as " Baby," aided Telles Jordâo in the torture and sometimes the murder of the prisoners. Apart from numerous nameless unfortunates guilty perhaps of no other crime than having read Bentham or subscribed to an encyclopedia, Borges-Carneiro, Melo Breyner, and the Marquis of Subserra succumbed to their incarceration.

Meanwhile the giddy Prince was once again sound in wind and limb. He rendered solemn thanks for his recovery at the Shrine of Our Lady of the Cave and soon, like the Emperor Commodus, was again earning tumultuous applause in the arena.

As for Dona Carlota Joaquina, she had suddenly grown old and ill. She passed her days in dreary immobility at Queluz, half-dazed with pain, stretched on a mattress. She could not bear to be touched. Her hair hung in unkempt wisps over her shoulders. Her cheap cotton gown grew soiled and rancid. As the weeks wore on her condition became almost too distressing to allow anyone to approach her. She spoke to no one ; she was never heard to moan. Only now and again, when an attendant crept to the door of her room to take a peep at her, she was heard to be muttering to herself the old rhyme that the Spanish gipsy had written for her in her remote childhood :—

> " En porfias soy manchega
> Y en malicia soy gitana
> Mis intentos y mis planes
> No se me quitan del alma."

On the 7th January, 1830, she died. Her exequies were performed in the chapel of the palace. The monk Joâo Boaventura—what more suitable orator ?—preached the funeral oration. " She has died," he concluded, " as she lived ; filled with peace, fortitude and resignation. May she be taken to Thy bosom, O Lord ! Our hopes are founded upon the heroic virtues which she displayed in many and momentous times of crisis."

Her body was laid to rest in a chapel at Cintra, and only in 1859 transferred to the royal pantheon of the Braganzas at San Vicente.

" The death of the old Queen of Portugal," was the Princess Lieven's cryptic comment to Lord Grey, " is no unfortunate event. The poor Portuguese must really be thankful." Many doubtless were.

Two days before her death she had made her will, leaving small but also valuable remembrances to all the servants of her household. This last act was in keeping with her life, for even in the days of her isolation and political disgrace her household, however shrunken, had always been a loyal kingdom to her. None of them was forgotten in her last testament. Dom Miguel was named executor and was left among other property the Quinta at Ramalhâo. She also left money to pay for masses—no less than one thousand and two hundred separate masses —a hundred of which were to be for the benefit of the soul of her husband. Was this a last futile gesture of reconciliation towards Dom John ? If so, it must have been inspired by some shadow of remorse hitherto foreign to her hard and revengeful heart.

She signed her will in a trembling, almost lifeless hand ; Carlota Joaquina, Empress and Queen.

Chapter XXVIII

FATE had not been kind to Dona Carlota Joaquina in her lifetime until her last two years. Uprooted from Spain at an age when other children have hardly begun their schooling and sent to live among a people whose character and humour were entirely antipathetic to her own, married willy-nilly to a husband she could not love, she had always been like a piece of grit in the machinery of her world.

But during those last two years her fortunes changed. In spite of Dom John, in spite of de Neuville, and Thornton, and Clinton, in spite of her personal unpopularity among the Portuguese—she saw her grand aim achieved. Her beloved Miguel was Absolute King *de facto*. His throne was cemented by the defeat of the Oporto Junta and the ludicrous fiasco of the " Belfastada." It was hardly likely that the great powers would or could withhold their recognition indefinitely. England, the ancient ally, though disapproving was not actively hostile. Wellington was remarking to Greville soon after this date that " the Government would be very foolish to interfere for Pedro, who was a ruffian, and for the Constitution, which was odious, and that Pedro would never have more than the ground he stood on." In fact, if only Dom Miguel had followed British advice and granted an amnesty to Dona Maria's supporters, the British government would have sent a minister to Lisbon there and then. Spain and France— Portugal's nearest neighbours—were still in enjoyment of régimes sympathetic to absolutism. All the Portuguese colonial possessions had acquiesced in the usurpation, with one insignificant exception : the island of Terceira in the Açores. Terceira was holding out for Dom Pedro. But of what importance was a tiny island ? Why, one could scarcely find it on the map. As for Dona Maria da Gloria, the latest news was that she had been ordered by her father to return to Rio de Janeiro.

Fate was particularly indulgent to Dona Carlota in the date of her death. For had she died two years later she would have seen her life's achievement menaced by a combination of dangers ; two years more and she would have seen it in ruins. The year 1830 was to prove itself one of the turning-points in history. In July there took place at Paris a liberal revolution overthrowing the Bourbons. Belgium erupted in sympathy ; Italy followed suit ; Poland rose against the Czar. Even in England, where nobody copied French example except in bonnets, the tide turned also. In September the Duke of Wellington asserted that the House of Commons did not need reform. But in November he was compelled to resign office and Lord Grey formed a ministry stipulating that reform must be a cabinet measure. Before the year was out the whole atmosphere of reactionary post-Napoleonic Europe had dissolved like a morning mist.

This swing of the pendulum exerted an effect on Portugal, where rival political parties during the three past decades had formed what was to become an inveterate habit of attempting to bolster up their own causes at home by identifying them with causes beyond their frontiers. Thus the Miguelists had willingly identified themselves with what until 1830 was the winning side in Europe. With the fall of Charles the Tenth they immediately felt themselves insecure, while the forces of opposition were correspondingly heartened. These exterior influences became even stronger in 1833, when Ferdinand the Seventh of Spain died. By a " Pragmatic Sanction " shortly before his death he had suspended the Salic Law and declared his daughter Isabela heir to his throne. Her claim was disputed by her uncle Dom Carlos, and to strengthen her position certain liberal features were introduced into the Spanish system of government. Dom Carlos upheld the reeling banner of Absolutism and Divine Right, and Spain was plunged once again into a bloody civil war.

While the Liberal current was steadily gaining impetus in Europe, an extraordinary sequence of events in the zone of the Atlantic exerted a profound effect on the destinies of the Portuguese nation and its monarchy. The despised island of Terceira repelled the attack of a Miguelist squadron sent to demand its capitulation. Palmella obeyed Dom Pedro's orders and went thither to become president of a government. The remnants of the Constitutionalist forces at Plymouth succeeded, after dreadful vicissitudes, in reaching Terceira also. The Liberal Cause soon boasted, besides the nucleus of an army, the possession of first-rate brains in Palmella, experienced generals in Saldanha, Sá de Bandeira and Vila Flor, and the sympathy of many public men in London and Paris. A single resolute, well-equipped expeditionary force from Lisbon could have nipped the movement in the bud, but in the dazzling blue above the bull-ring where Dom Miguel pranced was not Terceira merely like a little cloud the size of a man's hand ?

On the 7th April, 1831, took place an event even more important than the successful resistance at Terceira. Faced with an ultimatum from revolutionaries at Rio, Dom Pedro abdicated the imperial crown of Brazil in favour of his infant son. Assuming the name of Duke of Braganza, he sailed to Europe to join Dona Maria da Gloria and to proclaim himself her Regent. He held court among the liberal exiles in London at the Clarendon Hotel. He joined his supporters at Terceira. He announced his intention to conquer Portugal for his daughter. The Spanish jew Mendizabal, a strange financial genius at Dom Pedro's elbow, somehow wangled a loan of two million in the City. Ships were chartered, and mercenaries recruited. Dom Pedro's Odyssey opened.

That Odyssey belongs to the new liberal era, and has no place in a study devoted to the preceding epoch which terminated with Dona Carlota Joaquina's death. It is a tale rich in heroic action, not unornamented with comic relief. Dom Pedro's army effected a landing on the

Portuguese coast in July, 1832, and soon afterwards seized Oporto. Two years of civil war ensued, of which for a year the issue hung in the balance. As late as April, 1833, Palmerston was writing " as for the contest between Pedro and Miguel, it is anybody's race yet." Dom Pedro was now aged thirty-four, corpulent, diseased, but indefatigable, histrionic and unlovable, already a victim to consumption, execrated as Anti-Christ by the vast majority of the Portuguese, and disliked by his own supporters, whose intestine squabbles kept them, however, subservient to his authority. In contrast Dom Miguel's popularity among the masses was almost uninjured. When he went north to assist at the siege of Oporto he was enthusiastically acclaimed all along the road. But his government was chaotic, whereas Dom Pedro had better officers, more cash, and several hundred English soldiers fighting on his side—fellows whom Mendizabal's agents had rounded up in London pot-houses, most of them ex-soldiers temporarily out of a job ; very resourceful, handy men. In July, 1833, Admiral Napier, who the day before the news reached London had been struck out of the British navy, destroyed Dom Miguel's fleet " to the great delight of the Whigs " (wrote Greville) " and equal mortification of the Tories." On land the Pedroists raised the siege of Oporto and worked their way southwards. An expedition landed in the Algarve and seized Lisbon by a daring stroke. Dom Miguel's French generals Larochejaquelin and Bourmont were beaten in the field. He was forced to retire south of the Tagus to Evora. His final overthrow was hastened by the signature of the Quadruple Alliance between Dom Pedro, England, France and Spain confirming Dona Maria's crown. (Isabela needed foreign support for her precarious throne, and thus Spain deserted Dom Miguel's cause at last.) Confronted with this news, Dom Miguel realized that the game was up. On the 26th May, 1834, was signed the Convention of Evora-Monte, according to which the Pedroists accorded a general amnesty and Dom Miguel engaged to leave Portugal.

Palmerston was delighted. " Nothing," he wrote, " ever did so well as the Quadruple Alliance ; it has ended a war which might otherwise have lasted for months. Miguel, when he surrendered, had with him from twelve to thirteen thousand men with whom he could have marched into Spain, forty-five pieces of artillery, and 1,200 cavalry. Had he dashed into Spain and taken Carlos with him, there was only Rodil with 10,000 men between him and Madrid, and part of Rodil's army was suspected of Carlism. But the moral effect of the treaty cowed them all—generals, officers and men, and that army surrendered without firing a shot."

On 1st June, amidst the bitter lamentations of the country-people and fisher folk gathered on the shore, Dom Miguel went on board the English frigate *Stag* at the fishing village of Sines. The Duke of Cadaval, and numerous noblemen bearing names illustrious in Portuguese history, followed him into exile. He was never to see the sky of Portugal again. Dona Maria da Gloria reigned at Lisbon with her father's Charter over a people not merely exhausted but prostrate.

To the British public, totally ignorant of the Portuguese character and therefore of the real nature of the long sickness through which Portugal had passed, it appeared that Portugal had settled down at last to the smug enjoyment of a liberal régime. The young Queen's name figured from time to time in the London press. She was quickly married to a dull German prince called the Duke of Leuchtenberg, who died almost immediately afterwards. A widow and an orphan at sixteen (for Dom Pedro was carried off by a galloping consumption), Dona Maria then married another, even duller German called Prince Ferdinand of Coburg, who was a nephew of the Duchess of Kent.

"Dear Uncle Leopold," wrote Queen Victoria, "has managed a *great* deal of the business : he is ever ready and ever *most able* to assist his family. . . . I cannot say how happy I am to become thus related to the Queen of Portugal who has always been kind to me and for whom I have always had a great affection." A year later she was writing : "I read to Lehzen part of the *Directions and Advices* which dearest Uncle Leopold has written down for Ferdinand, most cleverly and beautifully done. . . . The part I have read is *affaires politiques* which is divided into headings of all the departments of Governments. Dear Uncle has studied the Portuguese Constitution, Government, People, Country, etc., etc., so completely . . . that he is as familiar with the whole as if it were his own country. . . . Dear Uncle Leopold is so clever and governs Belgium so beautifully that he is a model for every sovereign and will contribute to the happiness and reorganisation of Portugal as he has done to Belgium."

How revealing these congratulations are ! So Portugal was to be made prosperous and contented ! The mere fact that there was so little news from Lisbon was taken as proof that there were no complaints. Who in England understood that the silence that wrapped Portugal was the silence of a house where a parent lies dead ? The nation was in mourning for Dom Miguel, in mourning also for all the vanished flavour of a past utterly anachronistic in the nineteenth century, but the memory of which instilled deep melancholy into the people's hearts.

The spirit of Dona Carlota Joaquina lived after her. In a bad sense it had held sway as long as Dom Miguel's reign lasted. We discern her touch in the continued persecutions that had taken place from 1830 to 1834. We recognize her xenophobia in the scandalous maltreatment of respectable foreign business men which had contributed more than anything else to turning world opinion against Dom Miguel and which moreover had brought about a supreme national disgrace. In July, 1831, the French Admiral Roussin had sailed up the Tagus to avenge insults offered to French subjects and with his cannon trained on Lisbon extracted an apology from Dom Miguel's nameless, trembling ministers.

In a good sense, Dona Carlota's spirit survived in her descendants. Freed from the vindictiveness that sprang from her peculiar Spanish temperament and which had been irritated by political causes, her piety, her pride, her vivacity, her devotion to the principles of Legitimacy and the Holy Catholic Relig: her indifference to mundane considerations

of commerce and lucre, her unbounded affection for her dependants—
these qualities flowered with extraordinary nobility in Dom Miguel
during the remaining years of his long life in exile. Indeed, once
removed from the sphere of political conflict for which he had proved
himself to be so hopelessly unfitted, his character altered so radically
that in the whiskered silhouette of Dom Miguel at Rome, or in the
portly, heavily-bearded patriarch of Bronnbach, it is almost impossible
to find any traces of the cow-boy prince of the " Abrilada."

He refused to accept any pension from the Portuguese government.
He went on board the *Stag* with a single *vintem* (a penny) in his pocket.
His faithful eighty-years-old nurse—may her name be honoured:
Dona Francisca Vadre—attempted in September, 1834, to smuggle out
a few of his personal valuables by sea, but her ship was intercepted and
the things confiscated. She joined him in Rome, a destitute refugee,
and he took her under his own roof. Pope Gregory the Sixteenth put at
Dom Miguel's disposal an apartment in the Palacio Capponi, and
allowed him a small monthly pittance, five-sixths of which he spent
alleviating the penury of his fellow-exiles. For several years he went
actually hungry. Yet wonderful stories are told of his love and charity
towards the poor. One night in August, 1837, when Rome was visited
by a plague of cholera, Dom Miguel, who was driving in a carriage lent
to him by the family of Romaro Mencacci, came across a wretched man
dying in the street. He lifted him into the carriage beside him, indifferent to the peril of infection, and carried him to his own couch.
On another occasion he actually took the waist-coat off his back, like
Saint Martin, to give to a shivering beggar, buttoning up his own
coat-lapels so as not to excite remark.

In 1851 he married Princess Adelaide of Lowenstein-Wertheim-
Rosenberg and afterwards resided in Austria until his death in 1866.
His seven children in order of their birth were Dona Maria das Neves,
who married Don Alfonso Carlos, the brother of the Spanish legitimist
pretender; Dom Miguel, known to his Miguelist supporters as King
Miguel the Second; Dona Maria Teresa, who married the Arch-Duke
Charles Louis of Austria; Dona Maria José, who married the Duke of
Bavaria; Dona Aldegunda, by her marriage Princess of Parma and
Countess of Bardi; Dona Maria Ana, by marriage Grand Duchess of
Luxembourg; Dona Maria Antonia, by marriage Duchess of Bourbon-
Parma.

Of these children, all of whom were remarkable for their strength of
character and their extraordinary beauty, the eldest, Dona Maria das
Neves, personified in the highest degree the indomitable spirit of Dona
Carlota Joaquina, unmarred by its darker traits. On the outbreak of the
Second Carlist War in 1872, although not twenty years of age, she
proceeded at once to Spain and distinguished herself at the head of
her husband's army. She was in the forefront of every battle, urging
on the troops from her white charger. She wore uniform, and sported
a kind of Zouave jacket lined with astrakhan. Her tunic was covered
in medals, she carried a gilt riding-switch, and her head-dress was the
red beret of the *requete*. After two years' war it was evident that the

Carlists were fighting for a lost cause. At last Don Carlos and his brother Don Alfonso Carlos were compelled to cross the frontier into France rather than surrender to the forces of Alfonso the Twelfth. They travelled straight from the last battlefield and arrived at Brown's Hotel in Dover Street " still wearing " (to quote from Mr. Sacheverell Sitwell's " Background to Scarlatti ") " their stained and dusty uniforms and carrying the marks of battle upon them."

Dom Miguel's fourth child, who became Duchess of Bavaria, was the mother of Queen Elizabeth of the Belgians, whose brave bearing and unquenchable courage in the Great War of 1914-1918 need no description. The firmness of the reigning Grand Duchess of Luxembourg and her consort Prince Felix of Bourbon-Parma (they are both Dom Miguel's grandchildren) has been demonstrated in the Second Great War.

For the sake of those who take interest in historical links, it is worth recording that in 1940, when the German armies burst like an avalanche over western Europe, the Duchess of Parma, Dom Miguel's daughter, was among the many who found refuge in Portugal. Before crossing the Atlantic with other members of her family, she visited Queluz and looked upon the Ender portrait of her father, painted in the full bloom of his youth and manly beauty when he was resident at the Austrian court. Dom Miguel as a child of five crossed the seas to escape the clutches of a tyrant. In similar circumstances his daughter sailed from the Tagus for the kind shores of America after an interval of a hundred and thirty-three years.

The intimate association of the old Queen with the Palace of Queluz caused it to fall into disfavour with subsequent Portuguese sovereigns —a disfavour which was doubtless accentuated by the Coburg's well-known preference for architecture of a more Romantic style. The edifice fell into disrepair; weeds choked the once-trim paths; the long line of windows caught that strange, lost air of expectancy which is the peculiar attribute of deserted splendour. Fortunately in more modern times an enterprising government has attended to its repair, so that if ever the ghost of Dona Carlota Joaquina now stalks down the galleries of Queluz, she must find herself surrounded by a pomp almost in proportion to her pride.

The constitutionalist branch of the Portuguese Royal House came to an end in 1932 with the death of Dom Manuel at Twickenham. The Absolutist line of Dom Miguel flourished in exile, and his lineal descendant Dom Duarte Nuno, Duke of Braganza, is the present Pretender to the Portuguese throne. In 1942 Dom Duarte married the Princess Maria Francisca, of the Brazilian branch of the family and a lineal descendant of the Emperors of Brazil. It is to be hoped that round the cradles of their tender offspring, the discordant voices of old family feuds and of political passion may be stilled at last.

BIBLIOGRAPHY

" A Realeza de Dom Miguel "—Dom Miguel Sotto-Mayor.
" El Rei Dom Miguel I e a Sua Descendencia "—Caetano Beirâo.
" Travel Diaries of William Beckford of Fonthill."
" Dona Maria I "—Caetano Beirâo.
" Mémoires de la Duchesse d'Abrantes."
" Dona Carlota Joachina "—Cesar da Silva.
" Memorias do Marques de Fronteira e d'Alorna."
" Perfil do Conde de Barca "—Artur da Cunha Araujo.
" Account of the Escape of the Royal Family of Portugal to the Brazils "—
     Lieutenant Count Thomas O'Neil.
" Historia Geral "—José Acurcio dos Neves.
" A Corte de Portugal no Brazil "—Luiz Norton.
" Dom Miguel "—translated by J. B. Mesnard.
" Journal of a Voyage to Brazil "—Maria Graham.
" Dom Joâo VI no Brazil "—Oliveira Lima.
" Memoirs "—Sir Nathaniel Wraxall.
" Vida do Duque de Palmella "—D. Maria Amelia Vaz de Carvalho.
" The War in the Peninsula "—Napier.
" Revolutionary Europe "—Morse Stephens.
" El-rei Junot "—Raul Brandâo.
" Modern Europe "—Alison Phillips.
Memoirs of Sir Sidney Smith.
" A Corte de D. Joâo no Rio de Janeiro "—Luiz Edmundo.
Mémoires et Souvenirs du Baron Hyde de Neuville.
" Freimauer im Kampf um die Macht "—Paul Siebertz.
" Dom Joâo VI e a Independencia do Brasil "—Marquess of Larradio.
" Lisbon in the Years 1821, 1822 and 1823 "—Marianne Baillie.
" Sketches of Portuguese Life, Manners, Costume and Character "—London, 1826.
" A Morte do Marquês de Loulé "—Antonio Cabral.
" Historia da Guerra Civil "—Luiz Soriano.
" The Foreign Policy of Canning "—by Harold Temperley.
" Mémoirs of the Duke of Saldanha "—the Conde de Carnota.
" Dom Pedro e Dom Miguel "—Oliveira Lima.
" Memorias do Conde de Lavradio."
" Portugal Contemporaneo "—Oliveira Martins.
" Portugal and Galicia "—The Third Earl of Carnarvon.
" Portugal "—The Rev. W. M. Kinsey.
" Policia Secreta dos Ultimos Tempos do reinado de Dom Joâo VI."
" Dom Miguel no Trono "—Oliveira Lima.
" Historia do Cativeiro dos Presos d'Estado na Torre de San Juliâo "—Joâo
     Baptista da Silva Lopes.
" O Visconde de Santarem, Diplomata "—Conde de São Payo.
" Life of Lord Palmerston "—Evelyn Ashley.
Correspondence of the Princess Lieven.
Letters of Lady Holland to her Son, edited by the Earl of Ilchester.
Hansard : Parliamentary Debates.

INDEX

INDEX

INDEX